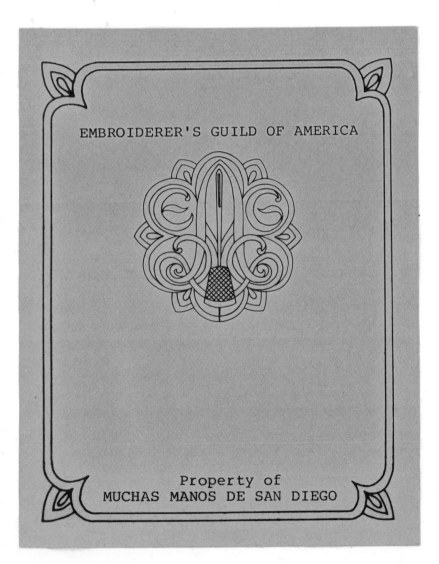

EMBROIDERER'S GUILD OF AMERICA

NEWNES COMPLETE
NEEDLECRAFT

NEWNES

COMPLETE

NEEDLECRAFT

HAMLYN

LONDON · NEW YORK · SYDNEY · TORONTO

First edition published 1969
Second impression 1970

THE HAMLYN PUBLISHING GROUP LIMITED
LONDON · NEW YORK · SYDNEY · TORONTO
Hamlyn House, Feltham, Middlesex, England
© Copyright The Hamlyn Publishing Group Limited 1969
ISBN 0 600 42037 x

Filmset in the Republic of Ireland by Hely Thom Limited, Dublin
Printed in Hongkong

CONTENTS

chapter   *page*

      FOREWORD

one   EMBROIDERY   9

two   DESIGNS FOR EMBROIDERY 12

three   SIXTY-FOUR USEFUL STITCHES 18

four   MANY KINDS OF EMBROIDERY 45

five   FINISHING, PRESSING, AND LAUNDERING EMBROIDERY . . 87

six   INTERNATIONAL EMBROIDERY 89

seven   HOME DRESSMAKING 99

eight   THE FOUNDATIONS OF DRESSMAKING 111

nine   MENDING 145

ten   PATCHWORK AND RAGCRAFT 149

eleven   KNITTING AND CROCHET 160

twelve   HOME UPHOLSTERY AND HOUSEHOLD LINEN 198

thirteen   NEEDLEWORK GIFTS 231

fourteen   USEFUL HINTS 240

      INDEX 245

The Editor acknowledges the cooperation of the following and offers her grateful thanks for their help in the illustration of this book:

The American Museum in Britain, William Briggs Limited, Mrs Jean Carter, Mrs Joy Clucas, J. & P. Coats Limited, Embroiderers Guild, The English Sewing Cotton Co, Fothergay Limited, Mrs Marcel Hellman, Mrs Olive Hill, Mrs Bertha Hollington, Mrs Moyra McNeill, Patons and Baldwins Limited, Miss Ann Mary Pilcher, Mrs Mary Pilcher, The Needlewoman Shop, Oelenschalgers of Scandinavia, Sandersons Limited, Selfridges Limited, Simplicity Pattern Book, Singer Sewing Machine Co Limited, Miss Anita Skjold, James Smythe of Belfast, Torres of Austria, The Victoria and Albert Museum.

FOREWORD

A great revival of interest in needlecraft has recently begun. Women with more leisure in their homes, created by the many modern improvements in housecraft, have suddenly found that they need a creative outlet. They want to make something beautiful for their homes; they find tremendous satisfaction in making clothes for themselves and their families. But for real satisfaction they need to know the 'how and the why'.

This book is intended to provide just that. It contains an introduction to each of the main branches of needlecraft: to embroidery by both hand and machine, to plain sewing, dressmaking, home upholstery and the making of soft furnishings, and to knitting and crochet. Though many readers may already sew, knit or crochet and even excel in one of these branches of needlecraft, it is unlikely that they will excel in all of them. With its comprehensive index the book is intended as a 'dip-in'. Many problems will be solved in its pages, many good and useful ideas, tested by experts, are introduced to readers.

EDITOR

EMBROIDERY

WITH mechanical aids and gadgets in most homes today, women are finding that they really need an outlet for their creative energy. To spend time on making something which may be useful as well as ornamental becomes a most satisfying hobby.

Some embroidery is purely decorative—an attractive design is worked on a plain piece of material to add ornament. But embroidery may also be an end in itself as in the creating of embroidered panel pictures; then it becomes a form of art as well as being a craft.

As a hobby it has many advantages over other crafts. For one thing it requires very little equipment. Also quite a lot of hand embroidery is worked in small pieces which can easily be carried around, or can be worked at in odd moments.

In hand embroidery there are a great many stitches that have been evolved over the generations. Some of these are very simple in themselves and are quickly learned. Others are slightly more complicated and need to be executed with great precision to get the desired effect. But this is merely a matter of practice. It is often in the combination of quite simple stitches that the greatest effect is achieved.

Though the sewing machine is now much used for embroidery it can only achieve certain effects. It does not set out to copy hand embroidery—rather it creates an extra dimension. Skill in machine embroidery comes with time and practice. But once mastered it has the added advantage of being able to be executed far more quickly than an intricate piece of hand embroidery.

EMBROIDERY EQUIPMENT

The tools you will need for hand embroidery are surprisingly few and inexpensive. They can all be stored in a very small space.

Here is all you will want for making any of the many forms of embroidery which are fully explained in this book:

Needles
Except for a very few stitches, such as diamond hemstitch, which are carried out in ordinary sewing cotton, sewing needles are not used. Instead, supply yourself with a packet each of CREWEL or EMBROIDERY NEEDLES (about the same size and shape as sewing needles, but with large eyes to take

the thicker thread used); WOOL NEEDLES (with blunted points, useful for wool embroidery or for doing canvas work); PUNCH NEEDLES (real giants these, with flattened blades, used for making the holes in the fabric in lace stitch, Turkish stitch, and punched embroidery generally).

These three kinds of needles may be bought inexpensively by the packet at most art-needlework shops.

Scissors

Your ordinary sewing scissors are rather too large and clumsy for most kinds of embroidery, especially where, as in scalloping and cutwork, part of the material has to be carefully cut away. So invest in a really good pair of slender, sharp-pointed embroidery scissors and keep them for embroidery purposes only.

A pair of curved manicure scissors is also a great help for cutting out neatly the points between scallops, but it is not essential.

Hoop Frames

Many kinds of embroidery are more easily and quickly worked if the material can be held well stretched, instead of having to stretch it over the fingers of one hand. Hoop frames consist of two rings of wood or metal, one of which fits closely within the other. The material is laid on the smaller hoop, then the larger one is pressed over it, holding the material stretched. It is useful to have two hoops, one of medium size and one small, but the medium one only will do very well. The best hoop to buy is one which has some kind of screw or tension arrangement to stop the material from slipping.

Stiletto

This is a piercing instrument set into a handle, and used for piercing the holes in *broderie anglaise*. You will get much better-shaped holes with its help than you can

ever achieve by using the points of your embroidery scissors to cut the material.

Tweezers

These are in no way essential, but they *are* a help in pulling out the threads of canvas after cross-stitch embroidery on ordinary material is done. They also handily draw out threads for hemstitching. Get the ordinary small toilet tweezers.

Corks

Keep a few corks of various sizes in your work-box. By putting the points of embroidery scissors, knitting needles, stilettos, and big punch and mattress needles into them when not in use you will save your fingers many an unexpected jab, and the lining of your work-box will wear far longer. (*See Fig. 1*)

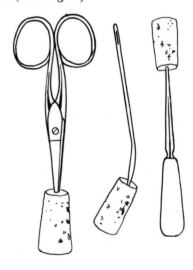

Fig. 1

Not a great deal to buy, is it, especially as everything except the needles will last for years? In addition to these permanent tools you will, of course, according to the work in hand, need from time to time supplies of suitable transfers (or a sheet of carbon paper for transferring your own designs), with material and threads suited to the particular job you are doing.

MATERIALS AND
WORKING THREADS

In the choice of materials for embroidery there is only one rule which should be observed—to have a successful piece of work the materials chosen must be suitable both for the use of the finished article as well as for the type of embroidery to be worked.

Today many very successful pieces of embroidery show the use of quite unconventional materials both as background cloth and also as threads. The embroiderer has enjoyed experimenting and the success or failure of the experiment is seen in the finished work.

So much depends on the type of work that is to be undertaken. Generally speaking, household linen, such as sheets, bedspreads and pillowslips, when embroidered, is kept for 'best' and will last a good while. By all means use good material for this. But to lock up money in expensive material for a quickly embroidered washable dress that will be out of date next year, or for some mat of the moment which can be made in an evening, would be rather wasteful of the cash available for your hobby.

For temporary embroideries of this sort a good quality of casement cloth, unbleached calico, glass-towelling, or some other sturdy cotton may be more suitable. And linen—certainly the most generally useful of embroidery fabrics—need not always be of the best quality. In fact, the thinner and cheaper qualities may be more suitable for some purposes.

On the other hand, *broderie anglaise,* cutwork and white work generally, are not quick to work, and they do wear extremely well—often longer than the fabric on which they are worked. So here it does pay to get the best material you can afford, so that it will wear and wash a very long time and repay the time and effort spent on it.

The same general argument applies to other embroidery materials—inexpensive material for quickly made or temporarily fashionable embroidery, and better fabrics for work which will not soon date or wear out. But material which is to be embroidered must be firm. Stretchy or springy material rarely makes a successful background for embroidery.

Canvas of different kinds is needed for some embroideries, such as cross stitch and tapestry, and the right type is obtainable at any good art-needlework shop. The same applies to the endless variety of silk, cotton, rayon and wool working threads. A good make of any of these is one which looks well, works well, wears well and is economical in use.

EMBROIDERY SHOULD BE
SPOTLESS

Embroidery is delicate, especially any form of white work, and as it is apt to be taken up at odd moments, rather than finished off completely in a short time, it is very easy for it to lose its charming first freshness before it is even finished. This is especially the case with any kind of white work.

For this reason do keep a bag made from washable material which will hold your work whenever you are not busy on it. In addition, if you do much white work or delicate embroidery for underwear, it pays to wear a clean overall or a sewing apron while embroidering, or to spread a clean white square of material on your lap. Try always to wash your hands just before starting work, even if they don't look grubby.

If, in spite of these precautions, your finished work isn't as spotless as you would like, turn to page 87 where you will find hints on how to clean, wash and iron embroidered items.

DESIGNS FOR EMBROIDERY

THERE are three ways of obtaining a design for embroidery. You can use a commercial transfer design, you can sketch out or draw your own design, or you can build up a design from the embroidery stitches as you work.

The first way, the use of a transfer, is obviously the simplest, but may be far less satisfactory if you have the wish to be creative. For a conventional piece of embroidery in cutwork, *broderie anglaise*, Jacobean and such like the ready drawn design is helpful. This type of work requires a stylised design which is probably much better drawn professionally. Transfers are also invaluable for those who find difficulty in making their own designs.

CHOOSING AND USING TRANSFERS

To get the best out of transfers there are certain points to remember. To begin with, from the very wide choice available, pick out a pattern which is suited to the fabric and to the type of embroidery you intend doing. Don't be caught by a charmingly pretty design intended for another kind of work.

Before you buy a transfer you must also decide whether you will have it printed in blue or yellow—the two colours available. Use blue whenever possible, as it is kinder to the eyes and obtainable in a larger range of designs than yellow. But yellow is necessary for all dark colours and for blue and mauve backgrounds, as on these shades a blue transfer will not show up.

Yellow is also best for dark greens or browns which have a decided yellow tinge; but it will not show too clearly on such shades, so work as far as possible by daylight.

The transfer must be correctly ironed on to your material if you are to have a clear outline for your work. A smooth padded surface, such as your ironing-board, is necessary, as any hollows, however slight, will prevent the transfer from marking properly. Lay your material smoothly on the ironing-board, right side upwards.

Cut away from the transfer any lettering, numbers, or parts of the design not wanted, and use these to make a sample stamping on an oddment of the same material. This is always advisable, because varying heating of the iron is required on different fabrics. If the transfer does not mark or only does so very faintly, the iron is too cool. If it marks blurred, heavy and thick, the iron is too hot—assuming in both cases that the material is a suitable one. An iron of the right heat gives a clear, firm outline. Uneven marking generally means an uneven surface under the material, or that the iron was allowed to cool noticeably between start and finish.

Arrange the transfer, face downwards, against the right side of the material, taking care that it is straight and in the right position. Pin it down, well away from the outlines, so that the iron need not go over the pins and leave marks of them on the fabric. Iron off with an iron of the tested heat. This applies to blue transfers. Lift a corner to see that the outline is good before removing the whole transfer.

As a rule yellow transfers require less heat to mark well. It is a good plan to put two thicknesses of newspaper over the transfer, to absorb part of the heat, when ironing it off. Press more slowly and evenly than for blue outlines. If the transfer does not mark well, press again, with only one thickness of newspaper under the iron.

Most smooth materials take a transfer very well, but there are a few fabrics which require special treatment.

Stamp organdie and voile on the WRONG side. The outline will show through clearly and not be so heavy as it would be on the right side. Thinner transparent materials, such as georgette, chiffon and net, should not be stamped at all. Instead, tack the transfer underneath the material, so that it shows through. Work through both transfer and fabric, afterwards tearing the paper away.

There are two methods for velvet and other pile materials. Pile will not take a transfer as it is, so the first plan is to press the material on the right side to flatten the nap. Let it cool, then stamp off the transfer. After embroidering, raise the flattened nap by steaming it from the wrong side.

If you do not want to flatten the nap on velvet or to mark a beautiful material with outlines, tack the transfer over the right side of the material, work through transfer and fabric, as for transparent materials, and afterwards tear away the transfer.

Sometimes you may want to remove a stamped outline ironed on by mistake. This can usually be done, though not from white and pastel satins. Different methods are successful, with different transfers and materials.

If the fabric is easily washable, first try washing and rubbing well with good soap flakes. If this does not succeed, or if laundering would hurt the material, rub the outlines hard with benzine. Methylated spirit works better in some cases.

DRAWING YOUR OWN DESIGN

Design for embroidery does not need to be elaborate. Many embroiderers who say they 'cannot draw a line' still manage to produce very charming designs which they can translate into embroidery. I have seen a delightful design built up from a memory of pebbles on a beach. The smooth, rounded

Plate 1

There are many variations for a design based on the circle which can be used in all kinds of embroidery. In the centre is shown a simply worked wool mitten for a child

but irregular look of the stones was easily translated into a design of uneven rounded shapes, which were worked in a variety of stitches in many subtle shades.

In the art schools students are taught to produce designs from sections of fruits such as a half pomegranate, a section of a marrow or an apple or orange. Nature has produced many fascinating arrangements of its seeds which lend themselves to pretty designs. These designs are not really difficult, though a little practice may be needed.

Autumn leaves gathered in the garden, on the common or in the woods can be arranged to suggest a design suitable for the border of a tea cloth, or an all-over pattern for a cushion. Their rough outlines are easily transferred to the material. But city dwellers too have their own sources of design if they will keep their eyes open. For instance, the unusual circular motifs seen on old manhole covers in many city pavements have often been used in embroidery. One of these in its entirety can become a design for a circular cushion or a round coffee table mat. But parts of the design can be used as a corner motif on a square or oblong such as in the four corners of a cloth, or cut in half and used across the ends of a runner or each side of a tea cosy.

These are merely a few suggestions that may lead the creative embroiderer on to working out exciting designs for herself.

You may see an illustration in a book which strikes you at the time as just the design which you might one day have use for. Trace it off and keep it by you until such time as you are going to embroider something on which it will look just right. Motifs for children's clothes can often be taken in this way from a child's favourite story book.

TO TRANSFER A DRAWN DESIGN TO THE MATERIAL

The best method of transferring your design to the material to be embroidered is by 'pouncing' it. First place the drawing on a soft pad of material and with a fine knitting needle prick holes all round the outlines. The pricked design is then placed in position over the material and secured with pins. (The best way is to lay the material on a drawing or pastry board with the pricked drawing fixed over it with drawing pins.) A fine powder (obtained for the purpose from art-needlework shops) is rubbed all over the holes. When the paper is removed the outlines are clearly shown in lines of tiny dots. These can then be 'fixed' by painting over them with water colour paint and a very fine brush.

Another method of transferring your own drawn design on to material is by using a special carbon paper. (Typing carbon should not be used as it is likely to smudge the material.) This carbon is available in black, blue or yellow (for dark fabrics or very delicate ones).

Place your material flat on the board as above, lay the carbon over it with your design on the top. Secure all three layers with drawing pins to prevent slipping. Carefully go over the outlines of the design with a knitting needle, embroidery stiletto or manicure orange stick, pressing evenly and rather hard, and you will find the design clearly marked on the material.

This method is also excellent if you want to use for a second time a transfer design which has been stamped off once. Trace its outlines through the carbon paper as many times as the design lasts.

BUILT-UP EMBROIDERY PATTERNS

The third way of producing embroidery designs is to draw the motifs directly on to the material and build them up with the stitchery. This is entirely suitable for very simple designs in which straight lines or circles are used.

The most charming patterns and small motifs can be contrived either direct on to the material in this way, or with such simple aids as coins, teacups, a ruler and a squared-paper exercise book.

Patterns which are evolved straight on to the material, without any drawing at all, are know as built-up patterns, because they are built up by one stitch being added to another till the desired effect is gained. At most, one or two pencil lines are ruled on the material to keep the first row of stitches straight.

Built-up patterns usually follow straight lines or circular forms. They are therefore specially suitable as dress trimmings or for straight-line work on rather small household items such as traycloths, tea serviettes, lunch mats, chairbacks and runners. Or the simpler of these designs may be used as borders to finish the edges of larger items embroidered from transfers.

You will find great interest in evolving your own built-up patterns by experimenting on a bit of fabric with one stitch and another till you get something that pleases you. Even using only three or four of the many stitches described in this book, literally hundreds of different patterns can be built up.

As a guide to pattern-making, a number of effective built-up designs are described below. Work them first, and you will be fired to invent others. Each is named so that you can identify it easily. (Instructions for making the stitches mentioned are in the following chapter.)

Clip-clop

This is so called because it somehow suggests horses' feet. A very simple border pattern using only one stitch—stroke stitch. Work blocks of touching stroke stitches $\frac{1}{4}$ inch apart, each block consisting of six horizontal stitches $\frac{1}{4}$ inch long. With thread of a second (preferably) darker colour, make a single diagonal stroke stitch in each space between the blocks. A variation would be to leave $\frac{1}{2}$ inch spaces (keeping the blocks the same size) and to add a second diagonal stitch at right angles to the first, thus forming a chevron in each space.

Climbing Roses

Running stitch, bullion and lazy-daisy stitches build up this flowery trellis pattern, ideal for a chairback, runner, guest towel, child's dress or pinafore. Run three lines of tacking across the material, the lines being 18 inches long and $\frac{3}{4}$ inch apart.

Pencil a dot on the middle line 1½ inches in from each end of the line; these are the points at which the diamonds begin and end. Put a dot along the middle line every 3 inches between. Along each outer line mark a point 3 inches in from each end of the line, and three more dots every 3 inches between. Rule pencil lines diagonally from upper to the next lower dots through the centre ones, and back the other way to form five diamonds.

Work the diamonds in running stitch— say blue—in six strands of stranded cotton, leaving spaces at each point and 'crossing' for the rosebuds. Work these in bullion stitch in two shades of one colour—say yellow. Finish the design by surrounding each rosebud at a point with four leaves, and each rosebud at a 'crossing' with eight leaves, four a side, in green lazy-daisy stitch.

Barbed Wire

This attractive border seems complicated, but consists only of three easy stitches. Work it between two parallel lines ½ inch apart. Inside each line, one end of each stitch touching it, work a row of herring-boning, making it less than ¼ inch in depth, so that a space is left in the centre, which you fill, between each herringbone cross, with a French knot. Resting along the guide lines and facing outwards from them, work the spikes of the 'barbed wire' in long-and-short buttonhole stitch, using long, medium, and short stitches in turn. The complete border should be 1¼ inches deep at its deepest point.

Cornerwise

This has many uses either for dress or household items. Place a ruler diagonally from corner to corner on a square or oblong of material, and mark a few inches near the corner along the ruler. This gives the line on which the centre of the five stems is based; just lightly indicate the two curved

ones each side in pencil. Work the stems in running stitch with stroke-stitch leaves. Put in near the top of the centre one, six satin-stitched dots clustered round a seventh of a different colour. To the top of each long curved stem add half a flower of lazy-daisy stitches (filled with two stroke stitches), also clustered round a satin-stitched oval. Put in the flowers by eye or with merely a pencil dot for the centre of each.

The next six designs described are not built up from straight lines, but are what might be called 'draw-round' designs. They are based on circles, because circles are so very easy to mark out. All you have to do is to place a cup, saucer or plate (according to the size of circle wanted) upside down on your material, hold it there firmly and draw round its edge with pencil or tailor's chalk. For quite small circles use copper coins or your thimble or cotton-reel. Half-circles are obtained by going half-round the circular object.

You will be surprised at the great variety of designs and patterns you can easily invent in this simple way, combining them, if you like, with straight-line effects.

Rainbow Wheel

Make a circle round a small saucer or bowl, and work it with running stitch. Inside the circle pencil round four pennies placed diamond-wise. At the centre of each circle work a French knot; from it, radiating outwards to the circle, stroke stitches to form a daisy. Darn the diamond shape between the daisies with open rows both ways. Rainbow wool may be used to give a pretty shaded effect to the daisies, or a rather thick thread all in one tone.

Forget-Me-Nots

Make a circle round a wineglass or small cup and work it in black outline stitch, leaving a space at the bottom. Fill this with tightly clustered French knots—about twenty-five of them—to give the impression of massed tiny blossoms. If all pale pinks and blues are used, the effect is of forget-me-nots.

Up-and-Down

Rule a straight line. Draw half round a penny, first on one side of the line and then on the other to form touching semi-circles. Work the curved lines in running stitch and the spokes of each half-wheel in stroke stitch. Overcast the half-wheels only half-way up the spokes. Use a dark colour for the spokes, a lighter one for the running and overcasting. A good border for children's clothes or household linen.

Eve's Apple

A useful spray for almost anything; it can be made in various sizes. A circle forms an apple. Radiate three leaf shapes round it on three sides. Work in rainbow or shaded silk entirely in chain stitch, coiling this round and round for the apple. Leave a tiny circular space unworked near one edge for the highlight. Work the leaves downwards from the tips, leaving a narrow centre space blank to represent the vein. (*See Fig. 2*)

Clover

An easy but very effective design for attaching a coloured hem to a white tray-cloth or tablecloth or to a child's frock. Join the hem to the white material with white long-and-short buttonhole stitch. At each corner and at intervals along the sides and ends, mark out trefoil shapes by pencilling

Fig. 2

partly round a halfpenny in three different touching positions. Work to match the join, with a feather stitch to cover the mitre at each corner.

Inner Circle

On a round or square mat, pencil round a saucer or cheese plate. Work the simple design by eye round this circle. Start with a tiny circle (round a button) in outline stitch, with a tinier round inside it filled with satin stitch, and surround it with French knots and lazy-daisy leaves. Running stitch, worked both along and across the circle, with more leaves and dots at intervals, completes the design. Mark the positions for the sprays beforehand, to get them even distances apart.

SIXTY-FOUR
USEFUL
STITCHES

THE first need if you want to do embroidery is to know your stitches—and to know them thoroughly. Never attempt to do a stitch, even of the simplest kind, with which you are unfamiliar, straight on to a piece of embroidery, or you run the risk of spoiling it. No one works a stitch as well as she might the first time she tries it, and you should always do a little practising first on an odd piece of the same or similar material, just to get your hand in.

The idea of the old-time samplers, which we now consider as curios, was to teach a little girl her stitches, and the first samplers were really 'samples' of different stitches. This is a good plan to follow today, at any rate with the dozen or so most used stitches. It gives you practice in forming the different stitches really well, and it serves as a reminder, for you can pack your sampler in your week-end suitcase, or take it about with you, when it would not be convenient to carry this large book for reference.

Linen is the best material for a sampler, and a good size, which will hold all the stitches you are likely to use often, is about 9 by 12 inches. To keep the edges from fraying, as linen so easily does, practise overcast cross stitch and various buttonhole stitches round the sides, while the centre can be devoted to rows or groups of such everyday stitches as outline, stem, chain, French knots, bullion, coral and feather stitches, and the simple hemstitches. Linen is suggested for this sampler, rather than a cheaper material, because it has threads which will pull, and so hemstitching can be worked on it as well as surface stitches.

If you haven't done much embroidery, don't attempt to fill your sampler all at once, for learning so many stitches too quickly will only muddle you. Practise two or three first, then do a piece of embroidery, using these two or three. Practise another, use this as well in your next piece of work and so go on gradually, always trying a new stitch first on your sampler and then using it on an actual piece of work. In this way you will learn a large number of stitches gradually and thoroughly.

Perhaps you will never learn all the sixty-four stitches described in this chapter. If you do, you will be able to work practically any type of embroidery you are likely to want to do—certainly all the types which are fully described here. Even if you master only twenty or thirty of them, you will be able to embroider a very wide variety of things for your home, and to decorate your own and your children's clothes.

If you use linen in a pretty shade for your sampler, and work your stitches in varying colours which harmonise or contrast with the background, the sampler will be ornamental as well as useful. Leave a space at the bottom where you can add your name and the dates of beginning and ending the sampler (these will give you practice in embroidering lettering and numbers). Then perhaps in years to come your grandchildren will frame your 'practice piece' as a treasured example of the beautiful work done at the present time.

By the way, when writing or reading about stitches, confusion often arises from the fact that many stitches have two, three, or even four different names, and that often any particular person only knows one of these names and her neighbour may only know another of them. Again, the same name may be applied by different people to two quite distinct stitches. All this often makes it difficult to identify a stitch that may have been read about or mentioned by someone else.

To prevent muddles of this kind as far as possible, in describing the stitches which follow I have mentioned their alternative names whenever I know them. Stitches are also given, in the index at the end of this book, by each of their alternative names, as well as by the one heading the description. So if you want a particular stitch and cannot find its name as one of the sixty-four titles in this section, just look it up in the index, and you are almost sure to find it.

One or two embroidery stitches mainly used for dress purposes, such as faggoting, are described in the Dressmaking Section.

For greater convenience, the stitches which follow are in alphabetical order.

BACK STITCH *(Fig. 3)*

This is an elementary and important

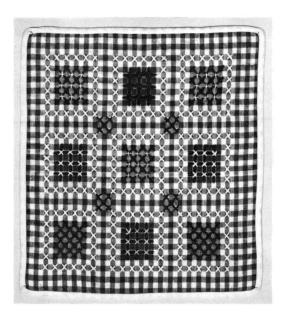

Plate 3

A simple cross stitch design can be worked with great effect on a checked material. The use of contrasting coloured threads helps to create the design

Plate 4

stitch both in embroidery and plain sewing. In embroidery it is used for outlines for which a definite, yet broken rather than smooth, look is required, and also for very indented outlines, as it goes easily round even sharp curves. It is a favourite stitch for quilting.

Fig. 3

To work Hold the work so that the outline to be back-stitched is across the fingers. Bring the needle out on to the line, not quite at the extreme end. Take a straight backward stitch along the line to the extreme end. Then take the needle under this stitch, on the wrong side and under as much more space as a second stitch the same length will occupy. Bring the needle up and take another back stitch from this point to the end of the first stitch. Continue similarly, alternating a short back stitch on the surface with a double-length one underneath. All the back stitches should connect neatly, be the same length, and be worked loosely enough not to pucker the material.

If short back stitches are worked in coarse thread, not quite touching each other, almost a beaded effect will result.

BARB STITCH

This is bold and handsome for borders and the veins of leaves. It is one of the buttonhole-stitch variations, enriched with a whipping stitch in a contrasting colour. It takes time to do, but it is not difficult.

To work Work a row of open or spaced buttonhole stitch (*see the entry for this stitch*) and then another row back to back with it, the spikes of both coinciding to form vertical bars. Whip over the double centre-line with

a second contrasting thread.

BARS *(Fig. 4)*

These embroidery 'bridges' thrown across a cut-away space are also known as brides. They are an important feature of most forms of cutwork (*see this heading*). Bars may be twisted, buttonholed, or needle-woven (darned) according to choice and the nature of the cutwork on which they appear.

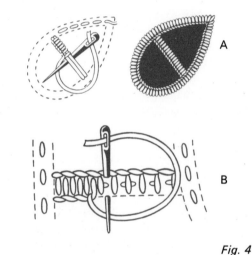

Fig. 4

Twisted Bars

To work these, from the main outline at the proper spot take a thread across the space to the other edge. Then return to the starting-point by overcasting loosely over the thrown thread with the remainder of the working thread, which forms itself into loose, spiral twists.

Buttonholed Bars

Take a thread twice across the space at the correct spot. Still with the same thread, closely buttonhole the double bar all across, placing the purl of the buttonhole along the edge that is to be cut away. (*See A in Fig. 4*) If the material is to be cut away from both sides of the bar, as sometimes happens, buttonhole with the purl along one edge first, leaving spaces between the stitches. Afterwards buttonhole again along the second edge, fitting this row of stitches into the spaces. (*See B in Fig. 4*)

Woven Bars

Work these just as for needleweaving (*see this heading*), but working on a made bar two or four threads thick instead of using the threads of the fabric as in needle-weaving.

N.B. When making any kind of bars, if you prefer to lay your threads across for these while padding, as suggested under Cutwork (*see this heading*), it is not necessary to use the same working thread for finishing the bars later on. Just fasten off the thread with which the bars are laid, and later take a new one to complete them.

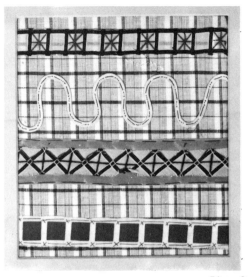

Plate 6

Interesting designs may be created by clever use of patterned materials as applied here with decorative stitches and a wavy couched line

Plate 5

BASKET FILLING STITCH

This is a very effective filling stitch, and gains its name because it suggests the weave of a basket. It is very useful for filling backgrounds of designs or monograms, for working baskets when these occur in flower designs, or as a dress or household linen border. When used as a border, the upright lines may be in a different colour from the horizontal ones.

To work Work short horizontal stroke or tacking stitches in pairs and in rows, leaving spaces between them rather shorter than their own length. Afterwards fill the spaces with pairs of vertical stitches the same

An appliqué of plain fabric on a checked gingham background may be further decorated with a double cross stitch pattern

length and distance apart. This stitch may also be worked in squares of four stitches.

BEADING

Either for home decoration or dress purposes, outline designs are often filled in with beads or sequins sewn over the outlines or filling the spaces or both. There are several variations of beading stitch: two are given here.

To work (*Method 1*) Bring the needle through from the wrong side, threaded with No. 50 cotton matching the fabric. Pick up a bead, then take a back stitch to secure it in place. This method is slow but very secure, as if a thread breaks in wear only one bead is lost.

(*Method 2*) Have two needles threaded with No. 50 cotton. One should be a special beading needle, as these are fine enough to go through very small holes in beads, yet long enough to carry a number at once. Bring up the needle from the wrong side, string on it enough beads to fill a short line or part of a long one, and slide them down to the end of the cotton. Stick the needle into the material so that the beads cannot slip off. Then with the second needle couch down the strung beads by taking a tiny bar stitch between every two beads over the cotton holding them. At the end of the line release any surplus beads, and fasten off the first or holding thread, as well as the couching one. Couching is the best way to apply bugle beads.

BLANKET STITCH *(Fig. 5)*

This name is often wrongly given to any form of open buttonhole stitch, but really it belongs to a diagonal type worked in groups of three stitches, which was originally used for blanket edges.

To work Fold and tack a hem on thin material. On woollens, especially if they are at all thick, turn only a single fold or work to the cut edge. Work as for buttonhole stitch, but take the first three stitches all into the same hole at their inner end. This

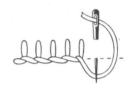

Fig. 5

means that two of them will be diagonal and only the centre one upright, the three forming a triangle with a line down its centre. Work all along in the same way in groups of three stitches, the end of each triangle touching the beginning of the next.

The illustration shows a conventional open buttonhole or blanket stitch.

BLANKET STITCH—LIGHTNING

As its name implies, this is a very quick method of doing a simplified form of blanket stitch, and was invented by a clever needlewoman.

To work Have a double thread in the needle. Make an ordinary open buttonhole stitch, but keep only one half of the thread under the needle, the other above it, and pull up. Continue in the same way, always passing the needle between the two thicknesses of the thread.

BRAID STITCH

This stitch has many uses both in dress or household embroidery, making charming borders or hem finishes.

To work Tack or rule two guide lines ¼ inch apart. Bring the needle up from the wrong side on the lower line and loop the thread, with the thread continuing under the loop. Take a straight downward stitch through the loop and pull up the thread, a little loosely, before repeating all along the two lines.

BRANCH STITCH

Also known as branching loop stitch. This is very effective for leaves consisting of a number of leaflets, and is, too, a very pleasing decorative stitch for children's frocks and underwear. It looks specially well as a trimming between tucks, and in modern copies of old-English crewel-work it is used for the veining of large leaves.

To work This stitch consists of single lazy-daisy stitches worked alternately on each side of a central line, which you form as you go along by working a back stitch to connect each loop with the next. If preferred, the back stitch may be separately worked in a deeper or contrasting colour. Avoid getting the loops too tight.

BULLION STITCH *(Fig. 6)*

Sometimes called long French knots, from the similarity in working of the two stitches; bullion stitch is used where an elongated French-knot effect is wanted. Grouped, in fact wrapped, closely round each other, several bullion stitches make an effective small raised rosebud, and are much used in this way in Italian coloured embroidery on linen. If several stitches are placed radiating outwards from a French-knot centre, a daisy-like flower in relief is easily made.

To work Bring the thread up from the

wrong side at one end of the line or space to be covered, picking up a stitch in the

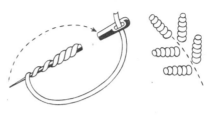

Fig. 6

material from this point the same length as the knot is to be, or picking up the entire outline. Do not pull the needle right through, but leave half of it in the fabric. Wind the thread round the exposed part of the needle from six to twelve times, according to the length of stitch required. Carefully hold down these twists with the left thumb and pull the needle through them all. As soon as it is clear, lay the twists on the spot they are to cover, still holding them down, and put the needle through to the wrong side close to the end of the twists. Bring it up again in position to begin the next stitch.

BUTTONHOLE CHAIN

This arrangement of buttonhole stitch is very useful for filling either backgrounds or part of a design, as it covers spaces quickly and not too heavily with a squared chain pattern. It is often used for filling scrolls in Venetian embroidery.

To work Make a line of ordinary open buttonhole stitch (*see this heading*). Work a second line into its purl edge, taking the needle *inside* the purl edge for each stitch, not through it. Work each new row into the previous one till the space is filled, keeping the upright stitches as much in line as possible.

BUTTONHOLE STEM STITCH

This is a striking variation of buttonhole stitch useful for bold stems, veinings of leaves or as a border on children's clothes.

To work To keep the stitch perfectly even, rule two parallel lines ½ inch to ¾ inch apart. Rule a third line down the centre. Make a line of open buttonhole stitches but set them on a slant, well spaced out, outwards from this centre line, with their purl edge along one of the outer lines. Work a second row on the other side, with its spikes meeting those of the first in the centre. When buttonhole stem stitch is used as a border, it gains in effectiveness if the spikes are more widely spaced, and a French-knot is placed between every two.

BUTTONHOLE STITCH (Fig. 7)

This, with its many variations, is one of the most important stitches in embroidery. In fact, whole pieces of work are often carried out entirely in this stitch, especially in cutwork. It is also very important in *broderie anglaise*, appliqué, and Hardanger, where it finishes cut edges firmly and prettily. Many small flowers in outline embroidery are quickly worked in open buttonhole stitch. It also, alone or with other stitches, makes innumerable pretty borders for dress purposes.

The open variety of buttonhole stitch, in which the stitches are well separated, is sometimes referred to as blanket stitch (*see this heading*). Actually blanket stitch is simply one variety of open buttonhole stitch—the kind used to edge blankets.

Every type of buttonhole stitch is best worked with a twisted thread.

To work If working over a hem, tack or crease this in place first. The best width for the hem is ¼ inch wide as a rule. Fasten the working thread inside the hem, where it

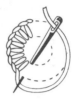

Fig. 7

will not show; then bring it up to the right side on the hem edge at the left-hand end of the hem. To start, make a straight upright stitch the width of the hem. Put the needle through to the wrong side at the end of this stitch, bringing it up again on the hem fold, where it originally came through. Make a second upright stitch, this time downwards towards the hem fold, ¼ inch or so from the first, holding the thread down with the left thumb so that it is *under* the needle. Pull up the thread, and it will form a bar along the hem edge, known as the purl—continuous, yet starting afresh with every stitch. This purl is the distinguishing mark of every type of buttonhole stitch.

Continue to take upright stitches ¼ inch apart all along, always keeping the thread under the needle. When turning a corner, make a diagonal stitch going, at its inner end, into the same hole as the last upright stitch, and take the first upright stitch on the new line also into this hole; this gives a symmetrical effect.

Sometimes in buttonhole stitch the stitches are worked close enough to touch. (*See Scalloping.*)

BUTTONHOLE STITCH—CLOSED
(Fig. 8)

This is a good edging stitch where a thick thread is used; it can be used instead of blanket stitch. The stitches are made in pairs forming triangles.

A cross-stitch motif worked as a border in three colours of stranded cotton on a single weave canvas where the threads are easily counted. (See plate 15 for full view of this tray cloth)

Plate 7

To work Bring the thread through at (A), insert the needle at (B) and with the thread under the needle, bring it through at (C).

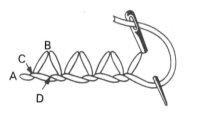

Fig. 8

Insert the needle again at (B) and bring it through at (D). Continue in this way keeping the stitches evenly spaced and well slanted to form the triangles.

BUTTONHOLE STITCH— LONG-AND-SHORT

This must not be confused with long-and-short satin stitch. Long-and-short buttonhole stitch is a simple and popular edge finish suitable for almost any piece of work. It should be boldly worked with a thick thread.

To work Make narrowly spaced buttonhole stitches which are alternately long and short. A bolder version of the stitch uses spikes of three heights, either going up from short to tall and then starting again with the short, or gradually descending from the tall through medium to short. The groups of graduated stitches may be continuous or with a noticeable space between each.

BUTTONHOLE STITCH—OPEN

This quickly worked and boldly decorative version of buttonholing is an effective way of working large stems rapidly. It also forms an attractive simple border for children's frocks or round the hems of such household embroidery as pyjama cases, runners and traycloths.

To work Rule parallel lines ½ inch apart for regularity. Along one line work buttonhole stitch, making the prongs ⅜ inch long and widely spaced, as shown in Fig. 5. Then down the other ruled line buttonhole similarly, arranging the prongs of the stitches to alternate with, and somewhat overlap, those of the first row.

BUTTONHOLE STITCH— UNDERLAID

This is a most effective edging when it is necessary to have a buttonholed edge, and yet something more solid than open buttonhole and with more variety of colour than close buttonhole, is wanted. It is useful both for general embroidery and for dress hems and edges, and specially good for cardigans.

To work Buttonhole with open stitches about ¼ inch apart. (*See Buttonhole Stitch.*) If several colours are to be underlaid, make the stitches rather deep. Use the principal colour in your embroidery for the button-holing. Then run underneath the stitches, but without penetrating the material, a thread of each of the other colours used in the work. Or, if a two-colour effect is preferred, underlay several threads of the same colour. The threads must lie side by side, flatly filling the space under the upright stitches.

To avoid catching the needle in the material when underlaying, it is a good plan to use a blunt rug needle or a fine bodkin.

CHAIN STITCH *(Fig. 9)*

For bold outlining or for filling the double outline of stems quickly and effectively, this stitch is excellent. It is also a good padding stitch to use under scalloping or satin stitch. Remember when buying working threads for a piece of work using chain stitch that it is rather extravagant of thread.

Fig. 9

To work Work downwards or towards yourself. Bring the needle up from the wrong side at the top of the line or design. Put the needle in close to where it came up, holding the thread down under the needle with the left thumb to form a loop. Pull up the thread. Now insert the needle inside the

loop, bringing it out again a little lower down the line. Pull up the thread to form a small loop as before; this gives the series of links from which the stitch is named.

Work chain stitch a little loosely or it will pucker the material. Keep the loops of even size.

CHAIN STITCH—TWISTED *(Fig. 10)*

This variation of chain stitch is more striking and elaborate. Use it for decorating hems of household embroidered pieces or as a dress decoration.

Fig. 10

To work As for ordinary chain stitch, with this difference. Instead of starting each stitch (after the first) within the loop already formed, place the needle to the left of the last loop. It may also be worked much more closely together, so that the links do not show up separately, and the effect is of a rope rather than a chain.

It is then called *Rope Chain Stitch.*

CORAL STITCH *(Fig. 11)*

This is also often known by the apt name of snail trail. It is effective for outlines, particularly curved ones, when a rather noticeable knotted and broken-up look is wanted. This stitch gives a pretty impression of beads at intervals on a thread. It is also much used in Teneriffe embroidery.

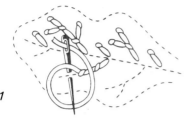

Fig. 11

To work Bring the thread up from the wrong side at the right-hand end of the line. Make a small slanting stitch, pointing forward and downward, a little farther along the line. The stitch should, as it were, pick up the line and a few threads each side of it on a decided slant. Take care that the thread goes forward ABOVE the needle and backward to the eye UNDER it, keeping it so while the thread is pulled up into a knot.

CORD STITCH

When a fine but prominent and raised outline is needed, this stitch, also known as whipped running stitch, is very useful. It belongs specially to the various types of white embroidery, such as *broderie anglaise* and fillette or punched work, but is very effective, too, in coloured stitchery. It is also known as fine satin stitch or roll stitch.

To work First make the padding by covering the outline with closely set, small running stitches. (*See Dressmaking Section for Running Stitch.*) Then closely across the running stitches, entirely hiding them, work very short satin stitches.

COUCHING (Fig. 12)

This is one of the simplest and quickest of stitches, very useful for emphasising a hem, outlining a bold design, or covering the edges of appliqués. It consists in laying a thick thread or cord on the material and holding it down with bar stitches worked across it at intervals with a thinner thread. This may match or contrast with the laid thread. Two or more thicknesses of thread may be laid, to give additional breadth.

Fig. 12

To work Bring the laid thread, in a large-eyed needle, up from the wrong side at one edge of the line to be worked. Remove the needle and let the thread lie loose. With the working thread in a smaller needle, work very short bar stitches at right angles across the laid thread, holding the latter in position with the left thumb. The bar stitches should be regular distances apart, usually $\frac{1}{4}$ to $\frac{1}{2}$ inch. At the end re-thread the laid thread, take it down to the wrong side, and there fasten off both threads. If the laid thread is too thick to go through a needle, poke a hole for it with a stiletto at the beginning and end of the work. Make sure the laid thread is long enough to complete the section.

COUCHING—TWISTED

This gives a more striking outline than ordinary couching, and is a good way to introduce several colours. Twist two or three thin threads together into a cord and use this as the laid thread, couching it down as described above.

CROSS STITCH (Fig. 13)

One of the easiest and most popular of all embroidery stitches, it has given its name to one type of embroidery, carried out entirely in this stitch. It is also often combined with other stitches in simple coloured embroideries or worked in rows or groups of joined or detached stitches as a trimming. (*See Pls. 3–7 for samples of this work.*)

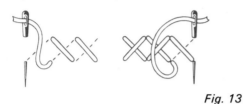

Fig. 13

To work Simply place two stroke stitches of equal length one over the other at right angles, so that a cross or multiplication sign (X) is formed. All cross stitches in a given piece of work should cross over the same way, and when a number close together are being worked, it is simpler to work one stroke of each cross all along the line, and then return crossing each stroke with a second. A line of touching cross stitches, worked X-wise, and enclosed in two rows of outline stitch in the same or a contrasting colour, makes a pretty decoration for babies' frocks.

CROSS STITCH—OVERCAST

Also known as criss-cross overcasting. This is a simple and very useful adaptation of cross stitch to a hem or doubled edges. It makes a bold and effective trimming for the joins of cushion covers or to finish the hems of runners and traycloths. When finely worked it is very pretty to hold the rolled edges of handkerchiefs or underwear. Tack down the hem or edges to be joined (with their raw edges folded inwards face to face) before starting the cross stitch.

To work Keep the right side of the material towards you, and start working from right to left. Make a row of slanting overcast stitches right over the hem or edge. Make them $\frac{1}{4}$ inch deep, or a little more (except on handkerchiefs and underwear), and keep the stitches an even distance apart. When the line is finished, return in the reverse direction, slanting the stitches the other way and working into the same holes as in the first row. Thus a series of cross stitches over the edge is formed.

Even working gives this stitch its effectiveness. A good way to ensure evenness is first to stitch the hem by machine, with fine cotton, loose tension, and a long stitch. Preferably use an extra large machine needle. This machine-stitching takes the place of tacking, and has the additional advantage of giving even spaces for the overcasting. Work the first slanting row through ALTERNATE machine stitches; when returning, use the stitches missed before. This makes the work very quick and regular. The machine-stitching may afterwards be pulled out, if liked; if left in, it will hardly show.

DARNING

In embroidery this quick stitch is simpler, and varies more than when used for mending. It consists of rows of running stitches, the in-and-out of the stitches alternating in each row. The term 'darning stitch' also sometimes denotes a single row of running stitches used to outline a design. Stitches do not run both ways, as they do in mending.

The chief use of darning in embroidery is to fill backgrounds or fairly large parts of the design. When a background is to be darned, this should be done before the design is embroidered, and the darning should be close enough for the rows to touch and strictly alternated. It may be either horizontal or vertical; the first is commoner. If petals or other parts of a design are first outlined and then filled with very widely spaced rows of darning, they will have more body and colour than if merely outlined, yet still look light and open.

To work Make rows of straight stitches with spaces between the same length as the stitches. In alternate rows go under where the previous row shows a surface stitch, and *vice versa*. Keep the lines very even. If a much-filled-up effect is wanted, pick up only a thread or two each time, leaving long stitches lying on the material. Thus almost continuous lines are formed with a minimum of thread and work.

EYELETS *(Fig. 14)*

These pierced and embroidered holes, round, oval, or leaf-shaped, form the basis of *broderie anglaise*, and are also much used in embroidering initials and monograms, and in Madeira and Venetian embroideries. They may also be used as slots through which cords or ribbons may be run.

Fig. 14

To work Use a firm material for good results. To make a round eyelet, pencil a small circle or use a transfer. Run closely round the outline with the working thread to give a firm foundation. With a stiletto pierce the circle inside the running stitches. Do not cut any material away, but overcast closely and tightly round the hole, over the running stitches, thus catching in the pierced ends of material. Round eyelets may be buttonhole-stitched instead of overcast, if preferred, and this method is usual in Venetian embroidery.

Sometimes several holes are placed touching each other. In this case the work will be less likely to tear in wear if the running stitches are taken along the lower edge of the first hole, crossing to the upper edge of the second, and so on, alternately. When the circles are to be thicker at the top than elsewhere, pad the top with several rows of running stitch, and overcast over them all.

Do not use a stiletto for oval or leaf-shaped eyelets, but cut down their centres with sharp, small scissors, catching in the cut edges tightly when overcasting.

FEATHER STITCH *(Fig. 15a)*

This is quick and pretty when a bordering effect is wanted, giving an open, rather lacy result. Use it to finish the hems or edges of embroidered articles, or work it inside a leaf outline when you want a natural veined look. It is also a favourite stitch for decorating in a simple way children's frocks and underwear.

Fig. 15a

To work The beauty of this stitch depends very much on its evenness. So if you are not used to it, a pencil line to work along will prove a help. Hold a line of feather-stitching upright, and you will see that it is really a simple form of buttonhole stitch, with the stitches below each other instead of alongside. Simply work a buttonhole stitch first to the left and then to the right, at different levels, placing your needle diagonally towards the guide line, which it touches at the bottom of the stitch. The thread must be always UNDER the needle.

FEATHER STITCH—DOUBLE AND TREBLE *(Figs. 15b and 15c)*

These are more elaborate variations of triangular feather stitch (*see below*), and are useful for making wider borders or as children's dress trimmings.

Fig. 15b   Fig. 15c

To work Work just as for triangular feather stitch but for the double variety take two stitches on each side before crossing over to the other, and place them so that their connecting lines slant, making the finished effect a series of right angles. Work treble feather stitch, shown in Fig. 15d, just as double, but with three stitches on each side instead of two. If ruling guide lines for these two varieties, place them $\frac{3}{8}$ inch apart for double and $\frac{1}{2}$ inch apart for treble.

FEATHER STITCH—TRIANGULAR *(Fig. 15d)*

This variation has a more formal look than plain feather stitch. It is particularly suited to use with embroideries with straight-line effects, and is the best type of feather stitch for crazy patchwork.

To work It must be very evenly placed, so use two pencil lines as guides, placing these lines about $\frac{1}{4}$ inch apart and parallel. Bring the needle up from the wrong side. Take a stitch exactly along the left-hand line, pointing towards you, and keeping the

thread UNDER the needle. Take the next

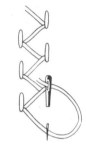

Fig. 15d

stitch in the same way down the right-hand line, making its top level with the bottom of the first stitch. Remember that, as in buttonhole stitch (of which feather stitch is really a variation), the thread must be kept always beneath the needle.

FLY STITCH *(Fig. 16)*

Many are the uses of this stitch as a simple hem or edge finish, or to build up borders in combination with other stitches. It may be considered as half a lazy-daisy stitch or as a form of open buttonhole stitch. Its beauty lies in its evenness, so guide lines should be pencilled or chalked until regularity in working becomes easy.

Fig. 16

To work Bring the needle up from the wrong side at the left-hand end of the work, and on the upper of the two ruled lines. Along the same line, a little distance farther to the right, insert the needle on a downward slant, so that it will emerge again to the left side at a point on the lower line midway between the two points on the upper line. Put the thread under the needle and keep it there while the stitch is drawn up into a V. Secure with a tiny downward bar stitch, as in lazy-daisy. Start the next V touching the first at its upper corner. Work loosely enough to keep the material unpuckered. Fly stitches can also be worked separately.

FRENCH KNOT *(Fig. 17)*

This is a favourite stitch with a great many uses. French knots, varying in number according to the size of the flower, make the best of all centres for small blossoms. Sometimes whole outline designs are carried out in French knots, giving a beaded effect. Clusters of small berries should be embroidered with one or more French knots for each berry. The stitch is also used in rows as a simple trimming for children's frocks, or to hold hems which are to be let down later, as it does not mark the material. When building up borders from simple stitches, French knots look well, worked inside ladder stitch, herringbone stitch, or the prongs of open buttonhole stitch.

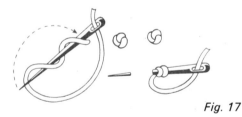

Fig. 17

To work Bring the needle up to the right side at the point where the knot is to be. Twist the thread once, twice, or three times (according to the size desired) round the needle, at the same time holding down the slack of the thread, above the part twisted. Push the needle through to the wrong side as close as possible to where it emerged, holding the thread down until it is all drawn through.

Should the knot be inclined to 'topple', it is a good plan to take a tiny extra stitch over the loose side of the knot after making it, thus: bring the needle up close to the loose side and put it down through the centre of the knot. The effect gained is particularly suitable for berries.

HEMSTITCH *(Fig. 18)*

This is the favourite of all drawn-thread stitches, and is extensively used as a fancy hem on linen embroideries, such as cutwork, Teneriffe drawn-thread work and Sicilian embroidery. It is also very popular as a simple trimming for linen dresses and coats.

Fig. 18

To work If it is being used as a hem, first turn in and tack the hem; then from the hem inwards draw consecutive horizontal threads to a width of $\frac{1}{8}$ or $\frac{3}{16}$ inch. If the hemstitching is to come in the interior of the fabric, where there is no hem, simply draw the thread at the right spot. When the hemstitching is not to go to an edge of fabric, but stops short at a given point, cut the threads at this point before pulling.

Hold the material with the wrong side towards you and work from left to right. With a fine thread in the needle, bring it through at the inner edge of the hem, hiding the knot in the hem. Take up on the needle four vertical strands in the drawn part; then insert it again diagonally behind the four strands, emerging in the edge of the hem. Thus the thread in order to pass behind the strands a second time will first pass in front of them, completely encircling them. Pull up the thread and the part round the strands will pull them tightly together.

Make a little stitch into the solid edge just beyond the four strands to hold the pulling thread firmly. Then put the needle behind the next four strands and repeat.

HEMSTITCH—BAR *(Fig. 18)*

This stitch is simply a more finished version of ordinary hemstitch, and is used for much the same purposes. It is also known as double hemstitch, owing to the double line of working.

To work Proceed exactly as for hemstitch. When the hemstitch is completed along the hem edge, turn the work and hemstitch the inner edge similarly, catching up just the same groups of four threads. These, instead of forming triangular shapes as in hemstitch, by the extra line of stitching are turned into straight narrow bars—hence the name.

HEMSTITCH—DIAMOND

This is a very attractive diamond-pattern hemstitch, used to adorn an area or surface, not a single row. It is quick and particularly easy to do on any material which is firm and has threads that draw readily. It makes delightful square, oblong, or wedge-shaped panels for decorating chairbacks, cushion covers, table linen, runners, or (in dress) for linen patch pockets, summer dresses or handbags.

Use a firm, close linen or tweed. The pattern is apt to drag on the soft, loosely woven makes.

To work (*Method 1*) This is the quickest in cases where the diamond pattern is to be lined, as for cushion covers and handbags, but the back is not neat enough to be used for items like table linen. Mark out the shape and size of the panel desired, and draw

threads both ways within this area, cutting them at the marking so that they do not pull away outside it. The number of consecutive threads drawn may vary according to the size of the pattern wanted, but always twice as many must be left as are drawn. A good average arrangement for linen is to draw six threads, leave twelve untouched, then draw six more and so on, both vertically and horizontally. This gives a check effect of small open squares alternating with bars of linen threads.

Do all the work on the WRONG side. The spaces form the pattern and the stitches are only to shape and hold the spaces firm. So work with ordinary sewing thread matching the material exactly, so that the stitches will be practically invisible.

Start by working a small open buttonhole stitch all round the edges of the panel. With the same continuous thread make a single buttonhole stitch round the nearest bar of linen, another over the next bar, and so on all along a row. Each stitch pulls the preceding one tight, narrowing the bars and so enlarging the spaces.

Reversing the work, take the thread along the buttonholed margin to a position where the next row of bars can be buttonholed, and continue so back and forth until the panel is finished. It puckers up rather, but will flatten out again when damped and well pressed. For a cushion or chairback, line the openwork with a contrasting shade.

(*Method 2*) Prepare and buttonhole the panel edges as already described. Working from the RIGHT side, whip over each bar twice, the second time catching up the first whipping thread and so centring the stitch nicely. Pull the thread very taut. Whip every row both vertically and horizontally.

HEMSTITCH—SINGLE CROSSING

This very pretty twisted hemstitch has many uses for decorating the hems of

Flower embroidery holds a special appeal — here an elegant rose design is worked in finely-shaded satin-stitch embroidery

Counted thread embroidery is another popular technique, and this fine example of traditional Assisi embroidery is worked from a guide chart

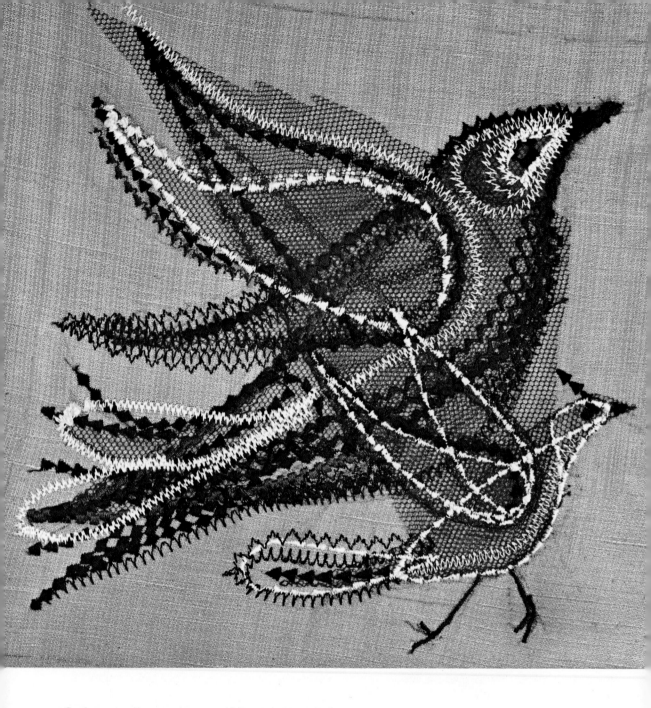

Swing-needle sewing machines have made possible a new form of speedy embroidery for busy women. This blue 'flying bird' has been created from scraps of net and zig-zag stitches

cloths and embroidered linen articles. It is simple and quickly finished.

To work Draw consecutive threads to a depth of $\frac{1}{4}$ inch. Bring the needle through from the wrong side at one end. Pass over, say, six vertical strands, but pick up the next six on the needle (pointing backwards) and double it backwards under not only these six but the other six missed previously. This gives the twisted or crossed look. Take the needle forward under the twisted strands, draw up the thread, and proceed to repeat the passing over and doubling backwards with the next six strands.

HERRINGBONE STITCH *(Fig. 19)*

This stitch has many uses. As an embroidery stitch it may be worked as a decorative line or can be used as a filling stitch. It is also used in dressmaking (*see page 102*). It is usually worked from left to right but may also be worked downwards.

To work Working from left to right along an imaginary double line bring the needle out on the lower line at the left side and insert on the upper line a little to the right,

Fig. 19

taking a small stitch to the left with the thread below the needle. Next, insert the needle on the lower line a little to the right and take a small stitch to the left with the thread above the needle. Continue in this way keeping the stitches evenly spaced and only picking up a small amount of material each time.

In Shadow Work (*see page 79*) herring-

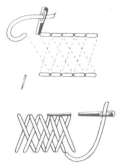

Figs. 20a and 20b

bone stitch must be worked very closely. It is then often referred to as double back stitch. (*See Figs. 20a and 20b.*)

HONEYCOMBING

This is one of the simplest of the various stitches used in smocking. Like all smocking stitches, it is worked on rows of gathers instead of on the usual flat surface. It is quickly made, and is a pretty stitch for trimming children's simple garments or for blouses or dresses of delicate material when in fashion.

To work Prepare the material in gathers as described in Smocking (*see page 80*). This stitch is worked on two rows at once, a stitch being taken alternately on the upper and lower rows. Bring up the needle from the wrong side through the left-most pleat of the second or lower row, starting with a very large knot that cannot possibly pull through. From the starting-point, make a back stitch which catches together the next pleat to the starting one, in the same row, and the starting one itself.

Insert the needle into the second of the two pleats (the right-hand one) behind the back stitch just made, and carry it up inside the pleat—so that it does not show on the right side—to the row immediately above.

Now, as before, back-stitch together this pleat and the one next to it to the right (actually the third pleat from the left, as this stitch was started on the second). This time put the needle downwards inside the third pleat, taking it down to the lower row.

Continue in this way back-stitching together two pleats alternately in the lower and upper rows, the second pleat in one stitch always becoming the first in the next (though higher or lower), so that a diamond pattern is formed.

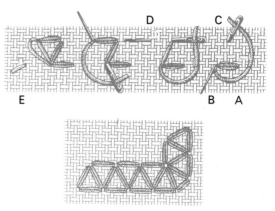

Figs. 21 and 22

LACE STITCH *(Figs. 21 and 22)*

Also known as three-sided stitch, punch stitch, Turkey stitch, double Turkish stitch, and Bermuda faggoting, this is a more elaborate form of Turkish stitch, giving a double instead of a single line of holes. It is much used as a background stitch (worked in continuous rows) in punch or fillette embroidery, and is also a very dainty way of joining lace to material in fine underwear—hence the name, lace stitch. Like Turkish stitch, it must be worked with a punch needle threaded with fine thread.

To work This is a double back stitch worked with a large needle which makes holes in the material, and worked in a

Plate 8

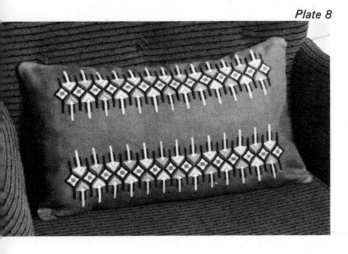

A crisp modern pattern worked entirely in satin stitch with a thick soft embroidery cotton on a coarse linen crash where the threads are easily counted

Plate 9

certain definite order to give a double line of holes in one operation.

The stitch is usually worked from right to left. If it is worked on linen or similar material the threads can be counted for each stitch so that the stitches are exactly regular. If it is worked on fine materials such as silks, lawn, organdie or other lingerie fabrics the points of the triangles must be gauged as accurately as possible.

Follow the working of the stitch as seen in Figs. 21 and 22; once you have mastered the sequence of the back stitches it is really very simple and can be quickly completed. To begin, bring your needle through slightly to the left of the end of the stitch at A and take two back stitches from A to B. Now take two stitches from A to C which is the apex of the triangle A, B, C. On the second of these stitches bring your needle through at D which is on the same line as C and take two stitches D to C. From D take two stitches D back to A to complete the three sides of the stitch. For the next stitch bring out your needle at E (which has taken the place of A in the first stitch) and continue the sequence as before. Pull all stitches firmly.

When joining lace in this way stitches taken into the upper row of holes go through both lace and material, those in the lower row through material only, just below the edge of the lace.

LADDER STITCH *(Fig. 23)*

This belongs to the very large buttonhole-stitch group. It is attractive as a simple border on household linen or children's clothes. For a more decorative effect a French knot may be added in the centre of each square. It also forms a very pretty way of joining lace to underwear, or contrasting borders to the main part of a traycloth, tablecloth or runner.

Owing to its pleasing square formation,

this stitch is a good one to serve as a basis on which wide borders composed of several combined stitches may be built up.

Fig. 23

To work Work as for ordinary open button-hole stitch but place the needle SLANTING instead of upright to form each stitch, and start that stitch from INSIDE the previous loop. When the thread is drawn up, a triangle is first formed, and this should be left rather loose, so that there is slack enough for the next stitch taken to draw it into a square.

LAZY-DAISY STITCH
(Fig. 24)

This is a very popular stitch for small flowers or leaves in designs embroidered in outline. It is specially suited to many-petalled, daisy-like flowers—hence its name, though it is also known as picot stitch or detached chain.

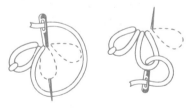

Fig. 24

To work Lazy-daisy is really a form of chain stitch in which each link in the chain is detached from the others and held down with a small extra stitch. (*Refer to Chain Stitch and Wheat-ear Stitch.*) Starting at the exact spot for the stitch bring the needle through from the wrong side. Hold down the thread with the left thumb, and put the needle back into the fabric where it came out, bringing it up to the right side again at the outer end of the loop. Keep the needle over the loop of thread just formed, and pull up the loop fairly loosely to cover the petal or leaf outline. Secure the loop down by making a little bar stitch across its outer end, which takes the needle back to the wrong side ready to start the next stitch.

LONG-AND-SHORT STITCH
(Fig. 25)

This variation of satin stitch has several uses. First, to cover large areas where satin stitches, if worked right across, would be too long and clumsy; secondly, to blend in several shades of one colour when shaded effects are wanted; thirdly, one thickness only of this stitch inside the outlines is effective when something heavier than an outline and lighter than a solid filling is wanted.

Long-and-short stitch is really satin stitch worked in several overlapping rows or layers.

Fig. 25

To work Work the first row of satin stitch from the outline, striking inwards to a suitable depth for this stitch. Keep the outline end of the stitches perfectly level, but on the inner side make them alternately short and long, or irregular in length. Then either in the same or a different shade work another row, also varying in length, but long where the first row is short, and *vice versa*, so that the two rows fit together without any obvious joining line. Work a third or more rows in the same way till the space is filled.

LOOSE LOOP STITCH
(See Fig. 26)

This little-known but very simple American stitch gives charming flowers, with looped daisy-like petals which are made in the hand, and afterwards attached to the material, at their centres only, with French knots or satin stitch. Standing away from the background like this, they give a bold and decorative effect with very little labour. They are usually made in wool.

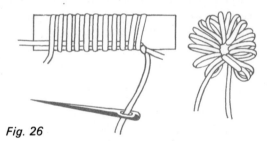

Fig. 26

To work Cut a slip of thin card 3 or 4 inches long, and the width that the length of the flower petal is to be—$\frac{1}{2}$ to $\frac{3}{4}$ inch is a convenient size. Thread a needle with 6 inches only of embroidery wool. With a separate piece of wool wind over and over the width of the card from twelve to twenty times, according to the size of the flower. Without letting the windings slip, pass the threaded needle through the end of the last loop, between the other loops and the card, and again through the end of the first loops. Slip the needle off the wool. Then, keeping the loops still strung on the short length of wool, slip them all off the card, and tie the ends of wool tightly together. The loops have now spread into a circular flower, which is sewn down as already described.

NEEDLEWEAVING (Fig. 27)

This · boldly handsome stitch is also known as Swedish darning stitch, though it figures in Italian as well as in Swedish embroideries. It is one of the most effective of the drawn-thread stitches, and makes a striking decoration worked in thick threads on crash or other coarse materials (tweed or linen in dress fabrics) for runners, cushions, chairbacks and dress accessories such as scarves and pochettes. Bright colours suit it best.

Besides being worked on the upright threads of a material when the horizontal ones have been pulled out, it may be worked on loose bars made with the needle and thread. The woven bars then serve as ornamental slots or casings through which bag strings or belts may be run.

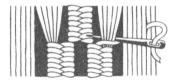

Fig. 27

To work Draw consecutive threads across the material to a depth of from ¼ inch to ¾ inch, according to weave and the thickness of the working thread. Leave a few strands of fabric untouched at one end, then at the top of the drawn strip bring your thread through to the right side. Avoid starting with a knot, securing it instead with a short end and a back stitch.

Pass the thread over a suitable number of threads—say four in a thick material—then under the next four. Turning back, pass over the group you have just gone under,

and under the first group. Continue darning back and forth in this way until the bar is filled. Fasten off by running the thread as invisibly as possible under the stitches of the bar. Wider bars may be made by darning twice over and under a larger number of strands before turning the needle.

OUTLINE STITCH

Perhaps the most popular of all outlining stitches. It is often confused with stem stitch (*see page 40*), but, although very similar, the position of the thread and stitches differs in the two.

To work Embroider upwards, starting at the bottom of the outline to be covered. Bring the needle through from the wrong side, and take a stitch, needle facing downwards, a little higher up. Keep the thread to the left of, and underneath the needle. Pull up the thread. Pick up a second stitch from above downwards, making the bottom of this come out just at the top of the first stitch. Continue thus till the line is covered.

RAMBLER ROSE STITCH

This offers a quick and easy way of making an informal-looking small rose in a design. Designs in which small flowers are simply indicated by a circle look well worked in this stitch. If roses so made are grouped in twos and threes, with a few lazy-daisy leaves, they make a charming scattered decoration for a little girl's dress or bonnet.

To work Start with a French knot in the flower colour. Then go closely round and round it in spiral formation with ordinary outline stitch (*see this heading*), until the rose is large enough or the circle on the design is filled. If an oval is to be embroidered instead of a circle, start with two French knots side by side and work round these. A pretty plan is to make the French knot and inner coils of outline stitch a deeper shade than those outside.

RUMANIAN STITCH *(Fig. 28)*

This is also known as Oriental stitch, but the two are actually the same stitch, worked with a slight difference. It is a good and quick filling, which takes less time and thread than satin stitch, and in its other form makes an attractive veining for leaves. It can also be used in building up decorative borders for trimming children's clothes.

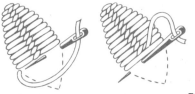

Fig. 28

To work Rule two parallel lines as guides. Bring the needle up from the wrong side on the upper line. Keeping the thread under the needle, take a short stitch upwards from the LOWER line, then a corresponding stitch downwards from the upper line, alternating in this way all along. The stitches may be worked close enough to touch or with narrow spaces between. When veining leaves take diagonal stitches instead of vertical ones.

SATIN STITCH *(Fig. 29)*

This is one of the half-dozen most useful embroidery stitches, and the most important of all filling stitches. So it should be practised until it can be worked to look as smooth and satiny as its name. It is used for filling where a solid, all-over effect is wanted, as in much flower embroidery. If

speed of working is wanted, combined with a more finished effect than is given by using only outline stitches, it is a good plan to work some of the smaller parts of a design in satin stitch. (*See plates 8 and 9.*)

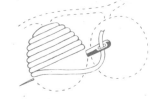

Fig. 29

To work Satin stitch is a series of stroke stitches lying side by side so closely that none of the fabric shows between them. Bring the needle through to the right side on one edge of the outline to be filled, and put it in again exactly opposite on the other edge of the outline, making a straight line of thread across the space. Bring the needle up again as close as possible to the start of the first stitch, put it in again beside the end of the first stitch, and so on till the space is filled.

The effect is often prettier if the stitch is worked slanting across the outline, instead of directly up and down and across. This plan is generally used for leaves and stems. If the space to be filled is so wide that the stitches would be very long and liable to catch in things, use the variation known as long-and-short stitch.

SATIN STITCH—PADDED

Sometimes important pieces of embroidery carried out in satin stitch look bolder and handsomer if a slightly raised effect can be given to the filling. In this case, before working the satin stitch, pad the design with chain stitch (*see page 26*), working just inside the outlines, and using the same thread. If the shape to be filled is a large one, more chain stitch may need to be worked inside the first line in order to fill the space.

When padding round shapes, chain stitch in circles, one within the other: do not work across and across the shape. If a rather flat padding only is needed, use a thinner thread than for the satin stitch, but keep it exactly the same colour.

SCALLOPING

This is almost the only embroidery stitch which will give such a firm finish to raw edges that no hem or other turning-in is necessary. It is actually a close, padded buttonhole stitch which, when used on edges, is called scalloping. Usually, but not always, the edge is shaped into a series of semicircles, either by marking half round a coin or with a scalloping transfer. Scalloping is a great feature of *broderie anglaise* and other forms of Cutwork (*see this heading*). Babies' flannels, too, are often finished along the edges in this way. It is best used on firm materials, such as linen, cotton and other fairly substantial fabrics.

To work Allow at least $\frac{3}{4}$ inch turnings on edges that are to be scalloped, placing the scallops that distance from the edge. Pad between the double outlines of the scallops with a line of chain stitch or with closely set running stitches—the chain stitch is much quicker. Then work close buttonhole stitch across the scallops, with the purled edge covering the outer edge of the curves.

When buttonholing is completed, with very sharp embroidery scissors cut away the turnings of material as close as possible to the buttonhole edge, taking great care not to cut the stitches.

SEED STITCH (*Fig. 30*)

This is also known as dot or mignonette

stitch, and is used when a broken filling is more effective than a solid one, giving a much lighter effect. Also, when surfaces or backgrounds are large, seed stitch can be worked much more quickly than satin stitch.

Fig. 30

To work Make very tiny stroke or running stitches at intervals all over the surface. They should lie in all directions to give variety and shading. If they are required to stand up rather more noticeably, make each stitch like a back stitch, but, of course, detached from its neighbours.

SPLIT STITCH (*Fig. 31*)

An extremely neat and close stitch for use when a fine outline is required. In appearance it is rather like a very slim version of chain stitch, but lies much flatter.

Fig. 31

To work Work upwards or away from you. Bring the needle up from the wrong side. A little distance higher up take a short stitch with the needle pointing towards you. As you pull the thread tight, let the needle pierce or split it, instead of passing to one side. As the thread must be thus divided, it should not be too fine; or two strands of stranded cotton may be used and the needle passed between them, giving an elongated chain stitch effect.

STEM STITCH *(Fig. 32)*

This very useful stitch for all kinds of outlines looks a good deal like outline stitch (*see this heading*), but is worked a little differently. Another name for it is crewel stitch. Strictly speaking, in stem stitch the stitches are overlapped more than in crewel stitch; but in practice the two are slightly different variants of the same stitch.

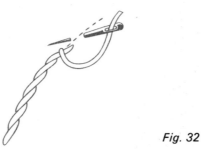

Fig. 32

To work Bring the needle through from the wrong side at the bottom of the outline, as working proceeds upwards. Work as for outline stitch, but keeping the thread to the RIGHT of the needle instead of to the left. Also, in true stem stitch each stitch should be started half-way down the previous one, whereas in crewel stitch it starts at the top of that just worked.

STROKE STITCH *(Fig. 33)*

Also known as *mille fleurs* (a thousand flowers) as it is so much used for clusters of many-petalled small flowers with a ray effect, such as daisies. This simplest of all stitches is also excellent for embroidering stars and for short, straight lines anywhere in a design. As it has only the single thickness of the thread, this should be a fairly thick one.

Fig. 33

To work Bring the needle up from the wrong side at the inner or centre end of the line to be covered (if a flower is being worked). Re-insert the needle at the other end of the line and bring it up again from the wrong side (in the same operation) at the start of the next stitch, unless this is too far away. Take care that each stitch exactly covers its transfer line, and is neither loose nor tight enough to pucker the fabric. Fig. 33 shows a large flower with radiating petals of stroke stitches.

TENT STITCH *(Fig. 34)*

This has a confusing number of names, being also known as *petit point*, needle-point, half-cross stitch, and tapestry stitch. Actually it is the best known of the many stitches used in canvas work or needlepoint, and many pieces of such work are carried out entirely in tent stitch.

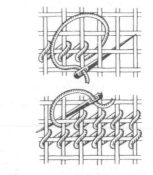

Fig. 34

To work The name half-cross stitch is an accurate working description. Simply make the first slanting half of a cross stitch (*see this heading*), working over either one or two threads of the canvas, according to the size of stitch desired. Work these slanting stitches closely. side by side, so that they cover the surface.

TENT STITCH—COUCHED

This variation of tent stitch is used in tapestry work when, owing to the large size of the canvas mesh or the comparative fineness of the working thread, tent stitch does not properly cover the surface.

To work Exactly as for tent stitch, but couching down with your stitches another thread, which lies under the stitches and pads them, giving richness and solidity to the result.

TURKISH STITCH

Sometimes known as Turkey stitch. This is a pierced stitch used in elaborate *broderie anglaise,* in punched work and to trim fine underwear.

To work The very large, flat-bladed needle known as a punch needle is essential for this stitch, to make the holes giving the open-work effect.

Work with a very fine thread such as No. 80 cotton or a single strand of stranded cotton, tying the fine thread into the giant eye. Work downwards. Pick up a short stitch at the top of the line to be worked, then make another stitch over it, pulling up the working thread very firmly so that a small hole is made in the material. This second time bring out the needle lower down, ready to begin the next stitch. In fact, what you actually do is to work a line of back stitches with a very large needle, but working over each stitch twice instead of once.

At this stage the work is very disappointing. The holes are shapeless and look a muddle. But put a very fine thread this time

into a fine needle, and go along one side of the line of holes, overcasting each hole twice and pulling the thread really tight each time. Overcast in the backstitching thread when doing this, so that it is not visible across the holes.

Return along the other side of the line, again overcasting twice into each hole, and you will have a very delicate pierced effect. It looks something like hemstitching, but as it is not dependent on the threads of the material, it has the advantage that it will go round any curve.

TWISTED FEATHER CHAIN *(Fig. 35)*

An attractive border or hem finish either for household furnishings or for clothes. It is somewhat like branch stitch, and is a combination of feather stitch and chain stitch.

Fig. 35

To work Mark two parallel pencilled or chalked lines, ½ inch apart, and work the stitch inside them. Work a chain stitch alternately each side, as in feather stitch, and link the chain stitches by short central stitches. The diagram shows the needle making a chain stitch, which is worked inwards towards the centre, and getting into position for the next slanting central stitch. In branch stitch the chain loops are worked OUTWARDS; in twisted feather chain from the line inwards to the centre.

VILNA STITCH

This is really more a narrow border than a stitch, as its other name, triple border, suggests. It is a dainty and quickly worked simple decoration specially suited for children's clothes. If neatly begun and finished off it is reversible and so particularly useful for 'both side' items such as scarves, handkerchiefs, and traycloths.

To work Make a line of running stitches (*see page 102*) with the stitches equal in length to the spaces between them. Run a similar line each side of the first one and quite close to it, making the stitches in these two lines alternate with those in the first one.

WAVE STITCH

This is a simple and particularly graceful variant of running stitch, using two separate threads, which look prettiest when of different colours. It makes an important-looking border for household linen or curtains; if worked all in one colour it gives a realistic effect of waves in a seascape or ship design. It is also useful for holding tucks on a child's frock in a decorative way, yet so that they are easily let out when the child grows.

To work Make a row of running stitches with the distance between the stitches about twice as great as the length of the stitches, which should be short. With a second thread, preferably contrasting with the first,

This easily planned design is ideal for a cushion as it faces both ways. It is quickly worked in six strands of embroidery cotton in easy stitches including chain and cable chain, stroke, running, satin and wheat-ear stitches

Plate 10

take the needle under each running stitch but without catching the material. Go under the stitches alternately from the upper and the under side and leave the thread loose enough to give the wave effect.

WHEAT-EAR STITCH (Fig. 36)

Very decorative as a rather elaborate veining for large petals or leaves, or for working ears of corn where they occur in a design. It also makes an effective border for children's clothes or furnishing accessories. It is much used in white embroidery and the more complicated kinds of cutwork. (*See Plate 10.*)

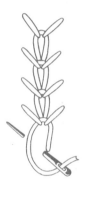

Fig. 36

To work This is a simple combination of lazy-daisy and buttonhole stitch, the two being worked alternately. First make a lazy-daisy stitch on the outline to be worked. After taking the needle through to the wrong side to complete the holding stitch of this, bring it up again ¼ inch to the left of the lazy-daisy. Put it in again ¼ inch to the right, and bring it out at the bottom of the lazy-daisy (the end with the holding-down stitch). By keeping the thread under the needle while drawing through, the button-hole loop is formed, giving the grain of corn its ears. Work another lazy-daisy immediately below, touching the loop, and so on. (*See Lazy-Daisy and Buttonhole Stitches.*)

WHEELS—DARNED (Fig. 37)

These, with their slightly more elaborate variation, overcast wheels, are used in many kinds of embroidery to fill effectively either round or square spaces. As they can vary very widely in size, simply by making the spokes longer or shorter, their uses are many.

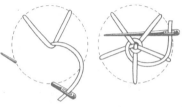

Fig. 37

To work Make a large cross stitch by placing a horizontal stitch over a vertical one. Work over these two diagonal stitches, so that you now have eight spokes of a wheel. With the same or a contrasting thread, start at the centre where the long stitches intersect, and darn round and round, over one spoke, and under the next alternately. The darning may be continued to only half the depth of the spokes or right up to their ends, according to the solidity of the effect wanted. The number of spokes may be varied as shown in Fig. 37.

WHEELS—OVERCAST

These have the same uses and much the same appearance as darned wheels (ABOVE), but take a little longer to work and have a more definitely wheel-like appearance. This stitch is a realistic way of working spiders' webs also, and these are sometimes worked on alternate squares of a soft canvas checked in two colours or on large-checked gingham.

To work Make the spokes just as for darned

Plate 11

A Christmas panel for a child's room worked in very simple stitches

wheels, but instead of darning them, go under two spokes (between spoke and material) and then overcast BACK over the last spoke. Continue round and round till the spokes are half or completely filled. For borders, half-wheels, with five spokes instead of eight, give pretty results.

WHIPPED RUNNING STITCH *(Fig. 38)*

Also known as twisted running stitch. This makes an attractive alternative to outline stitch for stems and tendrils or to finish hems on embroidered articles or children's clothes. It is very quickly worked, preferably in two well-contrasted colours.

To work First make a row of running stitches making the distance between the

stitches about twice as great as the length of the stitches. Then, with the same or a

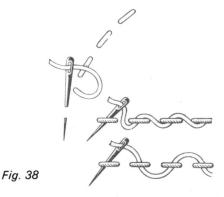

Fig. 38

second colour, pick up each running stitch by passing the needle between the stitch and the material. Always insert the needle from the same side of the running stitch, and leave the thread somewhat loose.

MANY KINDS
OF
EMBROIDERY

FROM the embroidery stitches in the fore-going pages you can now proceed to work many different embroidery techniques. You will find that many of the stitches figure in several kinds of embroidery and it is for this reason that they have been grouped in one chapter for reference, rather than given with any particular type of embroidery.

The only stitches which are given in this section, rather than in the previous chapter, are a few special ones which belong to the particular kind of embroidery and are in less general use.

APPLIQUE

No other form of embroidery is quite so boldly decorative as appliqué, which is the applying of one material, cut out to form shapes or parts of a scene, to another serving a background. As most of the colour effect is gained by the use of the super-imposed materials, stitchery is only used to hold these together and to embellish them and give added texture. Consequently appliqué is a quick form of embroidery for the area decorated.

It has so many variations and so much range of material and stitchery that it can be used on anything of fairly large size, such as bedspreads, pyjama cases, cushion covers, fire-screens, runners, lunch-mats, pram and cot covers, laundry and shoe bags. Unless the colours of all the applied materials used are fast, it is not so suitable for things which are continually washed, such as table linen. It has a limited use for dress trimmings, but is too bold for many dress purposes. It is particularly suitable for a decorative wall panel which can after-wards be framed (*see plate 12*).

There is hardly any fairly firm material which is not suited to appliqué, both for the background and the applied pieces. Linen, firm cottons and shantung silk are all good, while non-fray fabrics such as P.V.C. and felt have the great advantage that the edges

The Three Kings are a colourful subject for a wall panel in felt appliqué with embroidered detail

Appliqué may also be very successfully executed on the machine (*see page 72*).

Embroidered Applique

In this method the applied portions are held down to the background with embroidery stitches, and the interiors of the appliqués have their details embroidered. For instance, veins are worked on to leaves, stamens on to flowers.

There is a choice of two plans when doing embroidered appliqué. In the first the applied pieces are cut out roughly, buttonhole-stitched in place, and then their edges are cut away close to the purl of the buttonhole stitch, as in scalloping; in the second and more popular, the applied pieces are cut out exact to their outlines, which are then covered and prevented from fraying with buttonhole or some other stitch.

The first method is preferable for appliqués of material which frays very easily. Otherwise the second is better and easier. The first method requires two copies of the design. If a transfer is used one is needed for ironing on the background, the other for cutting up and stamping on the various appliqué materials. By the second method only one is needed, as the transfer may be first stamped off on the background and then the appliqué portions of the transfer may be cut out and used as paper patterns for cutting out appliqués (except where there are details to embroider on these).

Buttonhole stitch, worked closely, must be used to fasten down appliqués cut by the first method, as no other stitch has an edge that will allow the material to be cut away right up to it without fraying further. Work this outwards from the appliqué, so that the purl edge lies exactly along the join of the appliqué to the background.

In the second method, by which the appliqués are cut out to their exact shape from the start, lay each, as cut, precisely

need not be completely covered, thus saving much work.

The methods of working appliqué may be conveniently described under three headings, according to the stitchery used.

over its corresponding outline on the background, and pin or tack it down, taking great care that it lies perfectly flat and unwrinkled. To help in getting this result, it is a good plan with a large appliqué to put a thin coating of rather dry adhesive paste over the centre of the background. It is better not to paste the appliqué itself, as this sometimes wrinkles it. Be careful not to paste anywhere near the edges of the appliqué portion on the background, as the paste would be stiff and hard later for the needle to go through.

If pins are used for fastening down P.V.C. appliqués, remember that they leave permanent holes in this fabric, so they should only be inserted near the edges, where the holes can be covered by the applying stitchery.

Use a twisted embroidery thread for the buttonholing, either matching the appliqué in colour, or preferably a shade or two darker. Close buttonholing is needed for all fabrics which fray but P.V.C. material and felt may be appliquéd down with a well-spaced stitch which is much more quickly worked. The open stitch also gives a lighter effect.

Couching is also good, and is much quicker to work than buttonholing, but see that the laid thread is really thick and broad enough to cover and protect the edges completely. Several thicknesses of a moderate thread, laid side by side, will give a better and flatter covering effect than a single very thick one. Embroidery wool used double is generally satisfactory. Eight-ply or rug wool are good laid threads for really bold appliqué.

In most designs there are lines and small details, both on the background and on the applied portions, which cannot be rendered in appliqué. Treat these as ordinary embroidery, and work them in suitable stitches.

In a composite design built up in appliqué tremendous interest can be given

Two little mats in broderie anglaise *combine eyelet embroidery with satin stitch and scalloping around the edges*

Plate 13

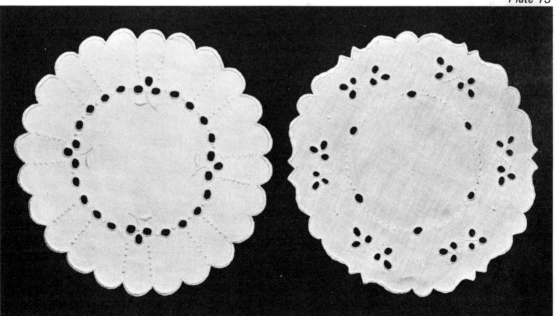

to the finished panel by the use of different textures of material. It may happen that parts of the design are two or three appliqués thick, a net or a transparent fabric being laid over a woollen or slub material. In this case the appliqués must be planned carefully before they are stitched down. Obviously the part of the design which is to be the focal point will be the last part of the appliqué to be stitched down, just as the background to the main design will be the first to be completed.

Chinese Applique

This is a special type of embroidered appliqué combined with a little simple cut-work. It is rather slow work, but is so particularly charming in colour and outline that it deserves to be better known and more used than it is. A neutral beige background is used, with the appliqué flowers and leaves in a number of bright shades (offering a good opportunity to use up scraps of material), worked with contrasting colours and outlined always with black.

The whole design is appliquéd (there are no embroidered parts on the background), and all embroidery is very fine, made with a single strand of stranded cotton. Fine linen is used for both background and appliqués.

Blind Applique

This is the name given to appliqué which is not embroidered (except in small details), but is secured to the background with slip-stitch or blind stitch (hence the name). Blind appliqué comes to us from the United States. It is suited to designs in plain materials which are so good in line and colouring that they need no added embroidery; also for those carried out wholly or partly in patterned materials, on which decorative stitches would be rather lost. It is particularly effective in cotton fabrics.

This is the simplest and quickest kind of appliqué, and so is excellent for very large pieces of work, such as wall hangings, bed-spreads, and cushions. To make it, cut out each appliqué piece with narrow turnings. Pin or tack the appliqué in position (keeping pins or tackings away from the edge). Slip-stitch down all round to the foundation, turning under the surplus edges with finger and thumb, or with the needle-point as you go along. Use sewing cotton matching the appliqué; afterwards press well.

BRODERIE ANGLAISE OR EYELET WORK (Pl. 13)

This is a very popular form of white embroidery which combines pierced work with outlined or solid surface stitches. Dress accessories, such as collar and cuff sets of linen or piqué, aprons and handkerchiefs may be embroidered in this way.

Broderie anglaise never goes out of fashion as a decoration for household linen—sheets, pillowslips, table linen, duchesse sets and so on—because it wears and washes better than almost any other form of embroidery. In fact, it often outlasts the material on which it is worked, and then may be sometimes saved and used as a trimming for something else.

The best materials for *broderie anglaise* are firm, closely woven ones—sheeting, linen, lawn and piqué. More skill is needed to work it successfully on flimsy fabrics.

Eyelets (fully described on page 29), either round, oval or leaf-shaped, are the characteristic feature of *broderie anglaise*. In fact, many designs are carried out entirely in eyelets, with perhaps the addition of a few stem-stitched stems and satin-stitched dots. Eyelets are simple in construction, but it takes practice to make them firm and true in shape, so that they will wash without losing their form. The beginner should practise making a few eyelets of each type on an odd

A classic garland of flowers in tent stitch on canvas

A minute petit-point landscape design

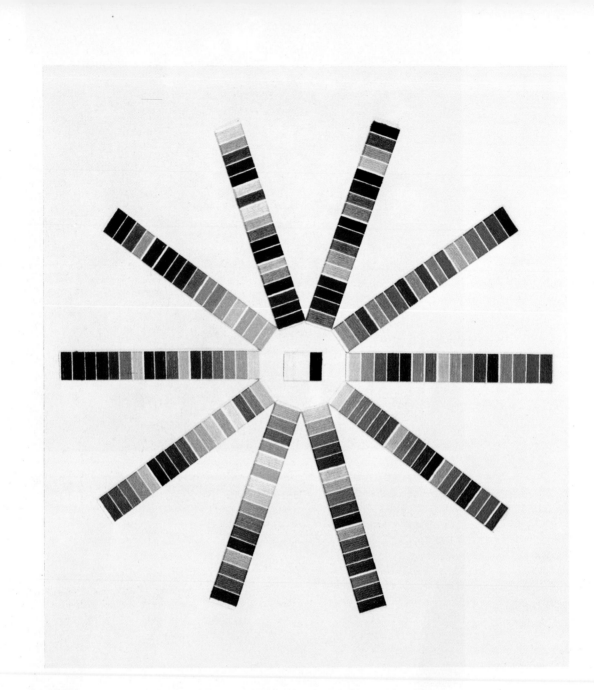

With a colour-range of wools like this, who wouldn't be encouraged to start embroidering. This is the colour choice offered in tapestry wools; there are many other delightfully subtle shades also to be chosen in embroidery silks

These pretty little flat pin cushions are worked in a variety of stitches for counted thread work including cross stitch and back stitch

Plate 14

piece of material before starting on a definite design.

It is easy to keep pricking the finger when making eyelets. This can be avoided if a small strip of coloured plastic is put under the work before it is held across the fingers of the left hand; green is the most restful colour for this strip.

In some *broderie anglaise* designs eyelets play only a minor part, and more or less solid white embroidery accounts for most of the design. The stitches used include satin stitch (generally well padded) and cord stitch (for stems and fine lines). Fine back-stitching may outline satin-stitched portions in elaborate work, and ladder stitch is occasionally used.

The edges of work adorned with *broderie anglaise* are mostly finished with scalloping, which goes most beautifully with this work. However, hemstitching is often more convenient for dress items and is much used.

As with all white work, *broderie anglaise*, especially the solid portions, is sometimes found rather trying to the eyes. In this case adopt the plan used by embroiderers in Madeira, whose work very much resembles *broderie anglaise*. They dip their working thread in a blue rinse before using it. The contrast of shade makes all the difference to the eyesight, and the blue tint disappears at the first washing.

Small bits of *broderie anglaise*, especially eyelets, are much used in working initials and monograms.

CROSS-STITCH EMBROIDERY
(Pls. 14 and 15)

Thanks to the great simplicity of its one and only stitch, and to the way in which it adapts itself to different materials and styles of design, this kind of embroidery never

49

loses its popularity. Almost any type of design may be translated into terms of cross stitch with good results. Consequently this work, in one form or another, may be used for most things a home needlewoman is likely to embroider, from a bedspread to a handkerchief.

Cross stitch should not be worked from a transfer as it is essentially a stitch for counted threads. It should therefore be worked ideally on a material with threads that can easily be counted such as canvas, scrim, linen or a flat plain tweed.

Cross-stitch designs are usually worked from charts. On these the motifs or design are clearly marked out on squared paper, each square representing a stitch. Depending on the weave of the material and the size of the stitch, each stitch is taken over the same number of threads each way. For a small stitch only two threads will be picked up each way, for a larger stitch, three or four threads may be picked up. But on a loosely woven material or where the threads of warp and weft are thick or coarse the smaller number of threads should be picked up for the cross stitch to give a neat and even result.

When the work is to be done on material on which threads cannot easily be counted it is still possible to work from a chart. In this case tack over the material some net or open canvas with mesh of a suitable size. The design is worked rather tightly over both net or canvas and the material beneath. When the embroidery is completed the net will not show. If canvas has been used it should be gently pulled away thread by thread leaving the perfectly regular cross stitches resting on the permanent ground.

Owing to the geometrical construction of the stitch, cross-stitch work really looks best if the design is rather formal and of a patterned and 'repeat' kind. (*Pl. 7, p. 25.*) However, it is often used for floral sprays, worked in several colours and even shaded in a fairly elaborate way. For these a colour chart, showing exactly where to place each shade, is often provided.

This bold design in cross stitch is all the more effective for being worked in four shades of the same colour

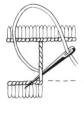
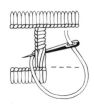
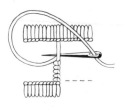

Fig. 39

Plate 15

Plate 16
A cutwork border worked in three colours of stranded cottons may be adapted for tray or trolley cloths, or place mats

Most canvas work and cross-stitch designs are interchangeable, as the working stitches are so similar. In fact, many embroidery designs of a fairly formal type can be turned into cross-stitch ones without much trouble. To do this, take a spare copy of the design or make a tracing of it on paper through a black carbon sheet. With a pencil fill in the design with crosses of suitable size, keeping them all the same size and in regular rows as far as possible. If the design is to be worked in several colours, mark the crosses with crayons of the correct shade.

When embroidering, use the cross-stitched paper as a chart, either putting the crosses in by eye, if the design is small and simple, or laying canvas over the material, as already described, and copying the chart on that.

Instead of forming the design, cross stitch may be used as its background, completely filling all the space not occupied by it. When it is thus used the design is of a geometrical type and is first outlined with back-stitching before the cross stitches are worked.

Cross stitch may also be used as a light filling for large monograms or parts of a small design which is outlined with some simple outline stitch.

Bright peasant colours are the most successful in cross-stitch embroidery; pastel tones are apt to give an insipid effect. Any sort of thread—wool, cotton or silk—may be used which accords with the type of material chosen for the background. It must be the right thickness to give substantial-looking crosses, neither spidery-looking nor so thick as to lose their shape.

Assisi work (*page* 65) is a special Italian type of cross stitch.

CUTWORK *(Pls. 16 and 17, Fig. 39)*

In many different forms of embroidery portions of the design or of the background are cut away, the cut edges being buttonholed to prevent fraying.

But what is generally known as cutwork by home embroiderers is a simple yet exquisitely pretty, lace-like type in which neither background nor design is cut away completely, but small parts of each are removed as a pleasant contrast to the solid remainder. The work is done entirely or almost entirely in buttonhole stitch, in all-white or natural colour, in white on a coloured material, or in a single colour on white. It looks complicated, but, like most one-stitch embroideries, is really very easy.

It washes and wears very well, and is particularly suited to household linens, such

Plate 17

An elegant example of cutwork with Richelieu bars across the open spaces

as sheets, pillowslips, tray-cloths, lunch mats, duchesse sets and chairbacks. Often the embroidery itself forms the edge of the article, but when it does not, the edges are usually finished with scalloping or Italian hemstitching. (*See pages 39 and 65 for these two stitches.*)

Though buttonholing is always the main stitch used, the characteristic bars of cutwork are sometimes needle-woven, and a few French knots or eyelets may be added for embellishment.

Use a special cutwork transfer, with the various parts of its rather formal flower or leaf design usually joined by bars.

Begin work by padding all the outlines with running stitch done in darning cotton or the working thread. Run a second row of stitches round the outlines, filling in the spaces left by the first, if the design is large and bold. Lay the threads for the bars (the making of which is fully described on page 20) but do not work them. To avoid mistakes, now mark all spaces that are to be cut away (if they are not already marked on the transfer) with pencil or tacking cotton crosses.

Closely buttonhole over all the padded outlines, working so that the purl of the stitch lies along the edge to be cut. If neither edge is being cut, place it along the outside of the design. Make the buttonhole stitching shallower than for ordinary scalloping.

Now cut away the fabric along the buttonholed edges with sharp embroidery scissors. Do not cut quite so closely as for scalloping. Finally finish the edge and catch in all loose threads by buttonholing again, or overcasting, over the purl edge of the previous buttonholing and over the cut edge of fabric. Use a finer thread for this, such as buttonhole twist. Cut the edges and do the fine buttonholing only a little at a time, to prevent any fraying.

Some workers omit this second buttonholing or overcasting and cut away the edges more closely. The result is as good when the work is new, but is apt to get ragged after laundering.

The last step is to work the bars (*see Fig. 39*). To save pricking of the fingers when doing this, use a blunt rug needle or put the eye end of the embroidery needle through first.

Sometimes the bars are worked with a picot half-way along each. These picots are often seen in cutwork and are very easy to make on buttonholed bars. Half-way down the bar leave a buttonhole stitch loose and pin it down to form a small loop. Take the working thread round under the pin, thus doubling the loop. Buttonhole over the doubled loop round to the bar, and then continue working along the bar to its end.

In some types of cutwork, such as Venetian and Catalan embroideries, petals and leaves are filled inside the buttonholed edge with seed stitch, triangular feather stitch or other filling stitches.

DARNED EMBROIDERIES

Besides being a simple and useful stitch in general embroidery, darning has given its name to a special type of needlework in which it is the only stitch used. In this kind of embroidery materials of open mesh or very distinct weave are used, such as canvas, net and huckaback, and are adorned with simple patterns or motifs darned in and out of the meshes, usually in bright colours or in white on a white background.

This easy work wears and washes very well, so is suitable for household articles which are frequently laundered.

Darning on Net (Pls. 18, 19 and 20)

This form of darned embroidery is done in embroidery wool on coarse-mesh curtain net for short pane curtains or for transparent net bedspreads. Conventional border designs are usually chosen, and these run

Plate 18

A short curtain of coarse cotton net shows a stylised white rose design in pattern darning

along the bottoms of the curtains and perhaps up the sides, or round the edges of a bedspread with, usually, a conventional motif of some kind in the centre or on the pillow portion.

Floral designs, such as orange blossom with true-lovers' knots, look fine darned on cotton net or silk on silk net, for bridal or confirmation veils.

Transfers will not iron off on net. For curtains and bedspreads choose a repeat pattern which can first be drawn out on squared arithmetic paper and used as a chart for copying. As the pattern repeats frequently, it is soon learnt and then can be worked without the chart. When a floral design is to be darned on fine dress net for a veil, lay the transfer under the net and tack transfer and net together. Then darn through both net and the tissue paper of the transfer, afterwards tearing the paper away.

In all darning on net, a thread should be used which is thick enough to fill the mesh well without distending or dragging it. It may be necessary to use wool double when darning a large-mesh curtain net. For dress net stranded cotton is good, as the right number of strands can be chosen to fit the mesh.

Before starting to darn in a border pattern, turn up the raw edge, several meshes deep, to the wrong side. Make a single turn only. Darn the bottom few rows through the turn as well as the main part of the net, thus making a neat hem and giving extra strength to the edge of the work. Darn continuously up one row and down the next. When taking a new thread, do not start with a knot, but lose the end

A detail of the border pattern on the curtain using woollen thread and mercerised cotton

Plate 19

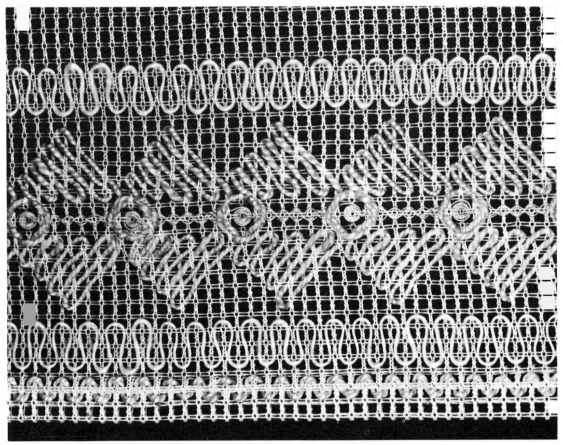

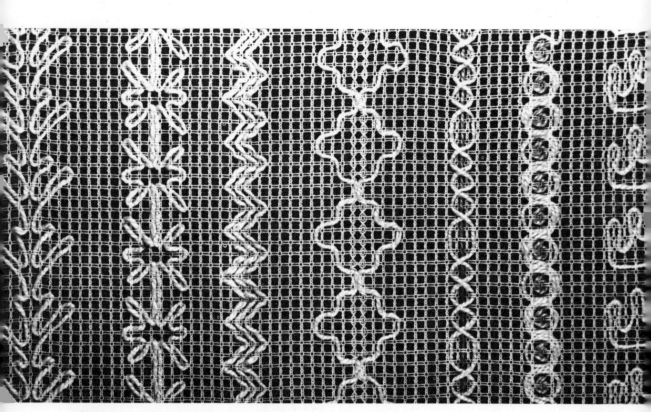

A sampler of different patterns darned on a coarse cotton net   *Plate 20*

among the last stitches taken with the old thread.

Darning on Huckaback

Huckaback, with its definite weave and surface threads just waiting to be picked up, is ideal for darned embroidery. Towels may be attractively embroidered in this way; so may duchesse sets and lunch mats if made from this hard-wearing material, bought by the yard either in white or colours.

The designs used for darning on huckaback vary much more than is possible on net. Geometrical patterns look well; so do flower or fruit sprays, little figures as in peasant embroidery, or small landscape or house scenes which look like a child's first drawing.

House and tree designs of this type are quite easy to darn in by eye, for they consist almost entirely of straight lines, which will be kept straight by the weave of the huckaback; but a transfer may be used if preferred. Put in conventional borders by counting the threads and working from a chart or the pattern which you have drawn out yourself on squared paper. Either stranded cotton or *coton à broder* are suitable and wash excellently. Use clear, definite colours, either one, two, or three in a design. Border patterns work out well in two contrasted shades of the same colour.

Huckaback darning is almost all on the surface, thus giving a great deal of effect for a little quick work. Pick up only the definite surface threads, which will hold the stitches without hiding them. These threads occur at regular intervals on the material and keep a pattern uniform.

Towels should have their decoration kept to one end. Mats and runners may be adorned on any part—ends, centre, edge or corners. Finish them by fringing out the edges. If a line of machine-stitching is first run the same distance away from the edge that the depth of the fringe is to be, and fringing out done as far as this, more threads will not come out accidentally in wear.

DRAWN-THREAD EMBROIDERIES

These are very numerous, for more or less drawn-thread work comes into a great variety of needlework. Some of the stitches used have been described in this section under such headings as *Italian Embroideries*. Here several more or less definite types of drawn-thread work are dealt with, although it must be understood that most kinds intermingle and overlap and are therefore difficult to classify.

Drawn-in Drawn-Thread Work

This is quite a distinct variety, used only by itself and in rosebud embroidery. It inserts lines of colour into the fabric so perfectly that they might have been woven in when it was made.

It may be used on linen, handkerchief linen, voile and shantung silk, or any fabric of which the threads will draw, as a simple, colourful trimming for household linen, underwear, babies' frocks, handkerchiefs

Most initials can be combined into a monogram and can be worked in a great variety of simple filling stitches

Plate 21

and so on. It is suited only for comparatively short lines of trimmings. It wears as long as the fabric and never gets out of order.

Use stranded cotton in one or more strands according to the weave of the material being embroidered.

The process is almost incredibly simple. Where the line of colour is wanted, completely draw out one thread. Start at one end to draw out the one next to it, but pull it only an inch or two. Have ready a single strand (for voile, shantung or handkerchief linen) of stranded cotton, twice as long plus one inch as the thread of material drawn out. Double the stranded cotton, and tie the linen thread partly pulled out to the loop thus formed.

Pick up the same linen thread *at the other end* of the line and draw it out gently and carefully. As it comes away it will pull through into its place the doubled coloured thread tied to it, weaving it perfectly into the material. Draw cautiously, constantly putting the pull on a different place, so that the drawing-out thread will not break. If it does, pull it right out and start again by tying the stranded cotton to the next thread in the material.

When the coloured thread is completely in, cut off the drawn material thread and trim off the surplus ends of the stranded cotton. By varying the numbers, colours, width apart, and length of the threads drawn in, endless different borders and simple trimmings may be evolved. Short lines not going from edge to edge may be finished off with a triangle worked in satin stitch, or interlaced squares may have a

This cloth and matching napkins are a typical example of Assisi embroidery

Plate 22

58

lazy-daisy flower at each corner as a final decoration.

Swedish Weaving *(Fig. 27)*

This is also known as Swedish darning or as needle-weaving, though the latter term properly belongs to the chief stitch used. The work comes from Sweden, and in its boldest form is done in vivid colours on canvas or coarse linen. Worked on finer linen and combined with other stitches not found in Swedish weaving, it is a feature of Sicilian embroidery and of Teneriffe work (*described on pages 68 and 60*).

Threads are drawn one way out of the material to form a 'run' and a coloured design is then darned into the vacant spaces, the darning going over and under the one-way threads left in the fabric. Various diamond and triangular repeat patterns may be formed by taking up more or fewer sets in each row. A set is the number of threads (generally from three to eight) which the needle goes over or under each time, and the set must be kept the same throughout a pattern.

Transfers are not required, as patterns are built up on the weave of the fabric. You will easily find effective ones by experimenting on an oddment of material, or can work them out first on a piece of squared paper, blacking in the squares which represent the pattern. To vary the design, intersperse bars among the darned sets, making the bars by overcasting the threads instead of darning them.

At corners work the windmill or spider's web, as it is variously called. This is also used in Sicilian embroidery and in Teneriffe work, and is much easier than it looks!

Windmill Corner Begin by first padding with running stitch and then closely buttonholing over the outer right-angle of the corner. Or, if making the windmill to fill an isolated square, run and buttonhole

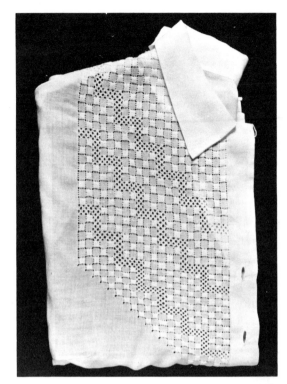

Plate 23

Italian hemstitching and punch work are combined in this finely worked block pattern for a blouse front

round the entire square. Now lay single threads (as when making cutwork bars) across the corner diagonally both ways, then again across twice—both vertically and horizontally. Take these threads into the buttonholed edge, into the inner edge of the material, or into the darned sets approaching the corner on two sides, according to the direction of the laid thread. For the windmill twelve laid threads are needed, three for each of the four arms.

Taking one of the diagonal corner threads as the centre thread of each set of three, darn these in the usual needlewoven way, starting at the centre where they cross, and ending the darning about three-quarters of the way along the threads.

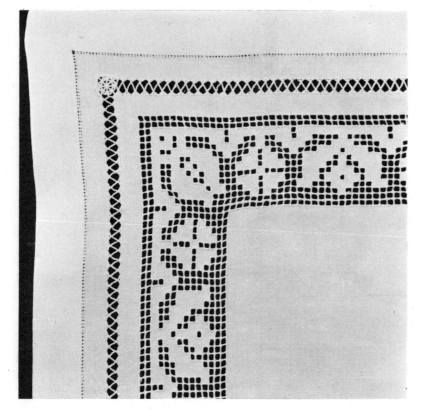

One of a set of napkins in Sicilian work embroidered nearly one hundred years ago

Plate 24

Fan Corner This is simpler, and suitable for a corner where the border design is quite narrow. After buttonholing the corner as described for the windmill, lay five diagonal threads, coming respectively from the corner itself and from two points along the sides that make it, and ALL going into the point of the inner corner of the border. Darn the fan shape so made, darning a little farther along the three centre threads than along the outside two.

Swedish darning wears splendidly and is particularly suited to furnishing items which will stand a bold treatment, such as chairbacks, table centres, and cushion covers. It is very effective, too, on many of the modern loosely woven tweed fabrics, the threads of which pull out readily.

Teneriffe Work

This is also known (in America) as Mexican drawn thread-work, and is Spanish in origin. Yet it uses the woven fans and windmills of Swedish weaving, not merely for corners, but also as repeat motifs in borders; and also the ordinary hemstitch for hems and for edging corners and borders.

Other stitches and patterns are peculiar to this work and give it its beautiful lace-like effect. Some are rather complicated; others, given below, are simple, lovely, and well worth trying.

The work may be done either on a rather fine linen or on a smooth cotton, such as casement cloth. All-white is usual, but sometimes blue working threads are used on a white ground, giving a note of colour and

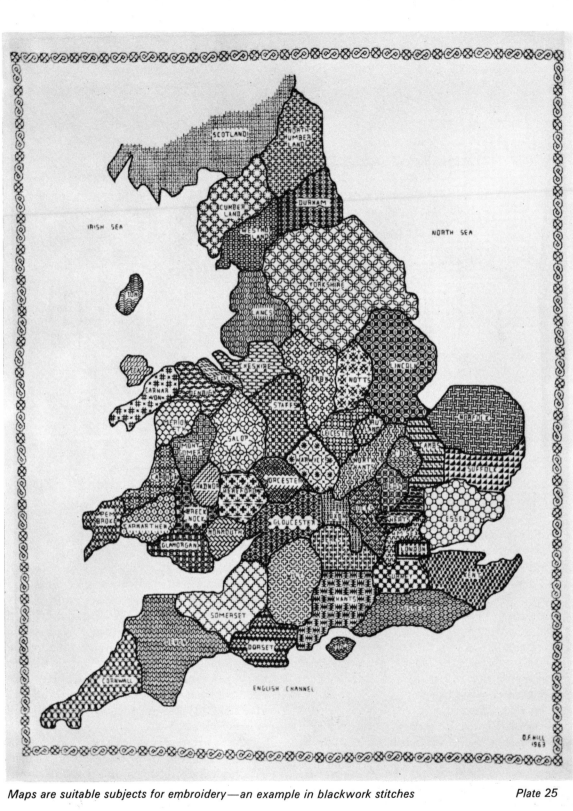

Maps are suitable subjects for embroidery—an example in blackwork stitches

Plate 25

Plate 26

One's home or some interesting piece of architecture seen on holiday may be reproduced in simple outline embroidery

making the work easier for the eyes. The chief stitch used is coral stitch. The work is arranged in borders and corners (often several, one within another, with plain fabric between), and makes charming table linen.

Some workers prefer, after pulling their threads, to do the work in an embroidery hoop, which keeps the added threads stretched all at the same tension.

Four-legged Stitch A wide, effective border. Draw threads to make a run $\frac{3}{4}$ inch

wide. Work ordinary hemstitch along each edge, taking up four threads each time. Now work a single crossing along the centre of the run, taking up sixteen threads, that is, four 'legs' of the ordinary hem stitch. With a fresh, long thread start again along the centre. Work a coral-stitch knot over the single crossing thread half-way between two crossings, take the thread up to half-way between crossing and top edge, and coral stitch across each of the four legs. Knot again over the next single crossing thread, then take the working thread down, and coral stitch across the lower four legs of the next crossing. Continue up and down in this way to the end, then return doing the legs missed the first time, and re-knotting over the centre thread. This makes a delicate hexagonal pattern superimposed on the single crossing—a very favourite Teneriffe device.

Stars These little motifs are easy and quick, and fill a nice lot of space. An inner border may consist of two rows of them, with extra ones at each corner. Divide the area to be covered into $\frac{3}{4}$ inch squares by drawing threads both ways, the squares to be solid material divided by runs from two to four threads wide. Using a thin strong thread, such as one strand of stranded cotton, stitch over from each corner into the centre of a square, and from two points along each side also into the centre. Pull the thread up rather sharply each time, so that the edges of the square are drawn into star-like points. Do not fasten off, but carry the thread to the next square. Work a line of coral stitches between the stars both ways.

The number of threads drawn must vary somewhat with the texture of the stuff. Experiment first, drawing enough to give the proper pull on the square without puckering it all up. Stars are best worked in a frame.

INITIALS AND MONOGRAMS
(Pl. 21, page 57)

If the necessary marking of household linen is done in embroidery instead of marking ink, it not only saves the material from the rotting caused sooner or later by the ink, but forms a dignified decoration. From time to time, also, embroidered initials or monograms are in fashion and appear on pockets, dress fronts, handbags and so on.

Initial transfers are obtainable in a great variety of styles and sizes, suitable for anything from sheets to handkerchiefs. Choose letters that are not too scrolly and ornamental in form. It is more modern to have clear, rather plain letters.

It is important to choose letters of the right size. Here are some tips as to sizes:

Top Sheets Letters 3 to 4 inches high, placed centrally above the hem.

Tablecloths Letters 3 to 6 inches high, according to the size of the cloth, placed half-way between the centre and the edge of the cloth.

Small Tea or Breakfast Cloths Letters $2\frac{1}{2}$ to 4 inches high, placed in a corner.

Dinner Napkins Letters $1\frac{1}{2}$ to 3 inches high, placed in the middle of one side.

Small Tea Napkins Letters $1\frac{1}{2}$ to $2\frac{1}{2}$ inches high, placed in one corner diagonally.

Pillowslips Letters 2 to 3 inches high, placed on the 'fall over' or in a top corner where they will not be lain on.

Bedspreads Letters from 5 to 10 inches high, placed in the exact centre.

Dress The size of the letters depends on fashion, but is usually between 1 and 2 inches high.

When the centre initial is larger than the other two, in a monogram, this large letter should always be the initial of the surname, although this would come last in a monogram of uniform letters.

Dress initials are usually worked in bright colours. For household linen allwhite, whether on white or coloured linens, looks smart though many people like the gaiety of colourful embroidery on white.

Many different forms of embroidery may be drawn upon for the working. Cross stitch is a favourite on material with threads that can be counted easily, while a mixture of this and darning makes a quick, simple marking for huckaback towels.

A padded satin-stitch letter, surrounded by a simple decoration of eyelets, always looks well. Sometimes a whole letter is made in touching eyelets. Chain stitch and ladder.stitch both make quick and not too heavy filling stitches for initials. Again, the outline may be back-stitched or outline-stitched, and the interior of the letters filled with seed stitch or lace stitch. Very large letters are sometimes worked in cutwork bars, and appliqué may be used for large monograms.

There is a very easy and effective way of working single initials without using a transfer.

Trace a letter of suitable size, taken from a newspaper or magazine heading or the printing on a box or packet, on to a piece of thin, firm paper. Thin typewriting paper does excellently and will take a direct tracing of a dark letter. Cut out the letter very carefully, taking pains to preserve the exact shape. Tack the paper letter in position on the article to be initialed.

Mark out a frame or shield comfortably larger than the letter. You can get a circular one by pencilling round an eggcup or other round object. Or cut a square out of paper and place it with one point upwards over the letter to mark out a diamond. Outline the shield in back stitch or some other suitable outline stitch. Then work lines of vertical darning, rather closely set but not touching, all over the shield except where it is covered by the paper pattern. Remove this, and the initial is found beautifully marked in the material itself and standing out boldly from its darned background.

INLAY EMBROIDERY

This delightful work is so simple to do, and wears and washes so well, that it is surprising it is not better known. The materials required are few and cheap— glasscloth towelling checked in red or blue, casement cloth or other cotton material matching the colour of the check, and a cotton thread—*coton à broder* is good—also matching the check.

The work is suitable for mats, runners, informal tablecloths, serviettes, traycloths and laundry bags.

Make up the item to be made in the ordinary way, but line it completely with coloured casement cloth. Make up your own pattern for your embroidery, working it out first on squared arithmetic paper. Inlay work is really a reversal of appliqué— instead of contrasting pieces being added to form a pattern, squares of the glasscloth are cut away, so that the coloured fabric beneath shows through with an inlaid effect.

Having decided which squares are to be cut away, do not cut them out right up to the checked lines, but leave tiny turnings inside the square. Secure each square to the coloured lining beneath with open button-hole stitch, the purl coming along the turning edge.

Instead of using the squares on glass-towelling, inlay work may also be done with a design. It is then known as *Découpé* (Cut-out) Embroidery.

Any appliqué transfer is suitable. Cut away and buttonhole down to the lining the appliqué parts of the design, working stems or other fine portions with suitable embroidery stitches. A bright colour may be used for the main material with a white or neutral lining or vice versa.

Very handsome table centres, cushion covers, lunch sets, chairbacks, and runners may be made in *Découpé*.

ITALIAN EMBROIDERIES

Italy produces many types of embroidery, brief descriptions of which will be found in Chapter 6. For convenience, those which you are likely to want to do yourself are described here under the general heading of Italian Embroideries.

Tendril Embroidery

This handsome work combines Italian hemstitching, used on so much Italian embroidery, with characteristic conventional motifs that always end in formal-looking tendrils, and little squares or diamonds in a form of cutwork. It is worked on natural linen with a mercerized cotton thread.

Suitable transfers can sometimes be bought; or the simple formal designs, based on straight lines, are not hard to design oneself or copy from an actual specimen.

When working tendril embroidery use the following stitches:

For the Tendril Motifs Work the solid parts in satin stitch (not padded), and the tendrils in cord stitch.

For the Cutwork Motifs Run round the edge of the little square or diamond, making a back stitch at each corner. Cut twice across diagonally inside the run outline, so that the material inside the outline is in four triangles. Whip closely over the run edge, whipping in at the same time these triangles of material. From the middle of one side take a thread across the space to the middle of the next side, bring it through from the wrong side upwards, continue to the middle of the third side, and so on back to the starting-point, thus making a diamond outline (in a square) or a square outline (in a diamond). If liked, these outlines may be twisted or overcast like cutwork bars.

A quarter-inch outside the motif, all round, work a line of *punto quadro* or Italian hemstitching (*given below*).

For the Edges of the Cloth Turn in a narrow hem and finish it with Italian hemstitching, which is worked as follows:

Italian Hemstitching

This is always eight threads in width. Draw two threads, leave in four, then draw two more, thus making up the eight. At the corners do not let the drawn threads run right to the edge, but cut them off at the right angle. If hemstitching a hem, mitre this neatly at the corner. Hold the linen with the wrong side towards you, and the hem, if there is one, to the left. Fasten thread in the hem at the top.

Holding the needle downwards, pick up four strands of linen and take a stitch into the edge of the hem. Continue all down the line—just an ordinary hemstitch so far. Turn the work to the right side. Bring the needle up in a space at the left, pass it to the right across the four threads left undrawn, and pick up four threads downwards in the drawn 'run' on the right. Re-insert the needle at the top of the four threads just picked up, bringing it out in the next space below in the row on the left, already worked. Now insert it four threads above or in the previous space, and bring it up in the same place where it came up last. Repeat to the length required.

Sometimes flowers of the daisy family appear in tendril embroidery. For each petal make two stroke stitches closely side by side, from end to end of the long petal; then use these as a bar over which to work buttonhole stitch which does not go through the linen. There should be the same number of buttonhole stitches—usually eight for a $\frac{1}{4}$ inch petal—used for each petal. They will curve prettily of their own accord.

Assisi Embroidery *(Pl. 22, page 58)*

There is no embroidery at once simpler and more effective than this, with its white design showing boldly against a coloured

background of continuous cross stitch.

This work originated in the Italian town of Assisi in the Middle Ages. Consequently the designs used for it are generally rather medieval in character—often of birds or dragons. Geometrical designs suit this type of work exceedingly well and are always obtainable.

Only two stitches are used—double running stitch and cross stitch. First outline the whole of the design in double running stitch—that is, two rows of running, the second filling the spaces left by the first row. Afterwards fill the whole background with touching, horizontal rows of cross stitch. Work a whole row at a time of slanting

Plate 27

This lovely pillowcase with its finely quilted centre from the Victoria and Albert Museum is dated about 1740. The silk flower embroidery is typical of the period

Plate 28

The feather design is a popular motif in traditional English quilting—part of a quilt in the Victoria and Albert Museum

stitches one way, crossing them all on the return journey.

A particularly effective colour arrangement is to outline the design in black, and make the background in some clear, strong colour, such as royal blue or deep leaf-green.

Another form of Assisi embroidery uses four-sided running stitch to outline tiny squares, instead of cross-stitching them.

The work is suitable for afternoon tablecloths, blotters, cushion covers, runners, traycloths and tea-cosies.

Sicilian Work *(Pls. 23 and 24, pages 59 and 60)*

This is more elaborate than other Italian embroideries, but so lovely and colourful that you will be repaid for mastering it. It is worked in bright peasant colours, in a mixture of needle-weaving, hemstitch, cut-work bars, and a special Sicilian openwork stitch called trellis stitch.

Sicilian work does not use Italian hemstitching, as might be expected, but for hems and outer edges of the motifs employs ordinary bar hemstitch.

On small items the embroidery is arranged in corner blocks. On larger ones, such as tablecloths, a double hemstitch border round the cloth encloses embroidered oblong blocks alternating with plain spaces of linen. In these there are no needle-woven 'windmill' corners, but five alternating rows of needle-weaving and trellis stitch. The stitch changes three times in each row; in the first row the order being needle-weaving, trellis, needle-weaving, in the second, trellis, needle-weaving, trellis, and so on.

Work the needle-weaving as described under that heading, but using more threads of material and darning a four-rib block each time, with an open space between each block.

Trellis Stitch

Trellis stitch is simplicity itself, being only coral stitch worked in rows across a 'run' of drawn threads instead of on solid material. Draw a 'run' of threads ½ inch wide. Along the run work four parallel rows of coral stitch, picking up four to six linen strands (always the same number, of course) at each stitch. Finish each edge of the run with bar hemstitch.

Cut the threads at each end of a drawing; do not let them run through to an edge. Finish the cut edge with a row of close buttonhole stitch, linking this to the edge of the trellis or needle-weaving, as the case may be, with a line of herringbone stitches. (*See page 33.*)

The making of the windmill is described on page 59 except that it has sixteen laid threads, four to each arm, instead of twelve.

LANDSCAPE AND MAP EMBROIDERY *(Pl. 25, page 61)*

Framed panels or unframed wall hangings made entirely in needlework are an interesting modern fashion. Though previous generations have had their needlework pictures such as the early stump work pictures of the seventeenth century and the later fine satin stitch embroideries of the eighteenth and nineteenth centuries, modern needlework panels are entirely of this age. The work is bolder, and achieves its effect much more quickly than the fine painstaking stitchery of bygone times.

It is the subject, rather than the treatment, of landscapes and maps which puts them under a separate embroidery heading, for actually they have no particular stitches of their own, but may be carried out in various well-known embroidery methods. But they do present certain special problems which are very interesting.

These landscapes and maps are intended for hanging on the wall. They will, therefore, be seen vertically and at a distance.

Under these conditions perfect or elaborate stitchery does not matter nearly so much as bold outlines and clear colours, so working methods are needed which will ensure these. There are several very suitable methods.

Really large hangings with large, bold designs are best treated on poster lines—in fact, some of the lovely modern posters are ideal to copy—and embroidered or blind appliqué is an ideal method. Use natural crash as a background, bound or hemmed with a contrasting colour. Linen may be used for the appliqués, but cotton satin which has a sheen that contrasts pleasantly with the dull surface of the crash, is better. It also keeps clean longer—an advantage in an unframed panel of this kind.

For smaller landscapes which are to be framed, work on natural linen or a good quality of creamy unbleached calico. A vivid impression is what is wanted, so the lines of the design should be clear and simple, and only very simple stitches should be used.

For example you might carry out a country landscape roughly sketched on an outing in which a group of trees, chestnuts in flower or tall dark pines are the focal point. These might be in a meadow in the centre of a rolling landscape of fields divided by hedges or low walls. For such a scene the maximum effect will be gained by appliqué of the different shapes of the fields, the hills in the background, and so on. The hedges or walls should be embroidered boldly in simple outline stitches. The main group of trees might be a combination of appliqué for the foliage, with embroidery stitches giving shape here and there. The tree trunks and branches should also be carried out in stitchery. In the foreground the meadow might be indicated again with the simplest and boldest of embroidery stitches on a background of appliqué.

Alternatively a landscape can be carried out in a combination of outline and filling stitches, the focal point and the foreground being worked more boldly and in brighter colours than the distance.

Maps, again, should aim at boldness and simplicity. They may be embellished with tiny pictures characteristic of each place shown, and with old ships and an elaborate compass, copied from ancient maps, shown in unfilled corners. Sometimes the names of places are given, as well as pictures representing them, and in any case lettering must be worked for the name of the country or district, always given in one corner and often surrounded by an ornamental border.

Work lettering in outline stitch (if large, 'lined' with another outlining in a different colour); or if the letters are very small, use back stitch. Narrow satin stitch or outline stitch, either of them with a line of fine running stitches outside it, makes a good coast-line. Running stitches are also suitable for county boundaries and lakes, with outline stitch for rivers. Satin stitch, darning, feather stitch and buttonhole stitch will work the tiny pictures. Use bright colours and a number of them—from six to ten different shades. Use fine wool or stranded cotton, not silk.

Both landscapes and maps are sometimes carried out in fine cross stitch all through.

Landscape and garden transfers are easily obtained; or it is an attractive idea to embroider one's own or a friend's home, sketching it first from 'life' or from a snapshot (*plate 26, page 62*). Map transfers are not so plentiful, but any worker who can draw at all can trace a map, or part of it, from an atlas or a large-scale walker's map, lettering the places neatly if she cannot draw pictures for them. Put in only the most important places, omitting all the small ones. Most school children love map-drawing, and would be delighted to draw an outline for embroidery. Transfer it to the fabric with embroiderer's carbon paper.

MACHINE EMBROIDERY
(Pls. 38, 39, 40 and 41, pages 81–85)

This is a fairly recent innovation in needlecraft but is becoming increasingly popular. Anyone who possesses a sewing machine, whether hand, electric or

Plate 29

A modern coffee cosy in padded-line quilting worked in back stitch

treadle can attempt it and will find enormous pleasure in the effective decoration quickly obtained. Machine embroidery is extremely useful to decorate clothes, summer dresses, party dresses and of course children's clothes. It is so much quicker and by being a continuous close stitch is practical for decorating frequently laundered everyday clothes.

Machine embroidery is also used today for much creative work in conjunction with appliqué and surface stitches. This is rather skilled work and requires a good deal of practice.

For much machine embroidery an electric sewing machine or a treadle machine is necessary as both hands are needed to guide the material. With the development of the swing needle so many more patterns and designs can be worked and with the automatic pattern attachments all kinds of effects can be achieved.

Sewing machines vary from one make to the other but each manufacturer supplies a handbook giving full working instructions. You should study the booklet carefully so that you understand about adjusting the tension of your particular machine and altering the size of the stitch to suit the material and thread being used. These are important points that need to be mastered as well as the basic details of threading up and working the machine, so that you can be sure of success. Time spent on experimenting and practising on sample pieces of the material that you intend to use is never wasted.

Plain Machine Stitching

You can achieve a number of simple designs made up of straight lines with plain machine stitching on an ordinary domestic machine. These patterns will look most effective on children's clothes and table linen. They are also invaluable practice in the art of machining which will help you in your dressmaking. Rows of stitching can be run on lightly pencilled lines using contrasting coloured threads. The lines should be spaced at varying widths, some close together, some at $\frac{1}{4}$ or $\frac{1}{2}$ inch distance, to create a pattern. A checked effect can be achieved by running the stitching across at right angles.

You will find that a No. 14 or No. 16 needle and a No. 40 mercerized sewing cotton are suitable for most purposes. When working on fine fabrics, such as organdie, use a No. 11 or No. 14 needle and No. 60 cotton. If working on nylon or Terylene use a fine needle and a Terylene machine thread.

Cable Stitching

Lines of cable stitching may be introduced to bring variety into the work. For this a thicker thread is needed in the spool, though the ordinary mercerized cotton will run in the needle. The two threads may match in colour or if preferred two different colours can be used to bring in another little touch of colour.

As the thread in the spool creates the thick cable effect the stitching must be done on the wrong side of the material. Any firm thread which is not stranded can be wound on the spool. For specially rich effects an untarnishable metal thread may be used but a little practice is necessary before embarking on this type of work.

Usually it is necessary to use a long stitch and the tensions of both upper and lower threads will need some adjustment. For instance the lower thread will probably need to be slackened to allow the thicker thread to run smoothly, though the upper thread may need a little tightening. Do experiment first so that you have stitch and tension correct before you begin stitching the actual piece of work.

As you become more proficient you will find you can develop all kinds of patterns. Straight lines may be made up into oblong shapes or triangles. Spirals and curved lines may be developed into patterns with circles or ovals.

Machine Filling

The same technique used for darning by machine can also be used to create attractive embroidery. For this you will need a small darning hoop and a darning attach-

Plate 30
For shadow work use a fine transparent organdie muslin so that the coloured threads of the embroidery show through on the right side

ment for your machine. With these you can make filled patterns for leaves, circles or any other shapes. These may be joined into patterns by ordinary machine stitching. A fine needle, No. 11 with No. 50 embroidery cotton will suit most materials.

Zig-Zag Machine Embroidery

With one of the new swing needle sewing machines many exciting patterns can be achieved. Though basically automatic the patterns can be arranged in so many ways that the effects are unlimited and you can create all kinds of exciting designs. Even straight lines of the different patterns in varying colours make an effective border pattern for dress hems, aprons, table mats, cushion covers and many other useful items. As you progress and you become skilled in the technique you can attempt any kind of pattern, working in the outlines of a drawn or transferred design, or creating the design as your fancy takes you.

Use a machine embroidery thread both in the needle and in the spool, either No. 30 or for fine materials No. 50. A firm closely woven material as a background will give the best results.

Machine Applique

Bold patterns, especially on large expanses such as curtains or wall hangings look particularly well if worked as appliqué. The applied pieces need not all be of the same fabric, and by using different textures including tweeds, cottons, synthetic materials and nets many exciting designs can be created. Hand embroidery or free machining may be introduced after the appliqué is completed to emphasize or pick out certain parts of the design.

Tack the pieces to be applied on to the background or apply them with a very thin coat of a dry paste to hold them in position. Stitch all round with two rows of plain machining as close to the edge as possible and trim off the surplus. If using a swing needle machine one row of satin stitch makes a firm edge.

Layers of transparent materials applied to overlap here and there will give you an unusual effect and create some fascinating shapes.

OUTLINE EMBROIDERIES

This simple type of embroidery is very popular because of the simplicity of the stitches used, and the quickness with which they are worked. These useful points make it the best kind of embroidery on which a beginner can start, and the best type to teach to girls who are just learning embroidery stitches.

Outline embroideries may be done on any material and with almost any kind of thread. Their characteristic is that the designs used are worked in outline only, and that no filling stitches are used. The most suitable stitches are the outline ones—outline stitch itself, split stitch, crewel stitch, running stitch, back stitch and coral stitch—supplemented by open buttonhole stitch (for edges and round flowers), lazy-daisy, couching and French knots.

Outline work of this kind gives a simple, light effect which is particularly suitable for children's clothes, for small objects which would be overweighted by solid embroidery, and for utilitarian things which are frequently washed, such as towels, teacloths, covers for hot-water bottles and so on. The material, the working threads and the design should be as simple as the stitches. This sort of work is out of place, for instance, on silk fabrics or done in gold thread.

As no light-and-shade effects are possible with outline work, and cotton threads without sheen are mostly used, there should be plenty of clear, vivid colour in the material,

Plate 31

An original smock front of 1827 from a
South Hampshire district

the working thread, or both. Pastel shades are to be avoided, as in the thinness of outline they give a weak effect; but touches of black, especially round the edge of the work, help to embolden it and hold it together visually.

If a piece of outline embroidery is more than quite small, it is a good plan to belie its name by working a small touch here and there solidly—preferably in satin stitch. Only an occasional detail should be filled in in this way. Thus the general lightness of effect and quickness of working is kept, yet

the solid touches give a little emphasis and 'body' to the work.

Remember that designs chosen for outline embroidery must be good in silhouette, and well distributed on the surface being embroidered.

QUILTING
(Pls. 27, 28 and 29, pages 66, 67 and 70)

This is one of the oldest forms of embroidery and can be traced back to very ancient times. Originally it was a way of adding warmth to bed-coverings by stitching a warm interlining firmly between a top ornamental cover and a lining, so that the stitches themselves made a pattern. The use of the thick padding gave a particularly pretty relief effect to the pattern, and this is so decorative that in modern quilting it is used for many items which do not require the warmth of the padding.

English Quilting

Both Wales and Northern England (Northumberland and Durham) have practised exquisite quilting for centuries and use traditional designs of their own. The same is true in America, where quilting is usually allied to patchwork. These crafts almost died out after the sewing machine was invented. Now, after being more or less forgotten for generations, of late years quilting has become very popular again, and has taken on up-to-date forms. It is a beautiful, quickly made, and durable decoration for tea-cosies, nightdress sachets, cushion and hot-water bottle covers, kettle-holders, chair seats for the home, and also for evening handbags.

In quilting, three layers of material are stitched together in a design or pattern. The top layer should be fairly thin. Silk, taffeta, a soft linen, cotton or organdie are all suitable. The lining, which is intended to hold the back of the stitches from sinking through into the padding, should be soft, cheap cotton, not too closely woven—cheesecloth is a favourite. The padding between may be a layer of wadding, preferably man-made if the article is to be washed and if a good deal of warmth and a high relief effect are wanted. When warmth is unnecessary, or less light and shade is desired, use a fluffy material such as wincey, flannel or flannelette.

The quilting transfer is often stamped on the lining material and the quilting stitches worked from the underside, so that the transfer lines will not show between the running stitches used for quilting. But as the transfer lines wear away during working, it is perfectly safe, and much more interesting, to quilt on the upper surface—if liked.

After the transfer has been ironed off, lay the three thicknesses together, the padding in the middle, and tack them *very* firmly to each other. It is very important that this tacking should be thorough and plentiful, for the work is spoilt if the layers shift during quilting.

The best plan is to machine-stitch all round the edges through the three thicknesses. Then hand-tack closely across the surfaces, vertically, horizontally and diagonally.

Quilting stitchery is of the very simplest. Only three stitches are ever used—running stitch, back stitch, and chain stitch—and not more than one of these in any particular piece of work. Chain stitch was a favourite in old quilting but is seldom seen in modern work. Running stitch is quick and very satisfactory, but back stitch is sometimes preferred for its more definite and solid effect.

Unless materials and padding are very thin, it is generally best to stab back and forth when quilting, rather than to take two or three stitches at once, to ensure that every stitch goes through all three layers. Do not work from end to end of a design, but either outwards from the centre or inwards from the edges.

Most quilting is done in one colour only, matching the top surface, two or three shades lighter or darker than it, or definitely contrasting. But if liked, each portion of the pattern may be in a definite colour. Use ordinary sewing cotton or silk or a thin, firm embroidery thread.

Unlike ordinary embroidery, the thread is not intended to show much, for the charm of quilting lies, not in its very simple

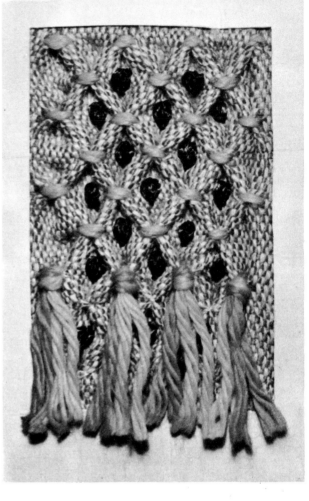

Plate 32a

Plate 32

Some new ideas in smocking by Margaret Thom, using thick wool and furnishing fabric and delicate silks and beadwork

stitchery, but in the relief effects obtained by the use of padding.

Sometimes, instead of a design being used, quilting is done in a geometrical pattern made by ruling diagonal lines across the surface both ways at regular intervals to form a diamond pattern, or by using a series of circles or semi-circles.

A very effective plan is to use a sprigged material and to quilt it in some simple pattern suggested by the arrangement of the sprigs.

Another variation is to quilt the floral pattern of the fabric itself, where this is large and bold enough, by padding and lining it and quilting all round the outlines.

Patterned handkerchiefs treated in this way may be made up into very attractive little handkerchief sachets.

When a quilted article is flat and not seamed round the edges, as in the case of a pram cover, the best way of finishing the edges is to bind them with bias tape or bias strips of fabric.

Italian Quilting *(Fig. 40)*

Italian or corded quilting, instead of being padded all over like the ordinary variety, pads the outlines of the design only. The design is worked in double lines for this purpose, and the padding inserted between them, giving a raised or corded

A stool top in an elegant tapestry design closely embroidered with tapestry wools

Plate 33

effect to the outlines. No warmth, of course, is added by this method, but the effect is very delicate and attractive.

The work is quick and has many uses for cushion covers, pram and cot covers, chair seats, pincushions, nightdress cases and handbags.

Silk, voile, organdie and soft cottons are suitable for Italian quilting.

Tack carefully together at various points the top surface and the silk or cotton lining, so that they cannot shift, having first ironed off the transfer on either the top surface or the lining—preferably the former. This transfer must be one specially designed for Italian quilting, or you can use a bold appliqué design by drawing in double outlines ½ inch or less inside the original ones.

Run or back stitch along both outlines in a matching or contrasting colour, using sewing cotton or fine silk. Then, to pad the double outlines, thread a large, blunt needle with 8-ply wool, oddments of rug wool, quilting wool, embroidery wool in four thicknesses or the special thick quilting wool sometimes obtainable

Turn the quilting so that the lining is uppermost, and with fine scissors carefully poke a hole, through the lining only (not through the top surface), between the two rows of stitching forming a double outline.

Run the needle into the hole, carrying it along the double outline as far as possible.

When a turn in the design makes further advance impossible, poke another hole to let the needle out, and start again with a fresh length of padding. Pad all the outlines in this way. (*Fig. 40.*)

Padding is usually done with wool the same colour as the top surface, but a particularly pretty variation, when this top surface is transparent and white or pale in shade, is to use vividly coloured wool for cording, so that it shows through the trans-

Fig. 40

parent top, outlining the design in colour slightly subdued by the material covering it.

If the wrong side of the quilting will show, as when the flap of a nightdress case is so embroidered, line the quilted flap additionally to hide the ends of the wool.

When a design for Italian quilting resolves

itself, as it often does, into enclosed spaces of various shapes, quilt in this way. Tack top and lining together only in the very centre, pinning them at the corners. Run or back stitch all round the *inside* outline of a space. Take out the pins, slip the padding wool between the two layers of stuff, close up to the stitched outline, and then make the outside line of stitching, thus enclosing the wool neatly.

This tidy plan avoids the poking of holes in the lining and therefore the need for any additional lining to hide them.

For the quilting of patchwork, see page 156.

RIBBON OR TAPE APPLIQUES

Small designs consisting of long narrow pieces may be effectively appliquéd in

Plate 34   *A traditional flower design for a stool top worked in tent stitch*

narrow ribbon or tape. Such appliqués have a ready-made edge, and there is no fear of fraying, so they may be very quickly applied by simple hemming (*see Blind Appliqué page 48*) without the work of holding them with embroidery stitches.

These appliqués are well suited to tiny designs for trimming underwear or needle-books, book-markers and other small items. They lend themselves to quaint or amusing designs such as are used for children's clothes. Where the narrow parts of the design are curved, as is often the case with stems, bias tape, doubled lengthwise, is a good substitute for the straight-cut variety. The small details of the design should be worked in ordinary embroidery.

Amusing designs of the 'matchstick' order (bodies and limbs indicated by straight strokes and heads by knobs) are very easy to draw—children love doing them—and can be carried out in narrow tape doubled lengthwise.

A handbag in fine 'petit point'   Plate 35

Lattice Work

This lightning 'embroidery' is merely darning done with ribbon. Room is made in the material for the wide 'thread' by drawing threads as for hemstitching.

It is an exceptionally quick and bold way of trimming rather large household accessories, such as runners, cushion covers, bedspreads and chairbacks. If used on things which are much washed, such as traycloths, thread narrow white tape into coloured linen. Linen is the best material to use, as the threads draw so well.

Suppose each end of a runner is to be ribbon-darned. Use $\frac{1}{2}$ inch nylon ribbon, say in brown and yellow. Start drawing threads right across the runner $4\frac{1}{2}$ inches from one of its ends, drawing enough to make a 'run' that will just take the ribbon flat. Leave $\frac{1}{4}$ inch, make a second 'run', then leave another $\frac{1}{4}$ inch and make a third 'run'. Thread the first and third 'runs' with brown ribbon and the second with yellow. Put it in with a ribbon threader or bodkin, and pass over twice as many threads as you pass under, so that the ribbon is well displayed. To pass over a $\frac{1}{2}$ inch width of threads and under a $\frac{1}{4}$ inch width is a good working rule.

A variation very suitable for bedspreads, cushion covers or traycloths is to make single 'runs' at even distances both ways over the entire surface, thus dividing it into large checks. A coloured linen checked with white in this way is particularly effective.

SHADED EMBROIDERY

When large designs are embroidered all over, usually in long-and-short stitch, it is known as shaded embroidery. It requires some skill and great patience and used to be very popular to reproduce naturalistic flower designs and charming silk pictures in the nineteenth century. It is still seen in Spanish silk shawls and on Japanese kimonos (though much of this work is now done by machine).

Shaded embroidery should only be used for items which have some permanence and do not require laundering, such as framed panels or firescreens, or a panel to be framed as a tray. Some church embroidery is worked in this way though gold threads may also be introduced into the working.

The threads used should be rich and soft, preferably of real silk, especially if the background material is silk. This is not an economical form of embroidery, and it is no use trying to do it cheaply.

Long-and-short stitch, which lends itself so well to shading, is the main stitch used, with satin stitch for smaller one-colour parts. If an all-solid effect seems too heavy, small portions of the design may be outlined in chain stitch or buttonhole stitch to give a relieving lightness.

A large number of shades of one colour are needed for successful shading—in fact, it is best to have one skein of every tone in that particular range. Generally speaking, the deeper tones are found in the centre of flowers or in half-opened buds, the colour becoming paler as it spreads outwards. Lighting must also be considered, as naturally the flowers look brighter where the light apparently strikes them, and darker when partly in shadow.

When choosing your shades you must consider also the colour of the background material. Black or a dark colour make the silks look brighter than they really are, while white dulls them down a little. When only one colour is used on a plain surface, effects of light and shade can be obtained by varying the direction of the stitches. On the

To work needlework tapestry success-fully the canvas should be mounted in an embroidery frame

turned-back part of a petal, the stitches should always go the opposite way from those on the main part.

SHADOW EMBROIDERY *(Pl. 30, page 71)*

This is aptly named, for the work consists of covering the design with a filling stitch worked on the wrong side of transparent material, so that the colour of the working thread shows through to the right side in a rather shadowy tint.

It may be used on sheer materials such as voile, organdie, and georgette with a charmingly delicate, almost fairy-like effect. It is best suited to comparatively small items, such as pincushions, dressing-table mats, tuck-in cushion covers, and handkerchief

Plate 36

The fish design in its wavy background is an exercise in a variety of canvas work stitches

Plate 37

sachets. Its extreme daintiness makes it ideal for a baby's Christening robe.

Nothing could be simpler or quicker to work than shadow embroidery. Choose a transfer which has no big surfaces, but is well broken up into small (especially NARROW) spaces. Designs featuring daisies and long narrow leaves are particularly suitable. Iron off the design rather faintly on the WRONG side of transparent material.

For working, choose a flat thread that fills well, such as stranded cotton. As its colour will be seen mainly through the thickness of the material, it should be a shade or two deeper than the finished effect desired. Work entirely on the wrong side of the material.

Only one stitch is used—the herringbone (*for working instruction see page 33*). Work this across the narrow petals and other spaces of the design, working closely enough for the stitch to show on the right side in a series of almost continuous short stitches marking the outlines. From a short distance the colour filling looks solid, and the effect achieved is almost that of a very softly shaded appliqué.

As the material is transparent, great care must be taken in disposing of the beginnings and ends of the embroidery threads. Tuck them neatly into the herringbone stitches and avoid the use of conspicuous knots.

SMOCKING
(Pls. 31 and 32, pages 73 and 75)

This decorative way of holding rows of gathers in place is never out of fashion. It gains its name from the fact that it was originally used for the smock-frocks or overalls worn by English farmworkers in the past.

Smocking is a special favourite for children's clothes, as, like all peasant crafts, it is essentially childlike. Also it has a great deal of elasticity, and smocked garments readily stretch as a child grows. It also has fashion appeal for dresses and blouses.

As much fullness is needed, smocking is most successful on fabrics which are firm but comparatively thin such as voile or some of the synthetic materials. It is sometimes used on woollens, but the effect then is always rather bulky, and should be employed only for narrow decorative panels rather than right across a dress front.

The evenness and regularity of smocking depend almost entirely upon the same qualities in the preliminary gathering, so this must be carefully and unhurriedly done. It is not safe to trust to the eye for keeping the rows level and equal distances apart. Either mark out a series of dots on the material, carefully measuring them with a ruler—or, better, iron off on the wrong side a smocking transfer, which consists of rows of dots ready spaced out.

Transfers may be bought with the dots various distances apart for different types of work, the distance between the rows being the same as, or greater than, that between the dots. An average space between the dots is $\frac{3}{16}$ or $\frac{1}{4}$ inch. Allow from two to four times as much smocking width as the width it is to be when finished, according to the distance apart of the dots. The further apart they are, the greater the width required.

To mark the material with dots, whether in pencil or with a transfer, stretch it quite taut on a drawing or pastry-board, and hold it down with drawing pins. If you are doing your own marking, prepare a long strip of cardboard with two complete rows of dots very accurately marked on it. Pierce each dot with a stiletto to make a hole through which the point of a pencil can be inserted. Lay this card on the material, make a pencil mark through each hole in the two rows, then shift it to mark the next two rows. Keep the card after use, as it will form a permanent marker.

When the material is dotted, start gathering with a long thread and a good knot, making a commencing back stitch in addition in case the knot pulls through. Gather by running the needle from dot to

Plate 38

Satin stitch worked on a swing-needle sewing machine

dot in a row, picking up your dots very accurately. At the end of a row pull up the thread to the width required. Do not cut off the surplus, but hold it by winding it round a pin placed upright at the end of the row. Gather each row on a separate thread and wind this on a separate pin.

For the smocking use a firm mercerized or cotton working thread.

The simplest smocking stitch is honeycombing. (*See page 33 for working directions.*) This is a little different from other smocking stitches in that most of it is invisible and hidden in the folds, whereas the usual smocking stitches are simply ordinary embroidery stitches worked on the surface of the gathers.

Here are some of the principal stitches used. As you will see by referring to *Pl. 32* various stitches may be combined in all sorts of ways, according to the worker's fancy and the depth to be smocked. These possibilities of original pattern-making are part of the fascination of smocking.

Outline Stitch

This is a favourite for the top row of a panel or to separate more elaborate stitches. Two rows in two different shades are often placed close together. Starting in the pleat at the extreme left, and holding the gathers sideways so that you work downwards, work as for ordinary outline stitch exactly over the gathers, taking one stitch in every pleat. Remember that in outline stitch the thread must be kept to the left of, and underneath, the needle.

Single Cable Stitch

A simple arrangement of backstitching. Take a back stitch in each pleat along a row of gathers, placing the thread alternately above and below the needle when making the stitches. Thus, first stitch, thread above needle; second stitch, thread below needle and so on.

Double Cable Stitch

Work a row of single cable stitch just above the gathering thread, then a second row just below it, reversing the thread in the second row, so that, where it comes above the needle in the first row, it will come below it in the second, and so on. This stitch gives a pretty linked chain effect.

Wave Stitch

One of the most decorative and imposing of smocking stitches, worked from left to right. Bring the needle through from the wrong side between the first and second pleats, and take up the first dot. With the thread BELOW the needle, now pick up the second dot and draw the two slightly together. Repeat with the third, fourth and fifth dots. Now you have finished the upward slant of the wave and must carry on, making a corresponding number of downward stitches, with the thread ABOVE the needle. Three rows of wave stitch are often worked close together.

Double Wave Stitch

Turn your single wave into a diamond formation by working another up to it, but reversed, so that it goes downward where the first went upwards, and vice versa.

Vandyke Stitch

This is much like honeycombing, but with the upward and downward threads kept on the right side instead of being hidden in the pleats. Work it from right to left. Bring the needle up on the first pleat of the first row, pass it through this and the second pleat, and make a back stitch. Descend to the second row of gathers, and there back stitch together pleats two and three. Return to the first row, back-stitch together pleats three and four, and so on, on alternate rows, the second pleat of one stitch always forming the first pleat of the next stitch on the row above or below.

Feather Stitch and Herringbone Stitch

These are also effective on smocking gathers (*see pages 29 and 33 for instructions for these stitches*). Honeycombing, owing to its rather different nature, is not often combined with other smocking stitches, but worked alone to the depth required.

When work is completed, remove gathers.

TAPESTRY OR CANVAS WORK
(Pls. 33, 34, 35, 36 and 37, pages 76–80)

This very old form of embroidery is also known as needlepoint. Both 'tapestry' and

Plate 39

A cutwork border is quite successful when a machine satin stitch is closely worked

'needlepoint' are rather inappropriate, for this work has no more to do with needle points than any other type of embroidery—and tapestry, strictly speaking, is a fabric woven on a loom. Needlework tapestry, as we might call it, is actually a cousin of cross stitch, and is an all-over embroidery worked closely on canvas. It often depicts pictorial subjects, but it is also much used for conventionalized flower patterns of the cross-stitch type.

As needlework tapestry is firm, heavy and extremely hard-wearing, while it will not wash, it is suited chiefly for furnishing uses of a permanent kind, such as chair-seats, footstools, firescreens and cushion covers. It is also used sometimes for smaller items such as handbags. It is slow work, but many needlewomen like to have a piece of canvas work going, and to do it a little at a time when opportunity offers.

The work is really best done in a frame (the upright, not the hoop kind, *see pl. 36*). But these are comparatively expensive, and take rather a lot of space, so many people manage their work in the hand. In this case a good plan is to weight the end of the work with dressmaker's weights, to keep it from puckering. If this is not done, and it DOES pucker, consult Chapter 5 for a remedy.

Two types of canvas are available for this embroidery—single-thread and double-thread. The latter is more popular, as its threads are counted more easily. This is an important point, because the usual method of working a design is to count it out on the threads from a chart, as in cross stitch. However, some modern pieces of work are printed in colours on the canvas, and it is only necessary to cover each portion of the design with its appropriate colour.

This sampler shows the variations of stitches that can be achieved on five makes of modern electric swing-needle sewing machines

Plate 40

Sometimes the design occupies the whole area. More often it is surrounded by a dark or neutral-coloured background. Most needlework tapestry is worked in wools which are specially dyed in a large range of subtle colours. On a fine canvas of say, 16 holes to 1 inch, the design may be worked in stranded cottons.

The most popular tapestry stitches are tent stitch (*petit point*) and couched tent stitch. Both these are fully described on pages 40 and 41. Cross stitch is also, strictly speaking, a canvas work stitch, but it is also used for so many other forms of embroidery. It fills up more than the tent stitches, so should be worked on a more open-mesh canvas or with a thinner thread.

There is a very large number of other needlework tapestry stitches; in case you want to vary your work, here are details of some of them.

Gobelin Stitch

A variation of tent stitch, worked so that it covers two vertical threads, but, like tent

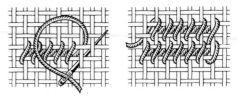

Fig. 41

stitch, only one horizontal one, giving slightly diagonal lines which are rather deep (*Fig. 41*).

84

Rice Stitch

This is very decorative, and may be done in two colours. First, make large cross stitches, covering four threads each way.

Fig. 42

With a finer thread, in the same or another colour, make small cross stitches over the intersections of the large ones (*Fig. 42*).

Tapestry Chain Stitch

Ordinary chain stitch worked on canvas was used for many old pieces of needlework, and is well worth trying. It is softer in effect than any of the other stitches, so is specially suitable for rather indefinite floral designs; also where many colours are used, as it is such a good blending stitch. Work it just as for ordinary chain stitch but picking up a thread of the canvas at each stitch. It cannot be worked to and fro, like most tapestry stitches. Begin each row separately and keep a different needle for each colour, to save constant re-threading.

WOOL EMBROIDERIES

There are many types of embroidery for which a wool thread is most suitable. For instance for a rather large and bold design around plain repp or furnishing tweed curtains, or for a quickly worked pattern

This garland of leaves has been worked in a free-running stitch on an ordinary domestic sewing machine

Plate 41

on a set of scatter cushions, wool threads will achieve an effect with the minimum of work.

The stitchery should be kept as simple as possible and definite outlines, often done with couching, will look best on a large piece of work. If a plain dark background is used then the embroidery may be carried out in bright contrasting colours. But on a coloured background, an orange cushion for instance, the design will look more interesting if worked in, say, two shades of light and dark brown, or in black and grey wools.

Wool Flower Embroidery

Simple abstract floral designs lend themselves to the elementary stitches best adapted to this thread. The work may be done on a loosely woven material, but is also often carried out on linen, linen crash, one of the heavier cottons or a firm mixture cloth.

A great number of home items, such as cushion covers, runners, workbags, nightdress cases and bedspreads, are very effective and hardwearing worked in wool embroidery. It is also a good decoration on curtains.

Keep the stitches very simple, relying on design, colour, and boldness for the gay effect. The design should be worked in stroke stitch, spaced buttonhole stitch, satin stitch or lazy-daisy, as seems most suitable. When the motifs are large and without definite spiky petals, the whole design is often effective if carried out entirely in outline or chain stitch.

Finish the edges of runners or table centres worked in wool embroidery with simply made borders—a line of couching or fly stitch or perhaps a right-side hem held down with running stitch or French knots.

When embroidering with wool, be careful to use a needle with a really large eye, or the wool will soon get frayed from being dragged through the material. It is a temptation to break the wool if scissors are not handy, but for good work it should always be cut.

Rug-Wool Couching

This particularly bold and quick form of wool embroidery for large pieces of work was originally designed for using up oddments of rug wool left over from rugmaking. But any very thick wool, even wool threads drawn from a novelty woollen cloth, can equally well be used as the laid thread, giving a softer, but not quite such a striking result.

Rug-wool couching is suitable for large surfaces which need broad and striking treatment, such as heavy curtains or portières, bedspreads, desk covers, chesterfield protectors, wall panels, firescreens and footstools. The designs used for it must be really large and bold in outline and minute detail need not be worked as this is wasted on this kind of embroidery.

Nothing could be easier or more speedy than this work. Simply lay rug wool or 8-ply wool over the outlines, and couch it down with either embroidery wool or embroidery cotton in the same colour, using different shades of rug wool, preferably, for the different parts of the design. If the ends of the laid wool are too thick to be put through the fabric with a rug needle, poke a hole for them with the points of scissors or with a stiletto and secure them neatly on the wrong side.

For a heavier effect on large pieces of work, the outline may be couched round twice in the same colour.

As this work is meant to be seen at a little distance and to stand out well, use strong vivid colours such as scarlet, emerald, and royal blue or black. It may be worked on any heavy cotton or linen material and especially on the wide range of furnishings, with their interesting textures and colours.

FINISHING, PRESSING, AND LAUNDERING EMBROIDERY

After you have taken a good deal of trouble to embroider a piece of work, please do not grudge a little extra effort to press and finish it nicely.

To begin with, look at the wrong side. Cut off all surplus ends of threads, and finish off securely and neatly any which may happen to have come loose. Naturally the wrong side, except in a very few kinds of embroidery, cannot be as well finished as the right. But the good embroiderer will neaten it as far as she possibly can, especially if the work is a flat piece, such as a traycloth or runner, which is to be unlined.

Carefully remove any temporary stitches, such as the tackings used to hold appliqués or the gathering threads in a piece of smocking.

Now for pressing. You will be surprised how much lovelier even the prettiest piece of work looks when it is well pressed. Have ready not only a clean ironing-sheet, but a piece of blanket or thick padding to go under it. The more raised the embroidery, the thicker this padding should be, so that under the iron the raised parts will sink into the blanket instead of being flattened out by the iron.

Lay the embroidery right side downwards on the padding and ironing-sheet, and damp it evenly with a damp (not wet) sponge. Then press with a moderately hot iron (linen generally needs a really hot one) on the wrong side till all creases and wrinkles are removed. If the foundation is of organdie, as in shadow embroidery, use only a cool iron, as organdie curls under great heat. Some delicate embroideries press best if a dry cotton press-cloth is placed between them and the iron.

Here are some special hints for particular types of embroidery:

Scalloped Edges on Cutwork, Broderie Anglaise etc. Press these twice, once after working the scallops, and a second time after cutting away the surplus edge.

Wool Embroideries Lay right side downwards. Press under a damp cloth, then without the cloth until quite dry.

Cutwork If it has puckered during working, pin it out carefully on a board, damp it, and leave it for several hours.

Then press the wrong side under a damp cloth.

Tapestry If puckered, lightly damp the wrong side, cover with a thin dry press-cloth and pass a hot iron very lightly over. Repeat if necessary.

Choose fast working colours. There are few modern embroideries, except those worked with metal threads, which will not wash if a little care is taken. For some reason it is popularly believed that quilting will not wash. This is a mistake. It launders beautifully, though the ironing presents a little difficulty if the padding used is a thick one. With thin paddings this does not arise.

Coloured embroideries, whether on linen, cotton, canvas, silk or fabrics of man-made fibres need a lather of pure soap flakes in moderately warm water. Wash them quickly, squeezing them lightly through the suds without rubbing or wringing—and remember that the work should be immersed as short a time as possible. Rinse twice in clean, tepid water, press flat between two towels with the hands to remove some of the moisture, and iron at once.

Do not roll up in a towel and do not leave it lying about damp. When ironing, place the work face downwards on a well-padded ironing-board, and put a dry cloth between the iron and the work. This prevents its acquiring a shiny, glazed surface. Use a moderate iron, and press outwards from the centre, pulling any scalloped edges carefully into position as you work.

Very fine, delicate *broderie anglaise* or Madeira work is best 'glass ironed'—that is, laid wet on a clean mirror, window pane, or other sheet of glass, pressed firmly and smoothly against it, and left in position until dry. This method is specially good for fine embroidered handkerchiefs.

When embroidery has been worked on material containing nylon, Terylene or similar man-made fibres it must, of course, only be pressed with a cool iron when dry. The wet article should be allowed to drip-dry and then gently pulled into shape, smoothing out the embroidery with the fingers. Press when dry on the wrong side of the work with a cool iron when a smooth and pleasing finish should result.

This wall hanging The Pied Piper *shows an example of built-up embroidery design. Plain coloured cottons are applied by machine to a black rep background*

Here is a sample of the wonderful choice of fabric for the dressmaker. Colours can be warm and bright or soft and shaded, while combinations of natural and synthetic fibres give endless variations in texture for evening-wear fabrics

Knitted toys are fun to make. Joey the rabbit, 11 inches tall, is easily made in plain knitting using double knitting wool

The attractive child's cardigan is quick to knit. The fluffy balls can also be made and instructions are in chapter 11

INTERNATIONAL
EMBROIDERY

IF you enjoy embroidery the chances are that you will also become interested in embroidery in general, even if you have not made it yourself. In the family attics, when talking to old people, in antique shops and museums such as the Victoria and Albert Museum in London, you will come across specimens of forms of embroidery which are rarely worked today but have left their mark on the history of embroidery. You will want to know a little about these interesting pieces and the correct names by which to call them.

Again, many fascinating forms of embroidery are brought home by friends from distant parts of the world, or you may buy them yourself on foreign holidays. Once more you will like to be able to identify these, and to have some idea of the people who made them. It makes embroidery so much more interesting if each English worker can know something of what has been made by other embroiderers in other

A tiny Victorian needlebook exquisitely embroidered, with delicate beads for the flower buds

Plate 42

Plate 43

The Family, *an amusing panel cleverly using a variety of blackwork stitches*

stems, and mingled with leaves, and worked in a great variety of beautiful, vegetable-dyed colours. Satin stitch, French knots, outline stitch and back stitch are the main stitches used.

BEAD WORK *(Pl. 42)*

The use of beads in embroidery is not new. Embroidery entirely in beads was worked in the eighteenth century as pictures and it flourished during the mid-Victorian period. Coarse beads were sewn on to a canvas background in floral or 'carpet' designs which were then mounted as foot stools or bell ropes. Sometimes the design was worked partly in beadwork and partly in wools or ribbons.

Beads and sequins are now often introduced into embroidery for the added effect and interesting texture. In this way they become an integral part of the design. In dress embroidery much use may be made of beads either as a 'collar' embroidered direct on a plain dress or on a band which is then made up as a belt. (*See page 22 for method of sewing beads.*)

BLACKWORK
(Pls. 43, 44, 45 and 46)

Originally known as Spanish work as it was brought to England during the reign of Henry VIII by the ladies of Queen Catherine of Aragon. The fine stitchery was worked in black silk on fine white linen. Sometimes dark green or dark red silks and gold thread were used. Today it is a popular form of counted thread embroidery. It is basically back stitch (*see page 19*) worked on a fine even weave linen over an exact number of threads vertically, horizontally or diagonally. The patterns formed are many and varied (*see sampler Pl. 44*).

countries or in the past centuries.

In this section it is not possible, of course, to include every form of stitchery of every age and nationality; but this list gives all which anyone interested in embroidery is likely to meet with in the ordinary way.

AMAGER WORK

A delicately beautiful form of shaded wool embroidery which hails from the Danish island of Amager, near Copenhagen. It is traditional, dating from the sixteenth century. It consists of wreaths or clusters of flowers, arranged 'full face' without

Plate 44

A sampler of blackwork fillings

Plate 45

A runner for a coffee table in an interesting black-work pattern. The detail shows the stitches, back and whipped back stitch and a diagonal back stitch

Plate 46

BULGARIAN EMBROIDERY

Worked by Bulgarian peasant women to adorn their clothes and household linen. Bright colours are used and separated from each other by a line of black; gold and silver threads are also employed. The background is white or black cotton, and the designs conventional patterns and borders worked in everyday stitches.

CATALAN EMBROIDERY

A very beautiful and elaborate Spanish embroidery in all-white, giving a lace-like effect. It combines stitches from punched work with satin stitch, buttonhole stitch and drawn-thread work, and has a characteristic mesh stitch of its own. It is used to adorn household linen and insertions.

CHURCH EMBROIDERY

Church furnishings consisting of altar frontals, pulpit falls, banners and such like require a special skill for their embroidery. Other pieces of church embroidery are

traditional priests' vestments, including the many beautiful copes worn for special occasions and the bishop's mitre. These are mostly undertaken by professional embroiderers as much of the work requires a knowledge of goldwork technique. Today untarnishable gold threads and cords are used. The background material is often a heavy furnishing silk, though sometimes velvet is used.

Though the designs incorporate the ancient ecclesiastical symbols the approach may be quite modern and in keeping with the new churches.

Smaller pieces of church embroidery often undertaken by less skilled embroiderers are offertory bags or a burse. Hassocks and altar rail cushions, in canvas work, are often carried out as a combined effort by a group of parishioners.

CREWEL EMBROIDERY

This term has been applied at different times to several forms of embroidery. (1) Floral embroideries for curtains and bed hangings made in Jacobean times, and usually worked in silk on linen. (2) A name used at the end of the nineteenth and beginning of the twentieth centuries for coloured embroideries on white, worked in outline mainly or wholly in crewel stitch. (3) In the United States today the name is applied to embroideries following the Jacobean ones in design, but worked on cream or natural linen in fine wools known as crewel wools.

CYPRUS EMBROIDERY

Whereas fillette or punched work (*see this latter heading*) has the background carried out in an openwork lace stitch, in Cyprus embroidery it is the design which is in openwork. It resembles cutwork and Richelieu in having the background cut away and the various parts of the design connected with bars. This form of embroidery came originally from the island of Cyprus in the Mediterranean.

CZECHOSLOVAKIAN EMBROIDERY

Like all Slav fancy stitchery, this is carried out in brilliant peasant colours, golden-yellow and scarlet combined in the same piece of work being a special favourite. Formal borders and corners are chiefly used, worked in cross stitch, solid embroidery or occasionally in outline. Stitches peculiar to this work include a number of unusual buttonhole stitches, known as *rivières*.

EGYPTIAN TENTWORK

This barely comes under the heading of embroidery, being really a form of patchwork or appliqué, originally made by a wandering Egyptian tribe to decorate their tents. Pictures of Egyptian scenes, showing pyramids, camels, donkey boys, priests and so on, are built up with coloured cotton appliqués on a cream ground, the appliqués being attached by blind hemming. A little embroidery is used for eyes and other details.

FILLETTE EMBROIDERY—
See Punched Embroidery

GAYANT EMBROIDERY

A variation of fillette embroidery in which the background is punched in the same way, but the design is darned all over not just outlined in buttonhole stitch.

HARDANGER WORK

A Norwegian embroidery which takes its name from the Hardanger Fjord in Norway. The work, handsome and bold, is done on an open-mesh canvas and combines simple cutwork and drawn-thread work with blocks of satin stitch. Geometrical patterns are used which can be counted out on the canvas mesh and are usually worked in white on natural canvas. The effect is rather that of a very bold and heavy lace (*Pl. 47*). The work is used for household linens, and less often for dress trimmings.

Three examples of modern Hardanger work

Plate 47

HEDEBO EMBROIDERY

This is of Danish origin and dates from the sixteenth century, being a special form of white embroidery worked for centuries by the women of a certain Danish *hede* (heath) on the linen they spun and wove from their home-grown flax. Old hedebo work was at its best about 1840, and afterwards greatly declined, till its former beauty was revived by a Danish art school in modern times. It is used for table and house linen, and combines chain-stitch embroidery in graceful designs with open-work motifs and satin-stitched flowers.

HUNGARIAN EMBROIDERY

In many ways this resembles Hardanger work, being worked on a canvas in a mixture of cutwork and satin stitch. Many of the same stitches are used.

LAID WORK

This term has two distinct meanings: (1) it is the old English name for couching; (2) a type of Oriental embroidery in which a solid background is made by laying down long threads, following either the weave of the material or the outlines of the design, each thread being couched down as it is laid.

MADEIRA EMBROIDERY

This is practically a variation of *broderie anglaise,* worked by the women of the island of Madeira. It is also called stiletto work, because the whole of the pattern, except for satin-stitched dots, is pierced with a stiletto or cut. In this it differs from *broderie anglaise*, in which much of the design is satin-stitched.

MEXICAN DRAWN-THREAD WORK

Teneriffe work (*see page 60*) as worked in Mexico. Both are of Spanish origin and practically identical.

PUNCHED OR RHODES EMBROIDERY

This came originally from the island of Rhodes in the Aegean Sea. It is also known as fillette, and in America is called punch or punched embroidery, the openwork stitch characteristic of it being worked with a punch needle. The design is usually carried out in solid or semi-solid stitches on a loosely woven material, and the whole background is worked over with lace stitch to give an openwork effect.

RENAISSANCE EMBROIDERY

This differs from Richelieu work only in

Plate 48

Part of a long sampler of the 17th century shows a variety of the intricate patterns used in embroidery of that period. Victoria and Albert Museum

twentieth century, in which flowers with narrow petals, such as chrysanthemums and daisies, were embroidered with a special narrow ribbon sold for the purpose. The rest of the design was worked in ordinary embroidery stitches in silk. A simplified version, which used ribbon in gathered-in circular coils to form flowers, was made at a later date.

RICHELIEU WORK

A beautifully bold form of cutwork in which the design is outlined in buttonhole stitch and the background cutaway. Twisted or woven bars with picots connect the various parts of the design. The designs used are less conventional and more varied than in the allied Renaissance embroidery, and include figures, animals and flowers.

SAMPLERS *(Pl. 48)*

These are strips of material, originally linen, on which little girls learnt their embroidery stitches. Samples of a number of stitches were worked on the strip, hence the name, sampler. As they are now valued antiques, it is useful to know enough about them to have some idea of their date when they are seen. In the reign of James I (first quarter of the seventeenth century) samplers were of linen and were short and wide. From about 1625 they grew longer and narrower, and patterns, instead of being dotted about, were arranged in horizontal bands. Towards the end of the century they became very long, and the patterns used were often Italian. During the Georgian era (eighteenth and early nineteenth centuries) samplers again became shorter and broader, and were soon square, and of woollen canvas instead of linen. The features we know—pots of flowers, little houses, and moral verses—began to appear, and most

having more formal designs and in using twisted bars without picots (except along the outer edge of the design) for the background. The designs used are of the type known as Renaissance, and consist largely of scrolls and arabesques.

RETICELLA

On the border between embroidery and lace-making, reticella is a lace made by embroidery methods. It is usually in square motifs showing star-like or diamond patterns, and using the bars (called, in reticella, brides or barrettes) of cutwork. Buttonhole stitch is the chief stitch employed.

RIBBON WORK

Modern forms of this are described in Chapter 4 but, strictly speaking, the name belongs to a type popular early in the

Plate 50 *The flowing lines on a piece of old Persian embroidery executed in fine silks of many colours*

Plate 51

*In contrast to plate 50 the Moroccan designs
were strictly geometric and carried out in red
silk on a fine cotton*

samplers were enclosed in a border. Gold thread and drawn-thread patterns were no longer used. Map and darning samplers also made their appearance. In Victorian times cross stitch was used throughout samplers, and the alphabet in both small and capital letters occupied much of the space, while both now and in Georgian times the little embroiderer worked her name, age and the date when the sampler was completed.

SPIDERS' WEBS

A form of embroidery which was very much in fashion in the early years of this century. The background material used was a special soft canvas with alternate checks of white and a colour. Either on all the white or all the coloured squares an overcast wheel (called a spider's web) was worked in thick mercerized thread. The work was made up as cushion covers, nightdress cases, and afternoon tablecloths.

TUFTING *(Pl. 49)*

Also known as candlewicking, because the thick white cotton spun for candle wicks was used for working it; this is an American embroidery of Colonial (pre-Independence) days. It was used for bedspreads, as it is bold and quickly worked. It consisted in covering an outline design with a knot stitch and leaving loops on the right side which were afterwards cut to form tufts. Tufting has been revived in the United States in recent years.

VENETIAN WORK

This is a near relation of Richelieu but differs from it in having the buttonholed outlines well padded, so that they stand out in relief. Inside the buttonholed outline the linen is not left plain, as in Richelieu, but is embellished with fancy filling or openwork stitches.

WHITE EMBROIDERY

This is a general term used to describe the class of embroidery carried out in white on white materials. It includes embroidery in which the pattern is wholly or partly cutaway, as in *broderie anglaise* and Madeira work; embroidery in which the background is cut away, as in cutwork, Richelieu, and Venetian; and surface embroidery which involves no cutting, such as much initial and monogram stitchery.

HOME DRESSMAKING

MODERN fashions, modern figures and modern paper patterns between them have taken all the toil out of home dressmaking. They have made it easy, quick and fascinating. That is why so many more women are making their own and their children's clothes than ever before.

First of all, modern fashions are so easy-fitting. We wear clothes which might have been specially designed for 'dressmaking without tears'—they are so simple, so casually fitted, so devoid of fussy trimmings.

Modern paper patterns, too, are a vast improvement on those our mothers used, for every kind of up-to-date knowledge and machinery are used to make them smarter in line and easier to work with. The variety, both in styles and sizes, is much greater, too. The old-time dressmaker fumbled with the pattern as best she could. We find, with every good pattern we buy, an illustrated leaflet giving a cutting-out diagram and clear instructions for making.

Home dressmaking is no longer a skilled art for exceptionally clever needlewomen, but a pleasant job that even the most inexperienced can take up with success. In these days it is no exaggeration to say that if you can sew, you can dressmake also.

Home dressmaking saves you money. Unless you are absolutely stock size, it gives you a better fit than ready-made garments. In everything you make you can combine exactly the material, exactly the style, exactly the trimmings and colour and price that suit you best. Your clothes have that slightly 'different' look which is the mark of the good dresser. You can renovate successfully too, combining two out-of-date garments into a smart, up-to-the-minute one.

And finally, dressmaking is SUCH a good hobby, giving you a pleasant outlet for the constructive ability and the love of beauty possessed by every woman.

YOUR DRESSMAKING EQUIPMENT

Every craft needs its own tools and for dressmaking the most important is a sewing machine. Not only does it save a tremendous amount of time but also it gives your dressmaking that professional finish which will make the garments a pleasure to wear. To speak of a home-baked cake means that it is especially good, but a garment that looks 'home-made' usually means that the finish is less good than if a professional dressmaker had tackled the job. Your aim should always be to give your dressmaking a professional finish.

Your choice of sewing machine is entirely a personal matter. There are today a great many excellent makes, some more expensive than others. In most cases the expensive machines give you extra gadgets or more power. But even the most expensive sewing machine will not automatically make the garment perfect if you do not know how to operate it correctly.

The first choice for most home sewers today is an electrically operated machine. It stitches smoothly and, most importantly, it leaves both hands free to guide the material. It is in these machines that the greatest variation of price exists; the swing needle machine on which you can do many fancy stitches with little trouble is of course fairly expensive. But a fixed needle machine, similar to a hand machine except that it is electrically operated, is still the most popular among the average home sewers.

The alternative, where electricity is not available as in some country districts, is a treadle machine. By being foot operated it leaves both hands free to handle the work.

Whatever sewing machine you buy it is wise to have one or more demonstrations from the expert in the shop to learn the various important points about your new machine before you begin to use it at home. Each new sewing machine is also supplied with its own book of operating instructions and hints on how to keep it clean and in good working order. To do good work your machine must be looked after (*see also page 240*).

As to the rest of the equipment—some is essential but there are other items which will make the work easier and these it is helpful, though not absolutely necessary, to have. Make sure of all the items in the first group to begin with, and add those in the second as opportunity offers.

Essential Equipment

You must have:

Needles (various sizes)

Sewing thread (cotton, Sylko and Terylene)

Large scissors (shears) for cutting out

Ordinary sewing scissors

A thimble

Tape measure

Yardstick

Pins ($\frac{1}{4}$ lb.)

A piece of tailor's chalk

Iron and ironing board

Optional Equipment

You'll work all the more easily if you also have:

A dress form or dummy with your own measurements

A tracing wheel

Buttonhole scissors

A stiletto (your embroidery one, if you have one)

A large firm pincushion (home-made)

A pressing roller (home-made)

Pinking shears

Sleeve board

Tweezers

When choosing equipment from either of these lists, remember these points:

Shears should be from 7 inches to 8 inches long, with bent shank and one bow (finger hole) larger than the other. Use them only for cutting out, and keep them very sharp, having them re-ground when the blades grow dull.

Scissors for ordinary sewing should be 4 or 5 inches long. Never cut paper with them, or they will soon grow blunt.

Pins should be of stainless steel. These will not rust and have fine, sharp points. Use brass pins for velvet.

Dress forms mean a financial outlay but last a long time. They may be bought in all the regulation bust, waist, and hip sizes. The most convenient are those which are adjustable. The most expensive adjust in all measurements and are fully padded.

Tailor's chalk may be bought very cheaply in white (the most useful); and one or two colours. It has a fine edge which gives a thin outline and, being slightly more greasy than blackboard chalk, does not rub off so easily.

Tweezers are very convenient for picking the short ends of tailor's tacking out of the material. Buy the ordinary small toilet tweezers from a chemist.

Folding ironing boards are not very expensive, and are better than using the kitchen table for the constant pressing needed in dressmaking, as a skirt or other tubular garment can be ironed on one of these tables without the under thickness being in the way. Pay enough for yours to ensure that it stands perfectly even and rigid, and is not less than 10 inches wide.

Tape measures are sometimes only marked on one side. It is worth paying a little extra for one which is marked both sides, and can be used from either end. You really need two tapes, as a second one is wanted when taking measurements.

Home-made Equipment

A large pincushion is a great convenience for general use in holding pins and the needle of the moment. Make it of firm material that will not soil easily, and be liberal as to the size. Stuff it very tightly with bran, or with coffee-grounds which have been saved and carefully dried. Coffee-grounds are said to prevent pins and needles from rusting.

A wrist or bracelet pincushion is a great convenience when cutting out, for you are constantly on the move then, and it is difficult to keep your pins within reach.

But worn on your wrist they are always handy, yet leave both hands free. Simply make a small round pincushion on a cardboard base and attach it to a bracelet of elastic large enough for your wrist. The cardboard guards your skin from pricks.

A pressing roller is a useful gadget which allows the turnings of silk seams to fall away on each side of it, so that they are not pressed against the fabric to form ugly ridges. A 30- or 36-inch length of any round rod, such as a broomstick, is suitable. Wrap it thinly and smoothly with cotton-wool, covering this with a white cotton cover tightly sewn into place.

So much for equipment proper. I am assuming that you will have available in your home a large table for cutting out and a full-length mirror placed in a really good light. You can't do really good work without either of these, though, failing the table, a large sheet of hardboard from a carpentry shop may be covered with P.V.C. cloth, and laid, at cutting-out times, on your bed or on a small table. You can store it in a cupboard when not in use.

I have not included press-cloths in either list, because any old clean white cotton rags will serve the purpose, and may be taken from worn-out sheets or pillow-slips.

STITCHES AND SEAMS

Most women, even if they have never done any dressmaking so far, know the ordinary plain sewing stitches. They are learnt at school and used so constantly for ordinary sewing jobs that they are never forgotten. For this reason such everyday stitches as hemming, overcasting and whipping are not included in this book. Back stitch, also much used for embroidery, will be found on page 19.

There are other very useful dressmaking stitches not quite so well known, and these you will find fully described in the following pages.

As for seams, even if you have done some dressmaking, you are probably rather vague about some of your seams, and especially just when to use each. You will also be glad of the simple tailored ones included here, as they add interest and variety to your work.

Remember, too, that practically all the stitches, and several of the seams, are just as useful for home upholstery as they are for making clothes.

Any stitch or seam which is new to you, or which you feel doubtful about, should be practised on a scrap of fabric before you use it in a garment. In fact, it is no bad plan to do with plain sewing what was suggested for embroidery stitches—that is, make a sampler of them which you can keep by you for reference.

Certain embroidery stitches chiefly used for dress items are included in the following list.

FRENCH RUNNING *(Fig. 43)*

This is actually running or gathering stitch done by a particularly quick method.

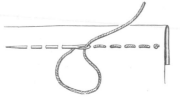

Fig. 43

The French name for it is *point turc*, from which it is sometimes called in English Turkey stitch. But it must not be confused with the embroidery lace stitch or Turkey stitch, from which it is entirely different.

Once mastered, French running saves a great deal of time when long rows of gathering or running have to be done. Use it for hand-sewn seams in underwear, for gauging and for putting in the gathering threads for smocking. It will need a certain amount of practice before it can be done quickly.

To work The material is held in a special way, with both hands alike. Place the thumbs towards you, at the front or right side of the work, and the forefingers at the wrong side, away from you. Take two or three preliminary stitches with the right hand. Then, without taking the needle out of the material or pulling the stitches through, steady the eye of the needle against your thimble, and with the left hand work the material on to it in tiny folds that resolve themselves into stitches when on the needle.

Never pull the thread right through until the line is finished. This is how so much time is saved. When the needle is crowded with folds of material merely push them off an inch or two on to the thread and push another group on to the needle. After a while you will French run twice as fast as you can gather in the ordinary way.

HERRINGBONE STITCH

This stitch leads a double life, playing a part both in plain sewing and in embroidery (*see Fig. 19*). In dressmaking it is chiefly used for holding down a hem made in flannel or other bulky material in which a double turn is not advisable. A single turn is made, and the raw edge held down by herringbone stitch, which prevents fraying.

This is the plan followed for turning in babies' flannels and sometimes in upholstery sewing when dealing with felt.

Ordinary sewing cotton is used on flannel.

Herringbone may also be worked in embroidery silk as a simple border trimming for children's garments, or may be used as an ornamental casing on underwear through which to run a ribbon or trimming band.

To work Work from left to right. Use two parallel lines to guide the stitches, and bring the needle through from the wrong side at one end of the upper line. Take the thread forward and downward to the lower line, on which pick up a small horizontal stitch with the needle pointing BACKWARDS. Pull through, take the needle diagonally upwards to the upper line and make another backward stitch there. Continue stitching alternately on the two lines, so that a kind of cross stitch is formed (*Fig. 19*).

When working herringbone over a raw edge, every slanting thread must pass over that edge, the upper line of stitches being worked on a single thickness of material, and the lower on the doubled turn.

TACKING (Fig. 44)

Ordinary running stitch when made large and used to join two edges temporarily for fitting or machining, is known as tacking or basting.

It is best made with the special tacking cotton sold in black and white on large reels.

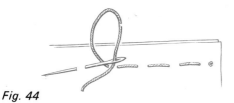

Fig. 44

To work As for running stitch, take stitches, parallel with the edge, in and out of both thicknesses of material, and making each stitch about $\frac{1}{4}$ inch long. Fasten off with two diagonal back stitches.

TACKING—ARROWHEADS
(Fig. 45)

Arrowhead tacks, often called arrowheads, are an ornamental tailored finish worked in tacking stitch in the shape of an arrowhead. They are useful for finishing each end of a pocket or for placing at the point where a pleat ceases to be stitched down.

As they are a tailored, not an embroidered finish, they should be worked in buttonhole twist or thick sewing cotton, matching the material in colour or a tone darker.

Fig. 45

To work With tailor's chalk mark a triangle on the material. The usual size is about $\frac{3}{4}$ inch high. Start at the lower left-hand corner. With the thread brought through at that point, take a small stitch across the top tip of the triangle, with your needle pointing to the left. Carry the thread diagonally down to the lower right-hand corner, and there take a long stitch right to the starting-point. Now repeat, making the tiny backward stitch at the top and the long stitch from the right lower point to the left, but this time working just inside the previous stitches, so that the two lines of thread lie alongside. Continue similarly round and round an ever-diminishing triangle until it is all filled up.

TACKING—DIAGONAL

This is a variation of tacking stitch which practically enables two rows of tacking to be made in one operation. It is used where two or more areas (as distinct from edges) are to be held together temporarily—chiefly round buttonholes and when interlining coats.

The stitch is sometimes called pad-stitch.

To work Tacking cotton is the best to use. Take a series of short vertical stitches, rather far apart, along a horizontal line, taking each stitch from above downwards. This gives slanting or diagonal tacking lines on the surface connecting the vertical stitches.

TACKING—TAILOR *(Fig. 46)*

Mark-stitching is another name for this stitch, because it is a quick way of marking pattern outlines and other pattern indications such as darts or pleats on both thicknesses of the material at once. Always use it for this purpose.

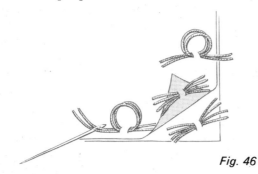

Fig. 46

To work Use a really long thread of double tacking cotton and with this tack in the ordinary way (*see Tacking Stitch*), but leaving each alternate stitch quite loose, so that it lies in a loop on the surface. Take care that all stitches go through both layers of material. When tacking is complete, gently pull the two thicknesses apart as far as the loops will stretch—usually about $\frac{1}{2}$ inch. Cut the stitches apart BETWEEN the two surfaces, and each will be found marked exactly alike with short ends of cotton.

VERTICAL HEMMING

This little-known version of hemming makes an inconspicuously pretty trimming for a right-side hem that is intended to be slightly ornamental. Use it for children's clothes or for underwear, working it with a rather fine embroidery thread in a colour deeper than, or contrasting with, the garment.

To work Turn in a hem on the right side. Take a series of tiny upright stitches, each holding down the hem to the material.

SEAMS AND THEIR FINISHES

So much of the wear and hang of garments depend on their seams that it is important that the right seam should be used, and that it should be well made.

In nine cases out of ten, seams in modern dressmaking should be made on the sewing machine, which gives stronger and much quicker work than hand-sewing. Still, you may have no machine, or you may be making gossamer underwear or fragile babies' things in which you wish for the extra daintiness of a hand-made seam. So you should be stitch-perfect with both kinds.

Remember, however, that hand-sewing is only suited to certain types of seam— plain, French, run-and-fell, hemstitched (*see Embroidery Section*), or faggoted. Lapped and tailored seams should be always machined.

Except in cotton or other firm materials, which may be pinned, seams should always be tacked before they are stitched. If this is not done, soft woollen seams may sag and silk ones may slip, in the stitching. Also tacked seams can be machined far more quickly than pinned ones, so the time spent on tacking is far from being wasted.

Be careful not to stretch bias-cut seams

when tacking or stitching them. Never strain them over the hand, but hold very lightly when tacking and, before starting even to do this, pin the two edges together at each end. Otherwise you may end up with one edge decidedly longer than the other.

Directly a seam is stitched, press it.

Now for the different kinds of seams:

Faggoting *(Fig. 47)*

This is both a seam and an embroidery stitch, being a form of mock hemstitch used to join two edges, whether seams or a hem added to the main part of the garment. It is a pretty way of joining on a yoke or insets decoratively.

For working it, use any embroidery thread suitable to the fabric of the dress.

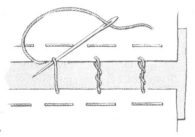

Fig. 47

To work Neatly crease-in hems on the two edges to be joined and tack them exactly parallel, but about ¼ inch apart, on to brown or other thick paper. Rule lines to make sure the distance is quite even everywhere, or use ready-ruled paper.

Bring the needle through at the extreme right of the lower edge and take a straight bar stitch into the upper fold just above, putting the needle through the fold from the right side to the wrong. Draw up. Put the needle under the bar stitch from right to left, pull up, then repeat, thus making two twists of the thread round the bar. Then insert the needle in the lower edge as close as possible to where the bar started, and take it through the thickness of the hem (so that the thread will be hidden) for ¼ inch.

Bring up there ready to start the second bar.

Flannel Fell

As its name implies, this seam is used for flannels for babies, for flannel and woven underwear and sometimes for jersey fabrics.

To make Make a plain seam (*see this heading*). Press both the turnings towards the back or bottom of the garment, according to whether the seam is vertical or horizontal. Narrowly trim the under turning, and tack down the wider one smoothly over it to the garment. Herringbone inconspicuously over the edge on the wrong side, taking light stitches that do not go through; or, on the right side, work feather stitch (*see page 29*) over the tacking, making sure that the stitches go over the raw edge on the underside.

Flat Fell *(Fig. 48)*

This stitch, also known as the machine fell, washes excellently, but has a more tailored and less dainty appearance than the equally washable French seam. Use the flat fell for boys' and men's laundered garments —pyjamas, shirts, underwear—and also for women's overalls and tailored blouses or jumpers.

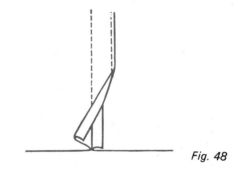

Fig. 48

To make Allow good turnings. Seam, press both turnings one way, and trim off the under one narrowly as for the flannel fell. Turn in the raw edge of the wide turning and stitch it down on the wrong side close to the fold. Then press again. It is a temptation to omit the first pressing, but please don't, for it makes a much flatter seam.

French Seam *(Fig. 49)*

Use this inconspicuous seam always for transparent material, except when joining two selvedges; for all washable garments which are not tailored, and every kind of underwear, as it washes so well. It is particularly suitable for nylon fabrics or other materials that fray easily.

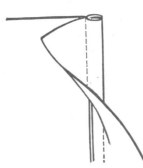

Fig. 49

To make Stitch a plain seam on the right side of the material. Cut off the turnings as narrow as possible—only just wide enough to hold except on nylon or other fraying fabrics. Turn the garment to the wrong side and stitch a second seam just far enough from the first to enclose the abbreviated turnings.

Lapped Seam

This is sometimes known as a ridge seam, as it gives a slightly ridged and raised effect like a very narrow tuck. It is used on 'pretty' joining lines which can stand being emphasized, such as the join of yoke to skirt or bodice, when setting in a godet, or for skirt and coat seams. In most cases the upper part of the garment is lapped over the lower part; but this depends partly on fashion.

To make Turn in singly the edge to be lapped, and apply it ½ inch in on the other

edge, first tacking the two together, then machining close to the lapped fold. If the seam is curved, slash the lapped edge freely so that it will set well. When a lapped seam comes to a point, work from both sides towards the point, not round it. Overcast the raw edges to prevent fraying.

Plain Seam *(Figs. 50–53)*

This is also sometimes called a flat seam, and is the most used type of all. Use a plain seam whenever any other kind is not specially indicated, and always for joining two selvedges.

To make Lay together the two edges to be joined with their right sides touching, and stitch a seam ¼ to ½ inch from the edges. Open the turnings and press them flat, one on each side of the seam. All plain seam turnings, unless selvedges, require to be finished in one of the following ways:

(*a*) **By overcasting** (*Fig. 50*) This is the most used finish and best for the average material, which frays if left unfinished. Overcast quite coarsely and not too tightly.

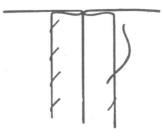

Fig. 50

(*b*) **By machine-stitching** (*Fig. 51*) This is quick and may be used for thin fabrics which do not fray much. Crease each seam, turning in once towards the garment and machine along the crease—through the turning only, not through the garment.

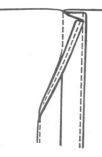

Fig. 51

(*c*) **By binding** (*Fig. 52*) Plain seams in heavy woollens and other fabrics, which fray badly, are best bound with seam binding, bias tape, or bias strips of self-material. Double the binding over lengthwise, slip the turning between the two halves, and machine down in one operation.

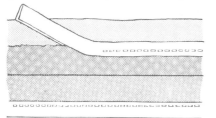

Fig. 52

(*d*) **By pinking or snipping** (*Fig. 53*) You can use this finish for velvet or bulky materials, which are almost non-fraying. Cut along the edges with pinking shears or with sharp scissors snip the turnings into a series of V-shaped gashes.

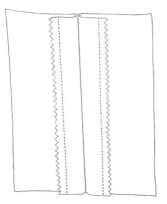

Fig. 53

Single-Stitch Seam

This is an attractive elaboration of the plain seam often used on tailored dresses or costumes.

To make Make a plain seam and press back the turnings, tacking them to hold them down to the garment. Now on the right side run a line of machine-stitching down each side of the seam, the width of the presser-foot away from it.

Finish the turnings as for a plain seam.

Welted Seam

You will want this when making tailored garments, such as skirts, coats or little boys' wear. It is decorative in a rather masculine way.

To make Make a plain seam. Cut away one turning narrowly and finish the wide one by overcasting or pinking. Then turn it back over the narrow one, and with your fingers push the material carefully away so that the seam is left clear everywhere. On the right side machine-stitch all down $\frac{1}{4}$ to $\frac{1}{2}$ inch away from the seam; if liked, add a second line of stitching just on the turn of the seam.

YOUR MEASUREMENTS

Before you can buy the size of pattern that will fit you, you need to know your exact measurements. The two most important for pattern buying are your bust size and your hip size, but for a perfect fit you need also to know your figure type. For this you need to know all your measurements to see into which category your figure fits best.

Most adult pattern sizes are grouped into headings such as 'Miss' which is the tall slender figure; 'Woman' which is the well developed figure; and 'Half-sizes' which are for the shorter woman, usually rather shorter from neck to waist. In the pattern catalogue of your choice you will find a chart showing you the various measurements for the different figure types and individual measurements. Check your own measurements against these to determine which pattern size approximates most nearly to your measurements.

Where there is any variation, and we all differ very slightly, choose a dress, coat, blouse or suit pattern by the bust size within your figure category. Go by your hip measurement for a skirt or slacks (unless your waist is much larger than the allowance on the pattern).

Taking your measurements is not something that you can do satisfactorily on your own and you will need the help of a friend. Write down the measurements in a notebook and keep this with your sewing equipment for reference. If your weight changes, when you buy your next pattern be sure to check the basic measurements, bust, waist and hip, and keep a note of the alterations.

You should have your measurements taken wearing your usual brassière, girdle or corset and only in a slip. If you take them over a dress or other garments the measurements would not be correct for the dress you intend to make.

To be measured you need to have two tape measures, tying one firmly round your natural waistline (or you can use a firm piece of string for this). Stand naturally but not stiffly with your weight on both feet. All measurements beginning or ending at the waist must be taken from the tied tape measure.

Bust This should be taken from behind, loosely over the fullest part of the bust and shoulder-blades.

Hips Take this not too tightly 7 inches below the normal waistline. If the widest part of the hips comes lower than this, take it at this widest part, making a note in your book of the distance this is below the waist.

Waist Measure tightly round the natural waist—that is, the smallest part.

Neck Round the base of the throat.

Front From the round bone at the centre-back of the neck forward and down in a slanting line to the waist centre-front.

Chest Across between the armholes, well above the bust.

Width of Back The back measure corresponding to chest. Take measurement 4 inches below the neckline.

Length of Back From the round bone at the back of the neck to the waist tape at the centre-back.

Armhole From the outermost point of the shoulder round the arm, close under the armpit and back to the shoulder.

Inside Sleeve With arm out straight, measure it from just above the armpit hollow to the wrist.

Elbow Rather loosely round the elbow when the arm is bent.

Hand This is for the size of the wrist of slip-on sleeves. Measure over the knuckles and held-in thumb.

Skirt Front From the waist centre-front to the floor.

Skirt Side From waist side (under the arm) to the floor.

Skirt Back From waist centre-back to the floor.

Skirt lengths vary according to the fashion, the type of garment and the age and figure of the wearer. Therefore skirt length measurements must be approximate, and should always be checked before a garment is cut.

ADJUSTING PAPER PATTERNS

This should be done with caution, for paper patterns are so expertly cut and in such useful sizes, that they will not need much, if any, alteration.

Note by your measurements whether your hips are about 2 inches larger than your bust. If they are approximately this, buy all full-length patterns by your bust size, and skirt, slacks and shorts patterns by your hip size.

A slight discrepancy can be met by slight adjustment. But if the hips are more than 3 inches larger than the bust, you must either buy the hip size and reduce the bodice part, or still buy the bust size and enlarge the hips. The latter is the better plan of the two, as it is more difficult to adjust bodice and sleeves than skirt, unless the skirt is of very complicated cut and the bodice a sleeveless one.

In nine cases out of ten, then, buy your pattern by the bust size. When you get it, measure the pieces against you (remembering, of course, that you have only half of most pieces) and judge if the fit is fairly good.

Do not attempt to alter the cut of a paper pattern. These have been expertly prepared so that the balance is correct. You can shorten or lengthen a bodice, skirt or sleeve and you can slightly widen these parts if necessary, or slightly narrow them when you find that one part of the pattern does not fit your figure exactly. A neckline may be cut a shade higher or a shade lower, but it should not be altered in shape from say, round to square, nor should the shape of a bodice be materially altered. There is, today, such a wide choice of styles among the various paper patterns available that you are sure to be able to find one to suit your taste.

If alterations are needed, these are most likely to be in the length of the sleeve, at the waistline (if this is close-fitting), or on the bust or hips (see Figs. 54–56).

The general plan in altering paper patterns is this:

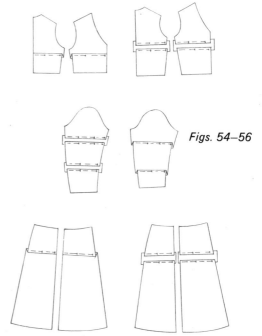

Figs. 54–56

To make smaller, fold a tuck or dart in the appropriate place.

To make larger, cut the pattern piece through or partly through, and pin in a piece of paper large enough to give the extra width.

Strip or tuck alterations are needed if the whole of a pattern piece needs altering; dart or wedge insertions if only part of it does.

To alter the waistline, pin darts or slash wedges in two or three places front and back downwards from the waist. If the back waistline is unusually hollow, so that a one-piece pattern wrinkles across it, pin up a long horizontal dart all across it, deep in the centre and tapering away towards the sides.

To alter the hip fitting, tuck or slash down the centre-back and centre-front.

An outsize bust generally needs both extra width and extra length. In this case you must slash and pin a strip into the front bodice pattern horizontally and vertically.

THE FOUNDATIONS
OF DRESSMAKING

ONCE you are provided with a first-class paper pattern, beautifully and expertly cut, and have made any small alterations your figure needs, you will find that successful dressmaking depends almost entirely on your understanding certain foundation or key processes. These are like the girders, walls and roof of a house, whereas the finishing of particular parts and the trimmings correspond to the interior fitting of the rooms. The most wonderfully fitted and decorated house in the world, with the best of doors and windows, will not be comfortable or lasting unless its foundations and general structure are laid and built soundly.

It is the same with dressmaking. See that your key processes—cutting out, putting together, fitting, stitching, and pressing—are as good as you can make them. In the following pages these foundations of dressmaking are described as clearly and fully as possible. Afterwards follow, in alphabetical order, briefer directions for handling the individual parts of a garment—sleeves,

collars, hems, and so on—and for the more important finishes and trimmings.

PREPARING TO CUT OUT

You cannot repair mistakes made with your cutting-out shears.

This is not said just to alarm you, but to make you careful and concentrated when you start on the first of the key processes in dressmaking. Choose for cutting out a day when you have plenty of uninterrupted time, and when, if possible, you can be alone.

Begin by putting everything ready. Have your large table or beaver board completely cleared, your wrist pincushion full of pins on your arm. Collect together your shears, your smaller scissors, your tape measure, your material, and your pattern, and see that that table is well lighted and placed so that you can move all round it.

The first step of all is to study your pattern and the cutting-out diagram on the instruction leaflet which comes with the pattern. Open out the pattern and identify the pieces (if you have not already done so to test the fit). Pick out, to place first on the material, the largest pieces and those which must go to a fold. Pin together and put on one side any pieces which are to be cut in another material or which you do not intend using.

If your material is the same width as that suggested on the pattern (and it is always wise to buy material that width AFTER choosing your pattern) you will be able to follow the cutting-out diagram exactly. It gives, worked out by experts, the best and most economical way of arranging your pattern pieces.

Lay out on your table as much of your material as there is room for. In most cases you will find that the diagram requires it to be folded in half lengthwise, so that the two selvedges lie together. Don't trust to a centre fold of the fabric, which is often not true, but lay one selvedge exactly over the other and pin them together every few inches so that they cannot slip.

Lay out your pieces according to the diagrams, taking great care that all edges marked 'Lay to fold' are so laid (if using a printed pattern lay printed line marked 'Fold' on the fold of the material). All good patterns have a turning allowance so cut close to the edges of a perforated pattern or exactly along the cutting line of a printed pattern. Sometimes you will find that the edges of a printed pattern overlay each other (especially if you have widened or lengthened the pattern pieces); so long as the printed cutting lines are clear you can cut through the various thicknesses of paper.

Beginners in dressmaking sometimes think that cutting diagrams are wasteful in the way they show the sleeve pattern. A little tilt to this, and it would fit into so much less fabric. Quite true, but that sleeve would never set right on the arm when

made up. A sleeve will only do this if, when you fold it seam to seam, the lengthwise threads run straight down it and the width-wise threads straight across it. So when placing it for cutting out, see that it lies straight down the material lengthwise, not even a little slanted across it.

When you are sure all your pieces are correctly laid out on the material, secure them down through both thicknesses of material with plenty of stainless steel pins.

Of course it may happen that you are using a different width of material from that indicated in the cutting-out diagram. In this case you must plan your own arrangement of the pattern pieces. Place first the larger pieces and those which must go to a fold, fitting in the smaller ones afterwards. Get every piece placed correctly and economically before cutting anything, to make sure you have enough material and the best possible pattern arrangement.

CUTTING OUT

All is now ready for the shears.

The chief things to remember in using these is to keep them moving along the table (not ABOVE it) as far as you can, so that the material is raised as little as possible; and to cut swiftly and cleanly, using the whole of the blades. Keep the broader blade above the work. Cut exactly on the printed out-lines or along the edges of the paper.

While cutting, steady the material by laying your outspread left hand firmly on the pattern piece you are cutting round.

Cut each piece out completely before going on to the next, even if it means more walking round the table. As each piece is cut, place it neatly aside, without unpinning the paper pattern from it.

Here and there on the pattern piece you will notice notches cut out of the paper edge. These have nothing to do with the shape of the garment, but are merely guides showing what edges must be joined later. So do not cut out these notches. On a printed pattern these are clearly shown.

This does not mean they must be ignored altogether. On the contrary, when the actual cutting out is finished, your next job must be to transfer these guides to your material in one of several ways.

PATTERN MARKING

Here is where tailor tacking comes in. It is far and away the most useful marking method, even though it is also the slowest.

Take each cut-out piece in turn, still pinned to its paper pattern. Begin by marking all the paper outline notches with tailor tacking. Do this with your material laid flat on the table, not held over your hand. This, as already explained, marks both thicknesses of material at once (*Fig. 46*).

Then indicate each internal mark by running tailor tacking from the edge of the fabric inwards to the narrow end of the notch.

Examine the pattern also for perforations or lines of tiny holes, for these have also to be marked. They indicate darts, pleats or slots, or perhaps the centre-front line of a cross-over bodice.

It is rather difficult to know how best to mark these, for as they are partly or wholly in the interior of the pattern, they are not easy to get at. In the case of darts, which come to an edge somewhere if they are wedge-shaped, partly unpin the pattern, fold it back along one of the dart lines, and tailor-tack along it. Then fold back along the converging dart line, and tailor-tack the fabric along this.

Where folding back will not meet the case, as with waistline darts to a one-piece dress and with slots, one plan is to tack through the pattern and then tear it away;

this, however, prevents the pattern being used again.

Another way is to pin along the perforation through both the pattern and the double thickness of material. Then turn the piece over to the patternless side and with tailor's chalk mark the pin line. Turn back to the paper side, remove the pins and the pattern. Turn once more to the patternless side and mark-stitch along the chalk line. It does not matter, you see, from which side tailor tacking is done.

All this tacking is apt to seem rather tedious when you are longing to pin your pieces together and see how they look. But some form of marking is absolutely necessary to good dressmaking and it saves time in the end, when you come to match the marked pieces of your garment together for fitting.

Sometimes it is possible to mark in quicker ways than by tacking. Chalk is often used for the purpose, and is fairly satisfactory on certain materials on which it marks clearly, or if a garment is to be made up very quickly after it is cut out. But the difficulty about chalking is that it is so very temporary and quickly brushes off if your material is much handled or fitted. Also each thickness must be separately marked, which adds to the preparation time before you can start stitching.

For cotton material the tracing wheel is quick and easy, which is why I have suggested that you should include it in your equipment. All you have to do is to run its spiked wheel along the pattern outlines, pressing rather hard as you do so, and on suitable materials a line of minute holes will appear through both thicknesses and be more or less permanent. Marking by tracing is a labour-saver for cotton frocks and underwear, overalls, and boys' and men's shirts; but on nearly all non-cotton fabrics the wheel either will not mark or it tears the fibres.

ASSEMBLING A GARMENT

Once the various pieces of a pattern are cut out and marked, those pieces must be correctly put together to make the garment. This assembling is a most thrilling business, as for the first time you begin to see what your dressmaking will finally look like.

Thanks to the care with which modern patterns are cut and notched, you won't find the actual pinning together and making up a difficult process. Study the leaflet with the pattern, with its helpful hints.

Remember in assembling that notches which you have marked are to be MATCHED. That is, an edge having two notches is to be joined to another edge having two, and a seam with, say, three notches, is to be linked with another seam marked thus.

Below you will find a typical assembling programme in twelve clear numbered stages for easy reference. It is for a dress of a usual type very often made by home dressmakers. You will find it a help to follow this programme in a general way, varying its details, of course, according to the particular design you are making up. Full instructions for stitching and pressing and for the individual parts of a garment and a number of trimmings, come after this programme and should be referred to for the detail work.

ASSEMBLING A BASIC
DRESS PATTERN

Here is a typical assembling programme in twelve clear numbered stages for easy reference. Though with every good paper pattern you will get a cutting out and assembling leaflet it is often assumed that the home dressmaker is rather more experienced and proficient than she is. This programme and the instructions which follow for stitching and making up individual parts of a garment will help to ensure success right from your first effort.

The dress described here is a basic style which may have many variations according to the fashion of the moment. It has only seven pieces in the pattern, bodice front, bodice back (cut 2), sleeve (cut 2), front neck facing, back neck facing (cut 2), skirt front, skirt back (cut 2). It has a centre back opening with a long zip from neck to below the waist.

1. After cutting out and marking lay the three skirt pieces on one side and make up the bodice. Stitch darts in front of bodice at shoulders and bust. Stitch darts in back bodice. Press darts.

2. Tack shoulder and underarm seams of bodice on the wrong side.

3. Stitch waist darts in front and back skirt pieces. Stitch the centre back seam to notch marking end of opening. Tack the side seams of the skirt on the wrong side.

4. Tack the bodice to the skirt carefully matching the side seams and the centre back opening. Try the dress on inside out and pin together the back opening. (Fitting oneself is difficult, so you will need either a good friend to help you or a dummy figure, *see page 101*). Fit the shoulders, bust, waist and hip, adjusting the seams if necessary. It is usually better to fit one side only of the body and then adjust the other side to match with the dress flat on the table. Measure the difference carefully so that the second side is identically fitted.

5. Unpick tacking of bodice from skirt at waist marking the line of stitching with tacks.

6. Stitch shoulder seams and underarm seams of bodice as fitted. Neaten the seams and press them.

7. Stitch side seams of skirt, neaten and press. Stitch waist seam joining bodice to skirt carefully matching the side seams and

centre back opening. Neaten and press the seam upwards.

8. Make darts in sleeves and tack the sleeve seam. Try on one sleeve and adjust for width. Stitch sleeve seams as adjusted.

9. Tack sleeves into armholes matching the notches carefully to get a correct set. (Any fullness at top of sleeve should be lightly drawn in with a gathering thread.) Sometimes it is necessary to adjust the depth of the armhole; it may be gently eased in the lower curve at the front by making small slashed cuts in the armhole curve of the bodice. Stretch the edge of the sleeve slightly to fit the lower armhole if necessary. Stitch the sleeves into the armholes, neaten the seams and press.

10. Join the front neck facing to the back neck facing pieces at the shoulder edges. Turn in lower edge of facing and stitch a single hem to neaten. Lay the neck facing to neckline of the dress right sides together and stitch round the neck edge taking care not to stretch the curve. Clip the turnings at intervals to ease and turn the facing over to inside of dress and press along edge.

11. Insert the zip fastener into the back opening of the dress.

12. Hem or face in the bottom of sleeves. Try on the dress and mark the hem. Turn up the hem as marked and tack. Try on the dress again before finishing the hem either by hand stitching or with the blind stitch attachment of the sewing machine.

FITTING FACTS

You will find fitting a friend or one of the adult children quite a simple matter, for you can see exactly what is happening all the time, and judge the effect of every adjustment you make. Fitting yourself can also be done and done well. Many successful home dressmakers always fit themselves. But as it is certainly much more troublesome than fitting another person, do try, whenever possible, either to get a friend to fit you or to do the fitting of your own clothes on a dress form with duplicate measurements to your own. (*See page 101.*)

If it is necessary to fit yourself, see that you have a full-length mirror in a good light and a good-sized handglass as well. Provide also for fitting, whoever is doing it, plenty of pins, a piece of tailor's chalk, a yard measure, and a yardstick.

In the early stages, when the main seams are being fitted, put on the garment inside out, so that the seams are easily accessible for alteration—except in the case of a garment to be French seamed, when tacking, of course, will be done on the right side.

Notice, first of all, if the garment hangs perfectly straight without any lopsidedness. If the material is striped or has a pattern arranged in regular vertical rows, you will be able to see quickly enough whether this really is vertical (not slanted or wobbly) when you stand in the dress. But if the material gives you no help of this kind, it is a useful plan, before tacking the parts together for fitting, to run tacking lines down the centre front and centre back of both bodice and skirt.

If these do not hang straight in wear, the two sides have not been tacked quite alike, or the two sides of your figure vary, or there is some other figure peculiarity which needs special fitting.

Try first if matters can be adjusted from the shoulder seams. Pin the dress to your underwear at the bust level, then you will be able to unpick the shoulder tackings without the dress slipping down while you alter them. Raise or lower the whole or part of one or both shoulder seams, or raise or lower the front or back edges only, until the tacking lines hang straight down both front and back.

If you find that to get the straight hang you have to adjust the two shoulder seams differently, then your figure is not quite symmetrical—a common occurrence—and you must fit each side carefully and separately. When the two sides of the figure match, you can, if you like, fit only one side and make the other to correspond after the garment is taken off. But actually it is less trouble to fit both sides while on, than to measure and match up the second one afterwards, even if the figure is perfectly even.

From the bustline, fit upwards. That is, if the material sags, strains, or wrinkles, between bustline and neck, pin the dress to the underwear at the bust, as already described, unfasten the shoulder seams, smooth the front upwards, and re-pin to the back. You will find that the depth of the front turnings has altered along some part of the shoulder-line, corresponding with the place where the fit was faulty.

The side seams should fit rather closely under the armpits, even if the dress is fairly loose at the waistline. That is, they should come well up under the arms, but not be tight sideways, or they will cause dragging across the bust and back. Sometimes an armhole which droops beneath the arm is best remedied by taking up the shoulder seam at the armhole end.

A common fault in a rather fitted style which is cut all-in-one is to find that it forms horizontal wrinkles just below the back waistline. This occurs on figures with rather a pronounced inward curve at this point, with a correspondingly pronounced outward curve below it (sway-back). Pin up a tapering horizontal dart along the back waistline—quite deep in the centre, but narrowing away towards the side seams. This will remove the wrinkles, and when the dress is finished it can be concealed by the belt.

The same fault where there is a join at the waist may be put right by making deeper turnings on the join along the wrinkled part.

If a skirt tends to shorten at the hem edge and to poke out at the centre-front there, probably the 'tummy' sticks out a bit. Let down the centre front as much as the turnings will allow; if this is not enough, lift the skirt front at the sides till the lower edge is level. This will shorten the front a bit, and you will have to shorten the back to correspond, either making a narrower hem, or facing up the lower edge.

An outsize bust may cause the same trouble, producing diagonal wrinkles at the armholes as well. In this case take up one or two horizontal darts on each front side seam just under the arm, to give the bust more room. Again this will cause shortening, so it is wise, if you are large-busted, to allow extra deep turnings on the bodice waist edge.

Wrinkles across the front or back neckline show that it needs cutting out a little. Do this while on by making slashes, rounding out the curve to the depth of the slashes afterwards. If the neck seems too loose-fitting, make the shoulder seam deeper at the neckline end only. Or, if only the back of the neck is loose, take up five little pin tucks running just an inch or two down the back to absorb the surplus material.

Naturally you want a good line which makes you look your best. Remember, however, that it is easy, if you fuss over fitting too much, to destroy the balance with which a good pattern is cut. So if, when you try on your garment, it hangs correctly and feels comfortable, without wrinkling or straining noticeably, it is wise to let well alone. Only attend to points which are definitely ugly or definitely uncomfortable.

When fitting children, allow for their rapid growth as far as you can without spoiling the grace of the garment by letting it become baggy and shapeless. For example, when girls are nearing the age of figure development, the paper pattern of the front bodice will allow for this, both in length and by having shoulder darts. There will be too much length in the bodice at present and the surplus must be taken up by means of deeper turnings on the bodice at the waist. But do not cut off these turnings or slit the fold of the (now) extra deep shoulder darts. Both may need letting out before the frock is discarded.

After fitting on the wrong side, try the garment on again on the right side, to see the general effect.

Professional dressmakers only fit twice, once for the main seams and a second time for the hem and smaller details. But it is far easier for the home dressmaker with little experience to try on more often, attending to only two or three points at a time. You will notice that in making out the assembling programme in the preceding pages I have suggested trying on the dress, or part of it, four or five times.

PRESSING

This is very important. Nothing so successfully banishes that home-made look from amateur dressmaking as plenty of good pressing.

Have your iron always handy and quickly available, for it is hardly possible to press too often. Make a rule of always pressing, as soon as it is made, any seam which has afterwards to be joined to another. For instance, a shoulder dart is impossible to press properly if you economize trouble by deciding to do it and the shoulder seam into which it is set at the same time. The reason is that each seam will get in the way of the other being nicely pressed.

Pressing AFTER stitching is the usual rule. But in some cases, especially if the material is rather bulky or springy, it is wise to press after tacking and BEFORE stitching. For example, press a lapped seam when you have made the fold on the upper or lapping edge, and press again after it has been stitched to the lower edge. Pleats also should be pressed after they have been tacked and before they are stitched.

Another instance where double trouble gives the best results is when facing the revers of a dress or coat. Seam the facing to the rever and press out the turnings flat, one each side of the seam. Then turn the rever inside out to the right side and press the seam again. You will get a much flatter result by giving the two pressings than if you left your ironing till the end.

To press open a plain woollen seam in a professional way, first press the closed seam under a thin dry cloth. Then open out the seam turnings by rubbing up and down hard with a damped sponge, a special soft toothbrush kept for the purpose or a bit of self-material. When the turnings lie flat, press heavily with a dry cloth between the seam and the iron.

Cotton and linen fabrics should be pressed after damping without a cloth over them. Silk should not itself be damped, but be pressed under a damped cloth. When pressing rayon or any mixture containing it, or other man-made fibres, test an odd piece of material first to see if it will stand damp heat—some shrivel under this treatment, so must be pressed quite dry. In any case, rayon and nylon fabrics will not stand as hot an iron as cotton, linen or pure silk.

For seams in thin silk, rayon, and other man-made fibres use your home-made pressing roller, described on page 101. Seam turnings in these thin fabrics are apt to mark through to the right side if pressed flat. But when the seam is laid on the roller, the turnings fall away safely below the iron and only the seam itself is pressed.

The centre crease of the material, down which the material was folded when bought, often needs really hard pressing to remove it. If the material will endure it, damp the crease well by running a wet finger-tip along it before pressing heavily under a dry cloth. Often one pressing is not enough, so it is a good plan to press the crease first on the uncut material before laying the pattern on it and to press again wherever it occurs on the finished garment when giving it your final pressing.

Use your sleeve-board for pressing sleeves and curved seams generally. (*See more details under Sleeves.*) In fact, as the sleeve-board, when placed on an ordinary ironing-board or table, is the right height to work at without any tiring stooping, it is a good plan to do all dart and short seam pressing on it and so save fatigue.

Velvet and other pile fabrics must never be pressed, as the weight of the iron flattens the pile. Instead, stand a hot iron upright and cover it with several thicknesses of a really wet press-cloth. While the steam is rising, draw the seam or hem to be pressed lightly up and down the covered iron, with the wrong side of the velvet next to the iron.

For the pressing of pleats, *see Pleats.*

MACHINE-STITCHING

After fitting, and sometimes before and sometimes after pressing, the various parts of your garment must be stitched together, preferably by machine. Use silk for stitching silk and velvet cloth, a mercerized thread for thin woollens, rayons and linen, and choose a cotton thread for stitching cotton. For stitching nylon, Terylene or other man-made fibres use a Terylene sewing thread. As threads always work up lighter than they look on the reel, use a shade slightly darker than your material.

Make sure before you do any dressmaking stitching that you thoroughly understand your sewing machine and how to work it. Instructions cannot be given here, as different makes vary; and they are unnecessary, because an excellent book of instructions is supplied with your machine.

Study this carefully and practise on scraps of material till you can stitch straight, true and rapid seams. *See also page 102.*

Before starting to stitch the seams of a new material experiment on a cutting to find the size of stitch, needle and thread that suit it best. Stitch all vertical seams downwards, not up.

Don't be scared of your machine attachments, for they will halve your work for you. The machine can crease a hem much more evenly than you can do. It can gather and gauge, pleat, tuck and bind with lightning speed. Find out just how each attachment works—and let it do the job. But do your preliminary experimenting with plenty of time to spare and only on a piece of material that doesn't matter—not on your new dress.

ORDER OF WORK

The specimen assembling programme (*see page 114*) gives the order of making up an ordinary dress and you should refer to it as you work. In the following pages the various dressmaking processes you will need are explained, not in the order in which you will need them (no one dress will require them all) but alphabetically, for convenience of reference.

BELTS

Cut a straight strip of material as long as required plus good turnings, and twice as wide as required plus turnings for seaming.

Belts are usually 1 inch to $1\frac{1}{2}$ inches wide when finished for grown-up garments. For children make them narrower—$\frac{3}{4}$ inch to 1 inch. Double the cut strip in half lengthwise, with right sides touching, and seam together the doubled edges.

If each end is to be attached to half a

buckle, the ends are left raw for the moment. But if the slip buckle, through which one end draws and fastens beyond with a press-stud, is chosen, one end should be seamed at the same time as the length. This end is usually cut into a V, but if left square, cut a triangular piece of the turning off each seamed corner after stitching. This is to avoid bulk when the belt is turned right side out.

To do this, use the bodkin method described under Rouleaux (*page 137*). Then press the belt flat, with the seam coming along one edge, taking care that the corners or V-point are well poked out and not left vaguely rounded. They may need careful prodding with the bodkin. According to the type of buckle, sew one end to it, over the centre bar, or the two ends to the two halves of the buckle. In the case of a slip buckle, sew half a press-stud to the under-side of the belt at the V end and the other half on the upper side of the belt, so that the correct size will be obtained when they are fastened.

Belt-holders are needed at the waistline under each arm to hold in position any belt which is not tight-fitting. These holders may be very narrow and tiny editions of the belt, made of self-material, about $\frac{1}{4}$ inch wide when finished and long enough to take the width of the belt comfortably. Each end is stitched firmly to the dress. Another form of belt-holder is the buttonholed loop—just three strands of sewing cotton laid across side by side in the correct position, and then closely buttonholed over to form a firm loop attached to the dress at each end.

BINDING

There is no more important finish than this for the edges of sleeves, necklines, collars, cuffs, underwear and the hems of dresses. It is often considered difficult, but is not really so if a few simple rules are remembered and a little care is taken. Good binding gives an 'air' to the simplest home-made garment.

When merely for neatness, binding is the same colour, often the same material, as the garment. But it becomes an effective trimming if carried out in a deeper tone or a contrasting colour or material.

If you are a beginner at binding or un-successful at it, get your hand in first by using ready-cut and creased bias tape. This can be bought very cheaply in either silk or cotton, in all colours, and saves you the problems of cutting and creasing. When you can bind beautifully with it, promote yourself to using self-material.

Here's a very easy way of binding to start with. It is quick, but distinctly unofficial, and not quite so neat as the ordinary method. So use it on something sturdy and everydayish, such as an overall or a toddler's rompers.

The bias tape already has each raw edge creased in and a crease down the lengthwise centre. Cut the edge to be bound, like all bound edges, without any turnings, and place it between the two halves of the creased tape, with the raw edge right up to the crease. Tack edge and crease together, through both sides of the tape. Then hem the binding down, taking your stitches through both sides of it at once, and hem-ming from the right side. Afterwards press the binding, when any slight wrinkles in it will smooth themselves out.

This is so easy that you will be able next time to put on your bias tape in the orthodox way. Lay an edge of the tape to your material edge, right sides touching, and stitch by hand or machine along the crease of the binding edge. Turn the binding over to the wrong side, covering the raw edge of material as you do so. Fold it down with its raw edge tucked under, and slipstitch the other crease down to the wrong side of the garment.

Now suppose you cut your own binding strips from the garment material. It is most important that they should be on the true cross, which you can obtain by laying a selvedge or lengthwise thread over to lie along a crosswise thread. Cut along the diagonal fold this makes, and use that diagonal as one edge of your bias binding strip.

An average width for binding strips is 1 inch. Keep them as even as possible, measuring at intervals or judging by eye.

Binding strips can be cut in short lengths from oddments of fabric and several can be joined together for a long bind. But you MUST join them the right way, with each joined edge along a straight thread of the material. As the strip itself is bias-cut, this means that the straight-cut join will slant across the strip. To join the strips accurately, lay them on the table in a continuous row, pin the ends together, and seam them as pinned. At each end one edge will stick out a little farther than the other. This is correct, though it looks wrong (*Fig. 57*).

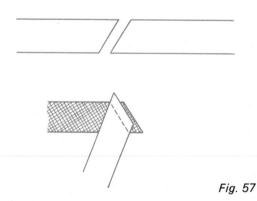

Fig. 57

Press each join very flat, pressing the tiny seam open.

Lay one edge of your binding strip to the material edge just as when attaching bias tape and stitch ¼ inch from the raw edges. (This time you have no crease to guide you.)

Turn the binding over the raw edge and slip-stitch it down to the wrong side, tucking in the raw edge neatly as you go along. Or you can crease in this turning with an iron before starting to bind, if you prefer.

When binding by any method, remember as you sew to STRETCH the bind slightly round an inside curve (such as occurs on a neck-line) and to EASE it slightly round an outside curve (such as occurs round a flared hem). For the binding of corners, *see Mitres page 133*.

Mock Binding

On SLIGHT curves or slants only, a binding may be simulated by allowing inch turnings on the edge to be bound. One inch from the edge make a tuck ¼ inch deep on the wrong side. Treat this tuck as if it were the raw edges of a binding, folding the ½ inch of material outside it over the tuck and slip-stitching it down, edge turned in, on the wrong side. This is known as a mock bind or French hem.

Centre-stitched Binding

This is a tailored-looking simulated binding suitable only for straight or nearly straight edges. Turn in a very narrow hem on the right side, making the first or raw edge turn as deep as the whole width of the hem. Machine-stitch along the centre of the hem, carrying the stitching continuously round any corner. This is a quick, neat and rather severe finish for square necks or for the top edges of slips.

BUTTONHOLES

These get so much friction and wear that they must be really well made if they are to last neat to the end. So do not hurry over a buttonhole. Modern clothes do not demand many, and it is time well spent to attend carefully to every detail. A pair of proper buttonhole scissors is a help in cutting the slits neatly. (*See Equipment.*)

Ordinary Worked Buttonholes *(Fig. 58)*

These are specially suitable for cotton blouses, dresses, overalls and children's wear. This buttonhole must always be made in at least two thicknesses of material, such as a hem or box-pleat. If there is only one thickness, tack a small piece of self-material beneath where the buttonhole is to come, work through it, and afterwards cut away any surplus.

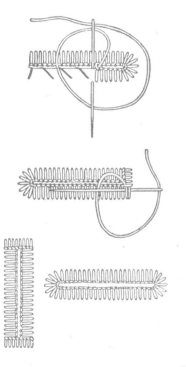

Fig. 58

Make buttonholes horizontal if there is strain on the fastenings, such as when they occur down the back; but vertical when they fasten a loose-fitting garment, such as the front of a blouse.

When doing a row of buttonholes, mark each carefully before starting, making sure

that they lie directly under one another at even distances apart.

Do not cut a buttonhole until you are ready to work it, as cut edges soon fray. The special scissors will prevent your cutting too far; but if you are using ordinary scissors, put a pin at each end of the slit marking (which should be a trifle bigger than the button) to prevent too long a cut.

To give extra firmness and ease of working, strand the slit before buttonholing it. To do this, lay a couching thread along each edge of the slit, quite near the edge, securing it from pulling up by a tiny back stitch. Then, to hold the couched thread and prevent fraying of the cut edges, without cutting off the stranding thread use the rest of it to take a few widely spaced overcasting stitches over both slit and stranding thread.

Buttonhole closely all round the slit, with the purl lying along the slit, of course. (*For buttonhole stitch, see page 24.*) Go round the outer end of the buttonhole, making your stitches form a semicircle, and at the inner end (nearest the edge of the hem or fold) either make the stitches form a straight line or work a tiny bar for extra strength. To make a bar, take three stranding stitches across the end of the buttonhole, and buttonhole-stitch them closely, not going through the stuff.

Use No. 40 thread for making this buttonhole. If possible, have a very long thread that will do the stranding, overcasting and buttonholing without giving out; but in any case the buttonholing must all be done with the same unbroken thread.

Bound Buttonholes *(Fig. 59)*

These are used on any materials which fray too readily to make worked buttonholes very successful. They are easy and quick, and can be made ornamental if they are bound with a different material or colour from that of the garment.

Carefully mark the slit on the garment as

for worked buttonholes, but DO NOT CUT IT. Mark the slit also on the wrong side of a piece of material, preferably bias-cut, measuring $1\frac{1}{2}$ inches longer than the button-

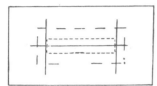

1st stage

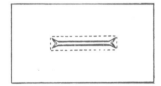

Cutting

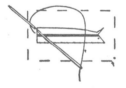

Finishing

Fig. 59

hole and 2 to $2\frac{1}{2}$ inches wide. Tack this down on the right side of the fabric, with the slit above and exactly over the intended slit on the garment. Frame all round the slit, $\frac{1}{4}$ inch away from it, with machine stitching or hand-running. Now cut the slit, through both layers of material, cutting each way from the centre to within $\frac{1}{8}$ inch of the stitched frame at the end. Finish the cutting by making the tiniest of diagonal snips each way from the slit just to (but not through) the corner of the frame.

Take out the tacking and bring the added piece through the slit to the wrong side, so that the raw edges of the slit are covered, as in a bind. Trim away any surplus material, turn in the raw edges, and hem them down. At each end arrange the corners neatly in a tiny pleat.

Bound Slots for holding ties, scarves or belts are made in just the same way.

This bound buttonhole should always be made on a double thickness. When used on coats, work it through the coat itself and the front interlining, but fold back the front facing out of the way. When the buttonhole is complete, replace the facing, cut a slit in it THROUGH the buttonhole, turn in its edges, and hem them down very neatly to the wrong side of the buttonhole.

Bound Buttonholes on a Single Thickness

These are made a little differently. Use this method for buttonholes on tailored jumpers and cotton frocks, overalls which button in front and washable coats or jackets which have no front facing.

Mark your buttonholes one below the other on the garment, keeping them mostly to the right of the tacking which marks the centre-front line. Then, allowing for the pull of the buttons in wear to the end of a slit, they will be centrally placed. Make the buttonholes before the edges near which they are worked are finished, and allow $2\frac{1}{2}$ inches of edge clear beyond the slit.

For each buttonhole cut a straight strip of material (preferably contrasting) which measures $2\frac{1}{2}$ inches long and $\frac{1}{2}$ inch wider than the length of the slit. On each long edge turn under and press a $\frac{1}{2}$ inch turn. Mark the slit across the centre of the strip and lay it, turnings uppermost, exactly over the slit on the garment. Tack it down through the turnings. Now machine-stitch, continuously through both added strip and garment, the broadened-out figure of eight. Begin in the centre, stitching a diagonal and horizontal line alternately. The distance between the two horizontal stitchings must be $\frac{1}{2}$ inch.

Cut the slit through both thicknesses horizontally through the centre but not beyond the turned edges of the strip. Remove the tackings. Now cut away the strip only (not the garment) in the two triangles. Finish as for ordinary bind, turning the strip through and hemming it down to the horizontal stitching. Turn in the raw edges of the garment beyond the buttonholes in a hem reaching to their outer ends.

Worked Tailored Buttonholes

These are too difficult for the average home dressmaker. When they are in fashion for coats and tailored dresses, send the garments to a working tailor, who will make the buttonholes for a small sum.

COLLARS AND COLLARLESS NECKS

Take pains with your collars, for they are a test point in home-made clothes. Also they come so near the face that they should be as flattering as possible—and good setting on is one way of ensuring this.

Collars fall into several different types, for which different methods are needed.

Detachable Collars

These are usually light-coloured ones on a dark dress, made easily removable for laundering. They are generally of the unlined type. Machine hem-stitching or picoting, done at a shop, are good finishes for such a collar. Slip the neck edge into a doubled bias tape or crossway bind; machine-stitch it in place, or use the hemming-both-sides-at-once method de-

scribed under Binding. Face in the neck edge of the dress with a matching bias strip (*see Facings, page 126*).

Lined Collars *(Fig. 60)*

These are usual on dresses and blouses. Their shapes vary according to fashion, but they are always of double material, the lining usually being the same as the upper portion. To make them up, lay collar and lining together, right sides touching, and seam them round, except along the neck edge. Notch the seam to remove bulk, then turn the collar right side out, and press.

Fig. 60

To set the collar on, except in the case of a cross-over garment, mark the exact back centre of the neckline with a pin and that of the collar (upper layer) with another. Match the two pins and tack from them each way to the collar fronts, with the collar proper lying inside the neckline, its right side against the wrong side of the neckline. Do not tack the collar lining, but leave it clear.

Try on, to make sure the collar is central, then seam along the tackings. Make a single turning along the free edge of the lining and fell this down to the seam-stitching on the right side. The collar itself will roll over and hide these stitches in wear.

Notched or Step Collars

These are the costume coat type, with small turnover collar at the back, joined to turn-over revers at the front. Simple linen or cotton jackets for summer wear are well within the home dressmaker's scope, either for children or adults, and always look well tailored with a notched collar. Here is an easy way of making it for a coat of this type.

Begin with the front facings. Down the inner edge of each, crease and machine-stitch a single turning. Tack up the shoulder and underarm seams of the coat. Join the under or lining portion of the collar (it is double) to the neckline, slashing the turnings so that they will lie flat when pressed. Similarly join and press the collar proper at each end to the top of one of the facings.

Place the facings with their joined collar inside the coat with its joined collar lining. Take care to match collar, neck seams and front edges exactly, and pin them together. Join the shoulders (and the tops of the facings in with them) with French seams. Crease in single turnings to face each other, and match exactly right round the coat fronts and facings and the outer edge of the collar and lining. At the right-angle join of collar and rever, slash the edges so that they will turn sharply. Machine-stitch two or three times all round the matched edges, making the rows of stitches the width of the presser foot apart.

Unlined Collars

These are mostly of a trimmed or fancy type. Finish their outer edges according to the pattern you are making up. Pin together the exact centres of the inner edge of the collar and the neckline, right sides touching. Over them place a bias strip wrong side uppermost. From the centre both ways tack all three layers together; then stitch them. Finally hem down the free edge of the bias strip to the inside of the neckline.

Dresses and cardigan coats are often collarless. In this case finish the neckline with a binding or facing, consulting these headings for details.

CUFFS AND WRISTBANDS

Do not attempt to finish off the wrist of your sleeve, whether with a cuff, wristband or otherwise, until the final setting in of the sleeve gives you its exact length.

Strictly speaking, cuffs, usually turn-back, are extras, and not part of the length of the sleeve; whereas wristbands hold the raw edge of the sleeve and ARE part of its length. But the word cuff is mostly used for all but the narrowest of wristbands, as well as for cuffs proper.

Most wristbands need plackets in the sleeves; most cuffs do not. (*For the making of plackets, see this heading.*)

Turn-back Cuffs

These may be single or double. If single, finish the edge with binding or braid, or according to the style you are making, and join the cuff into a ring with a plain seam. Place the cuff inside the lower edge of the sleeve, right side of cuff against the wrong side of the sleeve. Seam the two together. Turn the cuff over to the right side of the sleeve and secure its edge to the sleeve with an invisible stitch here and there, so that it will not flop down in wear.

If turn-back cuffs are double, lay the right sides of cuff and lining together, and seam them all round except along the edge which will join the sleeve. Turn the cuff right side out and join to the lower edge as for a wristband (*see below*), afterwards turning the cuff back up the sleeve and tacking it in position.

Detachable Turn-back Cuffs

These are useful when the cuffs will need

frequent laundering. They should have their wrist edges bound with bias tape, as described for detachable collars, and be merely tacked into the sleeve through this bind.

Wristbands

These are usually put on to a sleeve—blouse or otherwise—full enough to be gathered at its lower edge into the band. Provide the sleeve with one of the sleeve plackets described under Plackets, and gather it to fit the wristband.

Fig. 61

Make up the wristband of double material as for a double cuff. Set it on to the sleeve very much as a double collar is applied, thus: lay the upper layer of the wristband to the gathered edge of the sleeve, with the right side of the wristband against the right side of the sleeve, and seam. Each end of the wristband comes to one edge of the placket, of course. Turn the wristband through to the right side and hem down its lower layer to the wrong side of the sleeve (*see Fig. 61*).

Narrow Wristband with Tie Ends

Mark in the middle of one long edge the length that will be taken up by the sleeve being set in, arranging this so that one of the ends left over is slightly longer than the other. With right sides together, seam the two halves of the wristband together everywhere except along the part marked off for the sleeve. Turn right side out and press carefully, getting good corners. Set the sleeve into the open edges, as described above for an ordinary wristband.

Wrist Finishes

Many sleeves, especially in plain dresses are without cuffs. In this case, after the sleeve is set in, try on the dress and put a row of pins where the wrist end of the sleeve is to be. Turn in along the pins and face with a bias strip of material or bias tape. (*See Facings.*) Or in a thin material the wrist edge is sometimes bound. Short sleeves can be finished similarly (*see Fig. 62*).

For the wrist of a lined coat which needs a little extra firmness to give a nice tailor-made look, turn up the wrist edge over

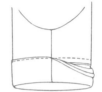

Fig. 62

2-inch wide bias strips of firm unbleached calico. First secure these to the sleeve with diagonal tacking, then hem the wrist turnings down over one edge of the strip and the sleeve turnings down over each of its ends. Remove the tackings. After the sleeve is lined, secure the upper edge of the strip, if necessary, invisibly to the lining.

DARTS

These are a very flat and neat way of disposing of surplus fullness in the interior of a garment, where it cannot be taken up by a seam, and where gathers would be too bulky or otherwise inconvenient. When darts gradually narrow down a portion of a garment, as at the shoulder or to narrow the waist of a skirt or blouse, they are wedge-shaped. When they narrow it at the centre, widening to nothing at each end, they are oval in shape, and are used chiefly to fit in the waistline of a garment cut down in one piece such as a sheath style.

Many dresses and coats have shoulder darts, which are quite deep at the shoulder seam and fade away downwards to give the extra width needed by the bust. Darts may also be horizontal, and start at the side seams at bust or waist level for fitting purposes.

I have explained in Pattern Marking (*page 113*) how to mark on your cut material the perforations by which darts are indicated on a paper pattern. Never cut out a dart till after it is stitched. Taking up the shoulder darts is the first job in making a dress, as they must be done and pressed before the shoulder seams are joined.

To take up the darts, carefully match and pin together the two lines of tailor tacking. Then tack them. Try on for fit, making the dart deeper or shallower, longer or shorter, as required. When correct, stitch along the tacking, starting at the wide end—the shoulder, in the case of a shoulder dart. Stitch in a tapering line towards the fold, so that by the time the end is reached the dart is hardly a thread of the material wide and tails off imperceptibly. (*See Fig. 63*)

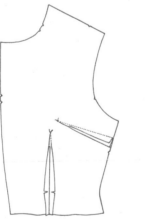

Fig. 63

If it is a wide dart and the material is thick cut the fold off, leaving only enough for turnings at the wide end. When the fold gets very narrow near the bottom, leave it uncut. Press the turnings back flat, one each way, pressing the narrow uncut part centrally over the dart. Overcast the raw edges of the turnings.

Oval interior darts must be tapered away at each end and the fold cut only in the thick centre part. As the turnings are curved, it will be necessary to nick them well before they will press out flat.

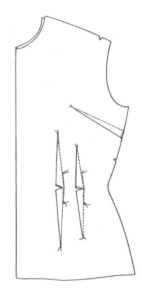

Fig. 64

Small shoulder or wedge-shaped fitting darts in thin material are not bulky and are often not cut open, but pressed towards the centre front. In transparent materials darts should be replaced by a group of narrow tucks. (*Fig. 64*)

FACINGS

A facing is really a hem made of an added piece of material instead of by double-folding in the edge of the garment. Facings may be straight-cut for straight edges, bias-cut for bias edges or occasionally cut to shape by the pattern used for the garment.

Front facings to coats and blouses are too wide and too much shaped to be classed as hems. They DO serve as hems for centre-front openings, but also provide the material which shows when revers are turned back and give a double thickness for fastenings.

Ordinary facings may be used to finish almost any edge, such as a neckline, arm-hole, panel, collar and so on. They are also used as hems at the lower edges of garments when there is not enough material to allow a hem being turned up. They are then often called false hems, and are convenient for lengthening children's outgrown clothes.

If merely required as a neat finish, a facing is of self- or nearly matching material, and is placed on the WRONG side. If used as a trimming, a facing is put on the RIGHT side, and usually contrasts in colour or material, or is cut bias on a patterned fabric to give a contrast of weave. This is particularly attractive in checked or striped fabrics.

Straight facings are simply straight-cut strips of material about $1\frac{1}{2}$ inches wide, or whatever width is in fashion—wider, of course, if they are to serve as false hems. Bias-cut facings are strips the same width cut on the true bias, as explained under Bindings on page 119. Wrong-side facings, especially, may have several joins in them to economize material; when they are bias, follow the rules for joining bias strips given under Bindings. For shaped facings, use the edges of the garment to be faced as patterns, but cut the facings only to a depth of $1\frac{1}{2}$ or 2 inches. They should be cut with the weave of the material the same way as in the garment.

Wrong-Side Facings

Cut the facing strip as just described. Lay the facing to the edge of the garment, right sides touching, and seam. Press the facing down along the seam; then treat its free edge as an ordinary hem.

Right-side Facings

Cut the facing strip as described above.

Lay it right side facing the wrong side of the garment and seam along the edge. Turn over to the right side of the garment and press down. Turn in and tack its free edge, and secure with a line of right-side machine-stitching.

Shaped Facings

Apply as a wrong-side or right-side facing, whichever it may be, neatly mitring any corners. (*See Mitres on page 133.*) Front facings for blouses are only stitched to the upper (rever) part, the lower half of the facing being cut as an oblong. This is not hemmed down to the blouse, but has its edges separately machine-stitched. Any buttonholes are worked through both blouse and facing.

FASTENINGS

In modern clothes fastenings are very few, so there is really no excuse for not putting them on as neatly as possible. They are details—but important ones.

Buttons

These may actually fasten some part of a garment or be merely ornamental. If the latter, there will be no pull on them and the chief question is to get them in exactly the right position; if in pairs, the pairs must match as to position and as to the way up in which they are sewn; if in a line, see that all the buttons are exactly below each other and even distances apart. The only way to ensure this is to mark the position of each beforehand with chalk or a pin.

If buttons are for use, not ornament, they must always be attached to a double thick-ness of material. Provide the second, if necessary, by putting a small square of material behind the spot where the button will be sewn. To give enough play for fastening and unfastening, when sewing on a two-hole button, slip a pin under the securing threads; for a four-hole, place two crossed pins between button and stitches. Finish with a 'neck' of thread wound round the loose stitches.

Hooks and Eyes

These are best for a close, tightly fitting fastening. Place these, again, on a hem or double material. Sew down the curves of both with neat buttonhole-stitching, and also oversew down the shank of the hook. If preferred, work buttonholed bars (like belt-holders but only just long enough to hold the hook) instead of eyes. (*See under Belts.*)

Loops

Loops are sometimes used for buttons instead of buttonholes. There are two kinds—rouleau loops and worked loops. Make the rouleau kind as very fine rouleaux (*see page 137*) attached in a semicircle to fit the button.

Buttonholed loops are made like buttonholed bars and belt-holders. If working a row of loops, carry straight on from one to the next with the same thread. To make the second exactly the same size as the first, cut a slip of cardboard that will just go through the first, and make the bar stitches of subsequent loops over this; or work them over a pencil.

Press studs

These are a most convenient fastening. Always sew the sunk half of the stud to the underside of the placket or other opening and the knob half to the upper side. Attach each half of the stud with several over-sewing stitches through each hole outwards. Sew the knob half on first, then press it against the under side of the placket and it will leave a tiny mark showing just where to attach the sunk half.

Velcro

This is another useful modern fastener. It consists of two tapes, one to be sewn on each side of the placket. One tape has a rough hairy surface and fastens to the other on the same principle as a burr found in country hedges. To open, the taped edges are merely pulled apart. This fastener is most useful in upholstery.

Zip fasteners

The most usual fastener today is the zip or slide fastener. This can be inserted in a side seam, or a long zip may run from the neck two-thirds of the way down the back of a slim fitting dress. Sometimes a short zip may fasten the back neck, and a longer one, about 9 inches, may be used at the side opening. Quite short zips are available for the edges of tight-fitting sleeves. Buy the zip fastener the exact length suggested on the pattern. (*See page 141* on how to insert a zip fastener, also *Figs. 71, 72 and 73.*)

Choose your zip fastener in the weight to suit the material and the type of garment. For thick material or a garment that will get much heavy wear you will need a heavier zip. On a light dress or a blouse a fine zip should be used. Match the colour as nearly as you can to the material of the garment.

FLARES AND FLOUNCES

Flounces are wide frills without any gathering, being cut on the bias so that they flare out naturally at the lower edge and give an effect of fullness. A whole skirt or an inset (often called a flare) may also be so cut that it gives this flared effect.

Flares and flounces depend on grace and lightness for their charm, so they should be finished rather casually. Make joins in flounces (and frills) with plain seams and leave the edges unfinished or overcast on a fraying material. A favourite and equally casual edge finish is to turn in the edge narrowly once only and machine along the extreme fold. Again the raw edges are left raw.

Never fit flounces by altering the seams, but always by lifting or lowering the top edge by which they are joined to the garment. In this way not only the length but the general hang and the distribution of fullness are controlled. Inset flares must also be altered, if required, by raising or lowering them where they join the main part of the garment. They are usually set in with lapped seams.

Read carefully the next heading Frills for most of what is said there applies to flounces and flared parts generally. A flared skirt is best finished at the hem with machine-stitching on a single turn, as described above, with binding or with picoting. Sew on flounces as described for Frills.

FRILLS

Frills are rather narrow strips of material gathered along one edge and sewn to a dress along the gathered edge only to form a trimming. The free edge, which flutters prettily, is finished with a narrow machine-hem, a bind or shop-made picot edging.

Frills fall more gracefully if cut on the bias; but as straight-cut frills are easier to iron, they are sometimes preferred in children's washable clothes. Cut straight frills across from selvedge to selvedge, not parallel with it.

The fullness required in a frill is generally $1\frac{1}{2}$ times the straight length to be covered by it. That is, to cover with a frill a space $\frac{1}{2}$ yard long, you should cut your frill $\frac{3}{4}$ yard long—more, if it is of very thin, flimsy material. Bias-cut frills may be a little less full, as they have a natural flare of their own.

If frills are long, for gathering divide them with pins into two or four equal parts, similarly dividing the space on the garment they are to cover. Gather each portion on a separate thread and pull this up to fit exactly the corresponding pinned space. In this way you ensure an even amount of gathering throughout.

There are two ways of joining a frill to a garment.

The first way is to lay the gathered frill UPWARDS on the garment, right sides touching, with the amount of turning allowed coming below the line on the garment to which it is to be fixed. Seam along the line, leaving the edges raw. In wear it will drop down, quite concealing the seam.

For the second method, crease a single turn along the upper edge of the frill and gather it through this turning. Or finish the upper as well as the lower edge with picoting and gather through the single thickness only. Lay the frill in position and machine-stitch in place through the gathers.

FUR TRIMMINGS

Fur is not at all difficult to handle, and every home dressmaker should accustom herself to it, for fur collars and other fur trimmings are among the cosiest and most becoming of all trimmings.

To cut a shaped piece, such as a collar, from fur, a complete pattern is needed, since fur cannot be folded for the two halves to be cut at once. If only half the collar pattern is given, lay it to a fold of newspaper and so cut it out complete. Then place it on the fur, laid out flat, with the skin side upwards, avoiding as far as possible any rough or badly coloured parts.

Put a weight on the pattern to hold it firm, and mark round it on the skin, using ink or tailor's chalk, and allowing no turnings.

Cut out with a sharp knife, never scissors. Lay the fur, skin side upwards, on a sheet of glass, holding it firmly with the left hand. With the right slash cleanly along the marked lines with a sharp penknife or a razor blade set into a handle. It is easier if a second person holds the fur while you cut.

Now the cut-out collar must be taped and padded. Both operations are very easy. Lay ½ inch tape to the edge of the skin, the right side of the tape against the fur, and oversew the tape and skin edge together all round. Next insert the padding.

Padding increases the wear and warmth of fur (especially the thin, cheap kinds) and gives it a richer appearance. A single layer of cotton-wool is the best padding, unless the fur is really thick, in which case you may prefer domett. Cut the padding the exact size of the fur, without turnings. Lay it smoothly against the skin side. Turn the free edge of the tape over its raw edge and tack the tape down to it.

If you are using small pieces of fur to make your collar, joins may be needed. In this case match up the pieces before marking and cutting the shape. Take care that the fur on joined pieces smooths the same way, and make the seam by laying the two cut edges together, skin side uppermost, pushing down any fur which pokes up between them and oversewing the edges firmly together.

Your fur collar will have a lining of the coat material. When sewing these together, it is a help to have a small piece of card with which you can hold back the fur as you sew, so that it does not get caught in the thread and hide what you are doing. The same applies when sewing on fur edgings, or ready-made collars and cuffs.

If the fur edging is a soft, narrow one, on the wrong side it will probably have a thin padded roll. In this case there is an easy way of sewing it on. Leave a turning on the edge being trimmed. The right distance inside this, diagonally tack the padded roll on the fur to the coat, working from the WRONG side. Then turn in and hand-stitch a hem that will cover the tackings. By this method the fur never gets in your needle's way.

HEMS AND CASINGS

The skirt hem is one of the last parts of a garment to be finished. On your paper pattern the hem allowance will be clearly marked and as well you will have checked the skirt length before cutting out. An average depth of a hem is 2 inches (but on dresses for a rapidly growing child it is better to leave at least 2½ inches to allow for letting down).

From your measurements run a row of pins or tacks around the hem at the required length. If you have a hem marker try on the garment, fastening the belt or any fasteners at the waist, and mark the hemline. Tack up the hem as marked and try on the garment again before stitching, adjusting if necessary.

Hems are usually best hand-stitched, especially on a thin or transparent material. If you have a blind stitch attachment to your sewing machine you can, with practice, do a near professional job stitching the hem turn almost invisibly. An ordinary machine stitched hem is only suitable for a skirt lining.

In dressmaking there are different hem finishes to suit different weights of material or types of garment.

Plain Hem

This is the one with the double turn. It is

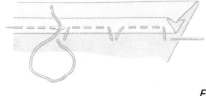

Fig. 65

correct for hemming more or less straight edges in cotton, linen, very thin wool and most silks (*Fig. 65*).

Flared or Gathered Hem

This is used for turning up an edge which is flared, bell-shaped or very definitely on the curve. This results in the raw edge being distinctly wider than the part to which it is to be hemmed, so that some method of disposing of the surplus fullness is needed. The usual plan is to gather ¼ inch from the raw edge wherever a curve occurs, to draw up that edge to the correct length. In thin materials these gathers will not be bulky, but in woollen materials they should be shrunk after gathering. This is done by damping the gathers and then pressing them with a really hot iron, without a press-cloth between.

In any material, fold and stitch bias tape or a bias strip over the edge all along. This is used instead of a double turn, as the gathers add bulk enough. Invisibly hem the fold of the bias down to the skirt.

In cotton materials use flat pleats instead of gathers.

The Skirt Hem

This is an even flatter variation of the gathered hem, and is used for tailored garments, such as costume skirts, and un-lined coats, which are made of thick, bulky woollens. Gather and shrink the gathers as described above. Then lap one edge of matching Prussian binding ¼ inch over the raw edge and stitch it on by machine, through the edge only, not the skirt. Finish by slipstitching the free edge of the binding to the skirt.

Other finishes besides hems may be used for the lower edges of rather flimsy dresses. They may be bound (*see Binding page 119*) or picot-edged at a shop which specializes in this work. For the latter finish prepare the dress by running a tacking just where the edge of the skirt is to be.

For hems in lined coats, *see Linings page 132.*

Casings

When hems have elastic, ribbon or tape run through them to draw them up, so that they will fit tightly round waist, knee, wrist or elsewhere, they are called casings. Casings, unlike hems, are nearly always machined.

It is advisable to make a casing ¼ inch wider than is needed to take the elastic, tape or ribbon comfortably, and to run a second line of stitching just inside the folded edge, thus making the tiniest of headings. This extra line of stitching prevents the edge of the elastic from wearing through the fold of material.

Casings are used chiefly on underwear and babies' garments.

If a casing is needed where there is no edge to turn a hem, as to draw in the waist of a dress cut out in one piece, then a tape or a straight strip of material with both edges turned in singly must be applied to the wrong side in the correct position to give the two thicknesses between which the elastic will be held.

To make the insertion of the elastic easy, when stitching the lower casing edge stitch the first inch through the casing turn only and not through the garment. This leaves a neat little opening for the elastic.

When ribbons are run through casings and tied ornamentally on the right side, two tiny vertical buttonholes must be made in the garment, through which each end of the ribbon may emerge. (*See Buttonholes page 120.*)

LACE TRIMMINGS

There are several ways of joining a lace edging or insertion to an edge of fabric.

One way is to roll the raw edge of the material inwards, very finely, between finger and thumb, and to whip the edge of the lace to the roll. As the roll does not 'stay put' well until sewn, roll only a little at a time as you go along.

Another plan—easier, but not quite so neat—is to place the straight edge of the lace along $\frac{1}{4}$ inch below the raw edge of the material, right sides touching, and the lace upside-down. Then overcast the lace to the fabric. This will result in a quite effective whipping of the raw edges down to the lace edge.

A very dainty method suited to fine hand-sewn underwear and babies' frocks is to join on the lace with lace stitch, *see page 34.*

If a garment edge is to be finished with both insertion and edging, join the insertion to the edge and then the edging to the free side of the insertion.

When lace is to be put on full instead of flat, first pull it up into gathers by the tiny thread which usually lies inside its edge and only needs drawing up to the required fullness. Allow extra fullness when turning a corner so that the lace will set well round the angle.

If the lace is set on flat, the corner must be turned either by gathering for $\frac{1}{2}$ inch or so each side of the angle, or a mitre must be made (*see Mitres page 133*). Match the pattern carefully, even if a little lace is wasted in doing so. Use a french or run-and-fell seam for the mitre joins.

Joining on Lace Yokes

A ready-made lace yoke is often used for the top of a dress or a nightgown. Tack the yoke in position well over the edges of the material to which it is to be attached, and secure it with a narrow line of satin stitch or cord stitch (*see pages 38 and 27 for these stitches*), or it may be machine stitched in place. Afterwards cut away any surplus material on the wrong side.

Inserting a Lace Motif

To set in a lace motif into a blouse or underwear so that it gives a transparent effect, lay and tack the motif in position on the garment. Closely buttonhole it into position all round its edge, then carefully cut away the material behind the lace close up to the buttonholed edges.

LININGS

Simple straight dresses made of flimsy materials are sometimes lined throughout to give them 'body'. In some cases the lining is made together with the dress (such as a lace dress over taffeta), the two parts being cut out exactly the same from the same pattern pieces and then tacked together to be made up as one. Darts or tucks may be stitched through both thicknesses if really thin, or they may be made in the individual pieces and then tacked together for the side seams to be stitched together.

If a dress is to have a loose lining it may be joined to the dress at the shoulders and armholes, but be cut less full to hang straight to the hem. The hem will be turned up independently.

A jacket of a suit or a coat may be lined depending on the material of which it is to be made. Follow the directions given with the paper pattern for these will give advice as to whether a material needs lining.

It may be, however, that a coat or jacket of a ready-made outfit needs relining as the material is still good, though the lining is worn. Or you may want to add a lining to an unlined coat to give it extra warmth. In this latter case you need, first of all, to interline the front facings of your coat. This may be done with unbleached calico or with one of the patent interlinings (some can be ironed on to the wrong side of the fabric to save tacking).

Interlining Coat Fronts

Using the pattern of your front facing, cut an interlining in firm unbleached calico. Place the inner edge of the pattern to the selvedge or straight lengthwise thread of the interlining and cut without turnings.

After seaming the front facing to the coat fronts, lay the interlining between the two. Fold back the facing out of the way, and diagonally tack the interlining to the coat down both long edges. This is to hold it firmly in position while you next hem the shoulder, neck and front edges of the interlining to the seam turnings of coat and facing. Leave the inner interlining edge free. Remove the tackings.

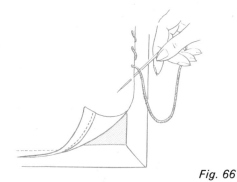

Fig. 66

Re-lining a Coat

Cut the new lining by the old one, which you have removed, completely unpicked, and well pressed. If you are making a new coat, use the coat pattern for the lining, but cut the back an inch wider all down and the fronts narrower by the width of the front facings, plus turnings. (When lining a hitherto unlined coat, you must use a similar pattern for the lining, or cut your own pattern by pinning sheets of newspaper down to each part of the coat and cutting at the seams. For the sleeve, however, a proper paper pattern will be necessary.)

Plain-seam the shoulder and side seams of the lining. Lay the coat out, wrong side upwards, or put it wrong side out on your dress form. Fit in the lining, matching and pinning the main seams and the armholes, and arranging the extra fullness in the back into a loose pleat at the centre back. Try on to make sure the lining does not strain anywhere. Then, turning the lining back a bit at a time, tack its shoulder and side-seam turnings to those of the coat. (*See Fig. 66.*)

Turn back the lining into position. Machine a hem along the lining lower edge making its length 1 inch shorter than the coat. If you are making the coat too, turn in a single-turn hem along the bottom and slipstitch it invisibly, quite separately from the lining. Slipstitch the lining fronts over the raw inner edges of the facings. Tack the lining to the coat round neckline and armholes. Make up the lining sleeves and slip them into the coat sleeves, wrong sides touching. Hem the lining wrists to the inside of the coat wrists, $\frac{1}{2}$ inch up from the wrist. Hem the armhole edges of the lining sleeves down over the coat armholes, covering their raw edges, and the collar down over the neckline edges.

MITRES (Fig. 67)

The diagonal joins made in two strips where they meet at corners, in order to form a true right-angle, are known as mitres. They occur in facings, bindings, lace, and other strip trimmings at the corners of square necks, also at the points of V-necks, though these are more acute than right-angles. Mitres occur frequently, too, in home upholstery.

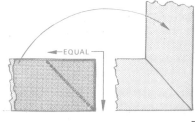

Fig. 67

A mitred corner must be a true right-angle, or fit and trimness are lost. When cutting the strips which will form the corner or face it, remember to cut them long enough to reach to the OUTSIDE point of the corner, plus turnings—not merely to meet at the inside angle.

To make the mitre, lay the two strips together, right sides touching; then fold them over diagonally, so that the end lies along one side edge, as when getting the line for bias cutting (*see Binding*). Mark the end of the diagonal line with a pin.

To get a perfectly straight seam, rule a line from the pin to the corner diagonally opposite, and seam exactly along this line. Unfold the two strips, when they will be found to be joined together exactly at right angles and can then be used for facing the required corner of the garment.

When binding, tack down the first edge of the bind to the garment in the ordinary way, and only mitre the corner as it is reached. To do this, at the exact corner (seam lines, not edges, of course) nip up a triangular fold of binding, so that the bind will then lie straight along the other angle of the corner. In tacking, put the needle through the fold and continue along the second angle. In stitching, lift the presser-foot and without breaking the thread swing over the fold and continue stitching. When the binding is finished a neat diagonal crease results at the corner.

This is for an outside corner. For an inside corner, whether a V-neck or a true right-angle, tack the bind along ¼ inch past the corner (seam lines, not raw edges), stretching it slightly at this point. Nick the corner diagonally almost to the tacking, and fold it down so that the two angles of the corner form one straight line. Tack straight on as if the corner were a single straight edge. When machining, at the corner keep the needle in but raise the presser-foot and swing the fold out of the

way, so that you can continue stitching along the second side. Finish the bind as usual.

PIPING

A good way to accentuate a pretty seam line and to add a touch of contrasting colour at the same time is to put in a piping. This trimming has a simplicity which makes it particularly suitable for children's clothes.

In dressmaking a piping is often merely a narrow fold of contrasting bias material inserted in the join, say, of yoke and skirt or round a patch pocket. Use narrow bias-cut strips of material or bias tape as for bindings, but only 1 inch wide. Crease the piping in half lengthwise, and place it between the two edges to be joined, so that the fold projects slightly beyond them.

Where a bolder effect is wanted, a corded piping is used. (*See page 199.*) In upholstery work, such as loose covers and cushions, corded piping is always used to give this more substantial effect.

PLACKETS

Openings, usually in a seam, to enable a garment to be taken on and off easily, are known as plackets. They are provided with fastenings to close them in wear, and as plackets should be as unnoticeable as possible, it is necessary to make them very neatly, particularly if the garment is made of a flimsy material such as lace, organdie, georgette or chiffon. Even though there are very fine zip fasteners available it is usually better to fasten delicate materials with tiny buttons and loops (especially for babies' clothes), or tiny hooks and bars. On most other materials zip fasteners are now preferred, and detailed instructions for setting these into position may be found on page 141.

Dress Side-seam Placket

Where a placket is to be fastened with press studs a wrap placket is simple and unobtrusive if made with matching fabric, or a fine binding tape.

Two strips of self or thinner material are needed. For an 8-inch placket one should be 9 inches long by 1¼ inches wide, and the other the same length but 2 inches wide. Lay one long edge of the wider strip to the back edge of the placket, right sides touching, and seam. Turn the strip over the raw edge and fell its folded-in other edge on the wrong side to the machine-stitching, as in binding. In fact, this wrap, as it is called, is actually a very wide bind.

With the narrower strip, face in the front placket edge, as described under Facings. Turn in and run together the raw double edges of the wrap at top and bottom of the placket, and sew the matching halves of press studs or hooks and eyes 2 inches apart down the placket. To prevent tearing down, the bottom fastener at the extreme end of the placket should be kept fastened.

One-Piece Placket

Here facing and wrap are cut together in one piece. This very neat and flat placket launders well, so it is specially suitable for thin or washable dresses and for underwear. Begin by cutting a strip of self or thinner material twice the length of the placket, plus turnings. For underwear it should be 1¾ inches wide; for dresses 2½ inches wide. Crease the strip in half lengthwise and then in half widthwise, thus dividing it into four equal quarters. Cut one of these quarters right away, except for ¼ inch turnings left next to the creases each way; then cut a tiny diagonal nick in the right-angle left, up to the 'cross-roads' of the creases.

Lay one long edge of the wide part of the strip (the edge which is continuous all the way down, not that which has the quarter cut from it) to the back placket edge, right sides touching, and stitch. When you reach the bottom of the placket, continue stitching the narrow part of the strip straight up the front placket edge. Press the seam and turn the strip through to the wrong side. There hem down the narrower half to form a facing. Double and hem down the wider half to make a wrap, stitching its base to the seam turnings to hold it. Finish with fasteners or tiny buttons and loops on babies' clothes.

PLEATS *(Fig. 68)*

On paper patterns the exact position of pleats is marked by perforations or printed lines, making pleating a very easy matter. After cutting out, tailor-tack the perforated lines as described under Pattern Marking. Then, when you are ready to put in the pleats, all you have to do is to fold and tack them along the tailor-tacked lines and they are ready for pressing.

Remember when matching up the tailor tacks that:

Side pleats are folded to lie all one way, usually facing outwards from the centre front.

A box-pleat is a pair of pleats placed so that they just touch, each pleat facing

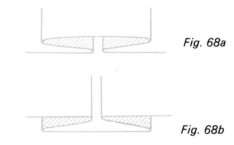

Fig. 68a

Fig. 68b

outwards away from the other. (*Fig. 68a*)

An inverted pleat is the exact opposite

of a box-pleat—that is, a pair of touching pleats which face inwards towards each other. (*Fig. 68b*)

It may happen that you must make pleats without perforations on the pattern to guide you—you may be renovating without a pattern or adding pleats to a design which originally had none. In this case, when cutting allow for each pleat three times its own width; thus a pleat 1 inch wide requires 3 inches of material. In some cases it is easier to fold and tack the pleats on the material before cutting it out.

The whole beauty of pleats lies in their complete regularity. To make sure they are all exactly the same width, the same distance apart, and perfectly vertical, measure very carefully along both top and bottom edges where the pleats are to come, and put in a pin at each folding point and at each point to which a fold is to reach. Or, better still, make yourself a pleat gauge.

This is an easy matter. Cut a strip of thin cardboard 1½ inches wide and as long as is necessary for your particular pleats. Out of one long edge cut two notches, having marked them very accurately first. The first notch shows the width of the pleat (measuring from the end of the card to the notch), and the second, exactly twice that length from the first notch, indicates where the next pleat is to start. By using this guide you ensure accuracy.

To Press Pleats

Place them, tacked all along, on your ironing-board. Have ready two press-cloths, one wet and one dry, and a hot iron. Press the pleats first with a vigorous thumping movement under the damp cloth. Remove it at once and substitute the dry cloth over the rising steam. Press back the steam into the pleats and they will always stay in well.

If the pleats are to be stitched part of the way down, do this next by machine, stitching the width of the presser-foot, or less, away from the folded edge. When removing tackings from pleats, never pull out the whole tacking from one end; this disarranges your careful pressing. Instead, snip the tackings every few inches, and remove the short ends with your fingers or tweezers. The free part of a pleat is sometimes stitched close to the fold to keep it well in place.

POCKETS

Only the simplest varieties of pockets are given here, for the more elaborate ones are not used except on strictly tailored garments and are not wanted by the average home dressmaker.

The Jumper Pocket

This is particularly easy and satisfactory for children's wear and washable garments. Use it for plain jumpers and blouses, play frocks, and little boys' blouses and rompers. This pocket is best made up on the front part of the garment directly after cutting and marking, before any seams are stitched.

Mark a horizontal line, 5 inches long, on the garment for the pocket opening. Centre exactly over the marked line a strip of self-material 10 inches long by 6½ inches wide, right side downwards. Mark the pocket line on this strip too, exactly over the garment marking, and frame it with an oblong of tacking, joining the strip to the garment well outside the marked line. In a long oval curve machine-stitch round the mark, touching it at each end, but being ⅛ inch away at the centre above and below. Start machining at the lower centre NOT at a corner.

Starting from the centre, cut each way along the pocket line to within two or three threads of the stitching. Take the two halves of the slit through to the wrong side, as for a bound buttonhole (*see Buttonholes*), and tack them twice to the edge of the slit— once close to the edge and again ¼ inch away.

Machine-stitch all round the opening $\frac{1}{16}$ inch from the edge. Along the outer line of tacking, stitch again, joining each end top and bottom with short vertical lines so that the whole forms a rectangular frame. Turn the work over to the wrong side. Form the pouch by pressing the upper half of the strip well downwards over the lower half. Cut off the lower edges of both to the same length, round off the lower corners; seam the halves together, and overcast the raw edges.

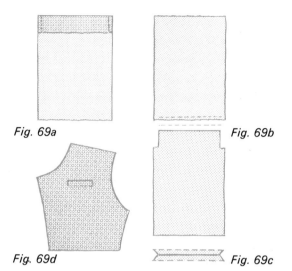

Fig. 69a   Fig. 69b

Fig. 69d   Fig. 69c

Patch Pocket

This is the simplest of all pockets, as it is merely a more or less square patch of stuff with its top edge hemmed, bound or faced, and its other three edges turned in singly and stitched to the garment. Make a patch pocket about 6 inches wide by 5½ inches deep—smaller for children's garments. This type of pocket is suitable for cotton dresses, jumpers, blouses, overalls, aprons and also for children's clothes. The lower corners are usually rounded off to prevent the accumulation of dust in them, or the bottom edge may be shaped to a point.

Simple Stand Pocket

The stand pocket proper, used for coats and costumes, is strictly tailored and not easy to work. But you can attempt this simplified version for tailored-looking dresses and unlined coats in washable fabrics.

Mark the pocket on the garment with tacking stitches. Cut two pieces of material, one 4 inches, the other 4½ inches long by the width of the pocket plus 1 inch. Turn over ½ inch on the right side at one end of the larger piece for the 'stand' and stitch the short seams (see Fig. 69a). Turn through and press. Lay the raw edge of the 'stand' along the tacking stitches but a fraction

below them, right sides together, and stitch. Lay the second pocket piece to the tacking but just above, and stitch (see Fig. 69b).

Now cut through the tacks and make a small diagonal cut at each side (see Fig. 69c). Turn the pocket pieces through the slash to wrong side of garment. Press the upper piece down over the lower one and trim the edges evenly, rounding off the corners, and stitch all round, catching in the tiny triangles at the corners of the pocket opening; overcast the edges. On the right side of the garment slipstitch the sides of the 'stand' in position and press well (see Fig. 69d).

ROULEAUX

These fine tubes of cross-cut material lend themselves to many dainty forms of trimming and are seldom entirely out of fashion, though their width and the way in which they are used may vary. Once you know how to make them lightly and neatly, you can adapt them to any style required.

Except that they are bias-cut and much narrower, rouleaux are made in exactly the same way as belts (see page 118). You will find the cutting and joining of bias strips fully described under Binding.

Strips for rouleaux must be very narrow —$\frac{3}{8}$ inch wide is the regulation width, but I advise you to practise first on strips twice this width. Double the strip lengthwise, seam along the edges with the narrowest possible turnings, and turn the tube so formed right side out.

To turn the rouleau, slip a bodkin into one end of the tube, with its eye sticking out a little. With needle and cotton sew the eye rather loosely to the end of the tube. Then push the bodkin straight through the tube. It will draw the attached end with it as it goes and so turn the whole tube right side out.

Rouleaux are generally required to look rounded, not flat, so press them only very lightly.

Sometimes rouleaux are made into a series of little bows to trim the front of a dress. Pressed out flat, like belts, they may be laid a little apart on stiff paper and faggoted together for collars, cuffs, and yokes; or woven into open or closed patterns; or plaited together and used as an edge trimming.

RUCHING

This trimming has many variations without much resemblance between them, except that all are formed of strips of material gathered or ruched up in some form. Ruching may be either delicate or bold, according to its width, its style and the material used.

Box-Pleated Ruching

This needs two finished edges, so it may be made from ribbon or from narrow straight strips of material picoted along each edge. Allow three times the finished length desired and box-pleat it all along (see *Pleats, page 135*) after first creasing it in half lengthwise. Tack down the pleats as made along the centre crease, and stitch to the garment to be trimmed along this crease also.

Corded Ruching

This is fairly heavy and striking, especially when made in velvet, as it often is. Consequently it is popular not only for dresses and evening coats, but for many upholstery uses, such as in trimming bedspreads and bolster cushions. (*See page 225.*) It is very pretty in dress or furnishing taffeta.

To make it, cut straight strips of material (usually about 2 inches wide), allowing two to two-and-a-half times the finished width needed—less in velvet, more in thinner materials. Crease a single turning along each long edge, place a fine piping cord under the crease, and seam so as just to enclose the cord without stitching it. Ruch up the strip over the cords to give a gathered effect, and stitch to the garment along each edge, concealing the stitches in the fullness. Although straight-cut, corded ruching will go round any curves by ruching more fully on one cord than the other. One end is often coiled into a spiral which makes an ornamental finish when the end is not enclosed in a seam.

In fine materials such as chiffon and georgette this ruching is often only gathered fully along each turned-in edge, without any cord being used.

Ruffled Ruching

There are two ways of making this. (1) Cut strips on the bias and fray out one edge slightly, giving them a fluted effect, if desired, by holding the edge every inch or so and making a rotary movement of the hand. Turn in and gather the other edge, and attach the ruching through the gathers to the garment. (2) Use narrow ribbon, or bias-cut strips with both edges slightly frayed out. Gather, and attach throughout the lengthwise centre. For each method allow one-and-a-half times the finished length desired.

SLEEVES

The way the sleeves are made up and set in to the armholes makes more difference to the look of a dress than almost any other single point. So it pays to take pains with them and to make any adjustments needed to get a perfect fit and hang.

Making Up Sleeves

The making of sleeves varies tremendously according to fashion and the style of garment you are making. Although the job is not a difficult one it does require a little trouble and attention to detail. Do check your pattern carefully, note any notches or instructions and follow them exactly: they are there for your guidance. Tailored sleeves of a coat or a jacket are slightly more complicated than on a simple dress, but here again by following the individual instructions for the particular style you are making and by NOT trying to take short cuts in this important part of dressmaking, you will certainly achieve success.

Bishop Sleeves

These are the rather full blouse type, set into wristbands. Stitch the sleeve seam and gather the lower edge to fit the wristband, providing it with a placket if required. Apply the wristband as described under Cuffs (*page 124*).

One-Piece Sleeves

If these are tight-fitting, elbow-room is given by allowing a little extra length on the back edge of the seam. Gather or pleat up this extra at the elbow before stitching the seam. If there is a fitting dart from wrist to

elbow, fit and stitch this, tapering it away to nothing at the elbow. Make a placket if required, but do not finish the wrist until after setting in.

Two-Piece Sleeves

These are used in tailoring rather than dressmaking. Here you have two seams and four edges all cut more or less on the cross and therefore easily stretchable. So take the precaution, when pinning the seams, of pinning at top and bottom first, and intermediately only after these points are secured. In this sleeve again, you will find a little fullness allowed at the elbow on one seam. Always tack a sleeve flat on the table, not held and folded over the fingers.

If the material has no right and wrong side, it is easy to make up both sleeves for the same arm. Take care to avoid this, and also to know which sleeve is for which arm. It sounds obvious but mistakes are sometimes made. When the sleeve is folded for seaming, look at the top curve. The side which curves in goes to the front and that which bulges outward a little goes to the back. Beginners should mark the right-hand sleeve with a cross in tacking cotton.

Even when sleeve-head darts or gathers are taken up, the top (armhole) edge of a sleeve is always slightly bigger than the armhole into which it is going to be set. This is to give ease in wear. It is adjusted to the armhole size during setting in by a slight easing of the sleeve edge.

Setting in a Sleeve (*Fig. 70*)

Hold the garment with its wrong side towards you and the armhole well opened. With the sleeve right side out, draw it just through the armhole towards you, so that its edges lie roughly flush with those of the armhole and you look into the wrong side of the sleeve. Start by carefully matching and pinning the notch on the under part of the sleeve with the armhole notch on the bodice front. According to the type of sleeve, this matching either results in the sleeve seam and under-arm seam meeting, or in the sleeve seam coming an inch or two forward of the under-arm seam.

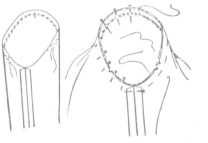

Fig. 70

Pin the lower part of the sleeve and arm-hole together, working both ways from the matched notches and easing the sleeve in very slightly. In the case of a gathered sleeve-head, adjust the gathers so that the top of the sleeve curve comes a little forward of the shoulder seam and the weave runs vertically down the sleeve. Now pin the top half to the armhole, putting all pins in ACROSS the seam, not along it. Tack over the pins, arranging any easing so that it is unnoticeable.

Remove the pins and try on the dress. The sleeve should hang well without twisting and feel comfortable when the arm is moved. When satisfactory, stitch in the sleeve and finish, as described in the assembling programme on *page 115*, stage 9.

When setting in a sleeve with a French seam on a thin fraying material this, of course, means pinning and tacking on the right side of the garment. In this case, hold the frock with its right side towards you. Turn the sleeve inside out and bring it through the armhole towards you, so that its wrong side touches the wrong side of the dress and you are looking into its right side.

Drop-Shoulder Sleeve

There is sometimes a fashion for an extra long shoulder which drops over on to the top of the arm, so that the sleeve is set in lower than usual. Be careful to match seams and notches exactly, then join the shoulder to the sleeve with a lapped seam. Stitch this close to the folded-over edge.

Magyar Sleeve

This type of sleeve is cut in one with the bodice and should always be a short or loose sleeve without any confining at the wrist. The under-arm and sleeve seam form one continuous line, curved at its centre.

Don't try to fit a magyar sleeve up tightly. It must always be fairly loose, with some bagginess under the arm. Stitch with a plain seam having good turnings. Afterwards slash the turnings every $\frac{1}{2}$ inch or so at the curved part, otherwise the seam will pucker at this point.

Raglan Sleeve

Here there is no definite round-the-arm armhole, because the seam joining the sleeve to the bodice runs up diagonally towards the neck at front and back. Stitch this diagonal seam first, the under-arm seam afterwards and slash the turnings of the latter as described for a magyar sleeve.

TUCKS

Tucks are rather narrow pleats which are usually stitched along their whole length. Some are very narrow indeed, taking up only the smallest possible ridge of material, and these are known as pin-tucks. Pin-tucks sometimes go both ways, giving a check effect.

Make tucks very much as described for side pleats, and cut a similar gauge, with notches nearer together, to guide you in making them perfectly even. Press them after tacking and again after stitching. If the stitching is done by hand, as often for baby garments, you will get the best effect if you start each tuck at the same end, not working back and forth.

Two or three tucks, made on the WRONG side, usually replace the shoulder dart in transparent materials, as on blouses.

Sometimes wide tucks running round a skirt or petticoat are in fashion and present the same problem as a hem on a curved skirt edge—that of surplus fullness on the under edge of the tuck. Dispose of this in the same way as for a curved hem, by gathering up the under edge of the tuck to fit the less full upper edge. Then stitch the tuck in the usual way.

UNDERWEAR

Though most of the underwear worn today is of nylon tricot or similar easy-care material and consequently rarely home-made, it is rather nice to make special trousseau items, for honeymoon or holiday. Woven nylon, seersucker, easy-care cotton batiste or even perhaps pure silk may all be used for delightful garments which might be expensive to buy ready-made. Pure silk should of course be entirely hand sewn with pure silk sewing thread (though the first, inner stitching of a French seam may be machine stitched). Nylon which frays easily is much better machine stitched and good turnings should be allowed.

Nylon fabrics are better sewn with a Terylene thread. All trimmings such as lace and braid should also be of nylon.

For a cotton fabric use a matching cotton thread and trim with cotton lace or *broderie anglaise*. Sometimes a contrasting bias binding is effectively used round the edges and as a trimming. This should be of cotton.

Scalloped edges are often popular, especially on cotton or pure silk underwear. To bind them, ease the binding round the outward curve of the scallops so that the bind curls over, more or less, at the inward corners. Slipstitch the other edge down to the wrong side in the usual way, and a neat, smooth bind results.

Darts in underwear are not bulky, so the fold of the dart should be merely pressed and not cut away. A very dainty plan is to tack a dart, sew it with Turkey stitch on the RIGHT side, and then cut away the back part. Darts are also useful in undies to remove the unsightly drop that often occurs under the arms of nightgowns and slips. Make them horizontal for this purpose, and place two or three, each about 2 inches long, running into the front part of the side seam a little below the armhole.

Finally try, while making, not to lose the freshness of your delicate, pale-coloured lingerie materials. It is a help to wear a clean sewing apron or light-coloured overall.

ZIP FASTENER *(Figs. 71, 72 and 73)*

To Insert a Zip Fastener

The length of the placket opening should equal the length of the teeth of the zip. First prepare the placket opening by turning in once and machine stitching the edge of the placket turnings to prevent fraying. Now turn in the sides of the placket to full seam allowance and tack in place. Lay the tapes of the zip fastener to the edges of the placket with the foot of the zip at the bottom of the placket opening. Tack the zip in to the placket so that it is almost concealed by the fold of the material. Edge stitch the placket in place by machine. As a general rule the zip should be kept closed while stitching to prevent threads of the material becoming entangled. On a closely woven fabric it may, however, be found easier to open the zip while stitching along the first side, then close it before stitching the second side. Cut away the tackings.

If a zip fastener is to be inserted in a skirt,

or at the back of the dress to the neck opening it is usual to take it to within ½ inch

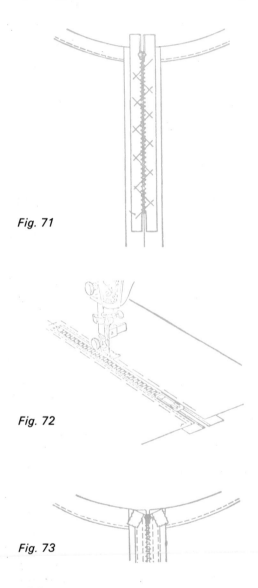

Fig. 71

Fig. 72

Fig. 73

of the top of the opening. Turn over the tops of the zip tapes and neaten under the neck facing of the dress (*see Figs. 71, 72 and 73*). On a skirt the tapes are inserted into the edges of the waistband. A hook and eye should be stitched to hold the top of the opening to prevent strain.

NEW CLOTHES FOR OLD

It sometimes happens that one has a dress or some other garment made from an exceptionally good and attractive material and when the fashion changes it hangs discarded in the cupboard. Sometimes it is worth renovating it or using the best part of the material to make some smaller garment. Children's clothes can often be cut out and made from something that was previously worn by father or mother.

Here are a few hints that will help to ensure the success of your work and make the new garment worth the trouble that has gone into it.

1. Convert or renovate only garments which may be faded or badly worn in places, but are SOUND AS A WHOLE. (It is sheer waste of time to spend hours and ingenuity on a fabric which is so thin generally from hard wear that the new garment will soon fall to pieces.)

2. Be as thorough with a conversion or renovation as you would be when making a new garment. Wash or have cleaned (according to its fabric) the old garment, unpick it carefully and use a paper pattern.

3. Plan for a new garment which is definitely smaller than the old one. Some fabric is always wasted—it is worn, torn or faded, or you want to save time by cutting away the seams instead of unpicking them. Allow generously for these curtailments and also for the fact that more material will be lost manoeuvring your pattern pieces. You are not working from uncut material, but from the various shaped pieces of an old garment.

4. Partly worn fabric never looks quite as nice as when new, yet you want your work to be smart as well as serviceable. Rely then, on careful planning and cutting, on good, unstinted workmanship, plenty of pressing and care over details. It is these that will

make your twice-cut dressmaking worth while.

New clothes for old divide into two broad groups. The first is altering a dress or other garment into something smaller FOR the same wearer—renovation. The second is cutting a garment in a considerably smaller size—say, for a child—out of an adult's dress or other item. This is conversion.

Let us take renovation first, as it is less drastic.

Renovation of Clothes

Pinafore dress from one piece dress The first signs of wear in many a dress is at the armholes. Sometimes it happens that there are perspiration stains which not only spoil the look of the dress but also help to rot the material. Sometimes it is that the sleeves of the dress were put in too close or too tightly and the material has been strained and split. If the dress material itself is good and you are fond of it, you can easily renovate it and turn it into a useful pinafore style to wear over jumpers or blouses.

Wash or dryclean the dress, then cut away all the soiled or split material. Carefully mark out with pins deep armholes each side, also mark out a deeply scooped neckline in front. Leave the back higher, taking your scoop 3 inches down from centre back neck, and tapering it up to meet the line from the front on the shoulders.

Draw a chalk line where you have the pins, measuring each side carefully so that it matches exactly. Slash down the material towards the chalk line (but not right up to it as turnings will be needed). Try on your new pinafore style and adjust curve if necessary making it deeper if required. Now cut out the curves of neckline and armholes within $\frac{1}{2}$ inch of the chalk line. Turn in to the lines and face with matching bias tape. If you are uncertain of your skill at cutting perfect curves use a paper pattern for a pinafore style.

Sleeves worn at cuffs or elbows This is a simple renovation and requires only the shortening of the sleeves. A long sleeve may be shortened to three-quarter length, if the cuffs are worn. If the elbows are worn the sleeves can be cut to above elbow length. A new three-quarter sleeve needs only to be faced up on the inside. A short sleeve may look better with a 'false cuff'. To make this, turn back on to the right side $1\frac{1}{2}$ inches from cut edge and stitch round $\frac{1}{2}$ inch from the fold. Turn the sleeve edge down and turn in the raw edge and hem to the edge of fold on inside. Press the 'cuff' flat.

Gathered or dirndl skirt into straight skirt Unpick the skirt before washing or having dry cleaned so that the fullness is pressed out before you begin your renovation. Recut your slim skirt using a paper pattern.

Refreshing a Frock When a dress is not shabby, but you are merely tired of it, much smaller alterations using only oddments of material can be made. A contrasting yoke inserted into a plain bodice, a new collar of a different type and colour, fresh buttons or other trimmings, long sleeves cut short above the elbow—something of this sort, according to what is in fashion, gives a fresh and up-to-date note with very little trouble and very little new material.

Conversions

The mother of a growing family or the aunt with small nieces and nephews can always find a use for her out-of-date shabby clothes. Some may be too adult in colour or texture or not washable easily enough for children, but most will convert delightfully into miniatures of themselves for a little girl or boy.

Here again, remember the rules given at the beginning of this section. Fresh trimmings, too, will often be needed, as buttons and zip fasteners may be too large for their new owners; but these are not expensive to replace in smaller sizes. When re-cutting, remember the extra hard wear youngsters give to their clothes and take particular care to use only sound material. It is a good plan to ring round with tailor's chalk any darns, holes, or weak areas and then lay the pattern pieces to avoid these ringed spots.

The following suggestions may be helpful when cutting down adult or teenagers' garments for children under ten.

Skirt Re-cut as little girl's skirt or pinafore frock, small boy's trousers, child's jacket.

Dress Re-cut, according to fabric and colour, as girl's frock or blouse, boy's shirt, girl's skirt, boy's trousers, dressing-gown for either (if woollen).

Blouse Re-cut as blouse or knickers for little girl or shirt for boy.

Slip Re-cut as knickers, slip or nightgown for little girl or (if of suitable material) as frock for a baby.

Coat Re-cut as coat for boy or girl, skirt or dungarees for girl, trousers or jacket for boy.

Man's Shirt Re-cut as shirt for boy, blouse or pinafore for girl, or rompers for toddlers.

Man's Trousers Re-cut as trousers for boy, skirt, slacks or coat for girl.

*Wool scraps can be utilised for knitting or crocheting gay
bed covers and rugs as shown above*

An excellent example of crochet is this
simple edging added to a breakfast cloth

MENDING

THE mending of household and personal linen is rather a dull job, and one is always tempted to let it accumulate till things get really bad. Do try to form the habit of doing each week's mending as soon as it is laundered, or, in the case of non-washable things, directly the need for repair is noticed. In this way holes and worn places never go very far and the work can be done in half the time.

Another good plan is to have a mending basket of strictly limited size. Put into this everything which needs attention, and as soon as the basket is full, sit down and attend to every one of its contents before doing any other sewing.

To reduce the time spent on mending as much as possible, remember that many repairs can be done on a modern sewing machine. Look through the attachments and book of instructions which go with your sewing machine and see if you are not neglecting some of its mending possibilities. At the same time, while machine-mending is quick and strong for household linen and knock-about garments, it is well worth spending the time on careful hand-mending for good dresses and coats.

Mending falls into three distinct divisions —darning, patching and miscellaneous.

DARNING

This form of mending consists in filling a hole or drawing together a tear by re-weaving the fabric with a thread resembling it as closely as possible. The re-weaving is done with a needle in darning stitch. Darning is suitable for small holes in most fabrics and for almost every type of hole in woollen stockings, socks and vests. It is also used for mending household linen.

A wooden darning ball or egg costs very little and is useful to put under the hole to hold it out while it is being darned. Otherwise the left hand must be used, which is rather tiring. When using a darning ball, do not strain the hole over it, or it will result in a bulging darn when the ball is taken away.

Darning stitch, as used ornamentally to cover backgrounds or large surfaces, is described in the embroidery stitches, *page 28*. As in mending, however, the object is to stimulate the weave of the fabric and also to fill the hole closely, the stitch is made rather differently. It still consists of alternating rows of running stitch. But the stitches in successive rows are worked as close as possible to each other, and a second set of rows is worked the opposite way (up and down if the first are across) and woven in and out of the first set, just as the original fabric was woven.

If the original threads of the fabric still remain one way, as is often the case, especially towards the edge of a darn, the new thread is woven in and out of them where it crosses them in regular alternations of in and out.

A little loop should be left at the end of each line when the needle is turned to start the next row. The idea of these loops is to allow for any shrinkage of the new mending thread. If this were drawn tight in the darn, after washing it might tighten the hole and cause further tearing.

The darning should also be carried some

distance each way beyond the edges of the hole, to give it a firm hold on sound threads. If a darn ends just outside the hole or in the thin, half-worn material which often surrounds it, the weight of the darn will soon tear the thin part and make the hole larger than ever.

When darning, match your thread to your material as carefully as possible in colour, thickness and actual texture, using a matching wool thread on wool, cotton on cotton, silk on silk and so on. Many sock and knitwear firms sell with each garment a card of the same thread for mending as that used in making it. When socks or stockings are hand-knitted, again a little extra wool should be bought and saved for mending them. Then any darns they need will be almost undetectable.

Never try to save work by using a coarse thread much thicker than the threads of the worn fabric. This may fill up the hole rapidly, but the darn will be clumsy and the weight of it will soon cause further holes. For a large hole a better plan is to darn with a finer thread doubled, but even this way of labour-saving should be sparingly used.

To give substance to a big hole and mend it more quickly, cheap net may be used as a foundation for darning. Cut and tack over the hole a piece of net amply larger than the hole. Then darn in the usual way over it. It is quicker and smoother and takes less thread than the ordinary method.

Darning a Tear

Tack the tear, right side out, over a piece of paper. This will hold the slit together while you darn across it. Alternate your stitches bringing the needle up on one side of the tear, down through the tear and up on the other side so that only small slanting stitches are seen. If the tear is triangular, draw the edges of the slit together in the same way. (*See Fig. 74.*) To make a firm

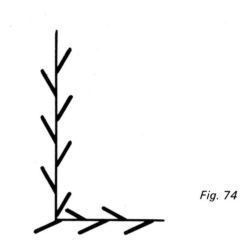

Fig. 74

repair darn under and over the threads of the fabric across the slit take the darning beyond the slit at each end.

Darning a Glove

Gloves, when of fabric, should be darned on the finger, which makes the best possible darning ball. To mend a hole in a skin glove, a special method is used. Use a three-sided glove needle specially made for sewing leather, and thread this with silk or strong thread exactly matching the glove. First buttonhole all round the edges of the hole, then fill it with closely worked buttonhole chain (*described in the Embroidery Section, page 23*), worked, round and round in narrowing circles. Such a mend has just the right elasticity. Repair splits between the fingers similarly, but work lengthwise of the split instead of round and round.

PATCHING (*Fig. 75*)

This mending method consists of applying over the hole a new piece of material matching as closely as possible. Patches are used for holes which are too large to be darned, and the art of patching consists in placing and stitching the applied pieces so that they show as little as possible.

To put on a patch, first find a suitable piece of fabric for it, if possible a piece of the same material. (Here you see the value of keeping dressmaking left-overs.) It is better not to use new material for patching, as it may be too strong and heavy for the worn garment; so save the best parts of old garments or linen for patching. If the garment has faded more than the patch, wash the latter in soapy water containing a little baking soda before applying it.

Cut all frayed and ragged edges off the hole, trimming it to a square or oblong shape. Then cut the patch the shape and size of the hole, but an inch or two larger all round, so that it will reach to firm fabric beyond the hole and allow turnings also. Tack the patch in position over the hole, on the wrong side. Turn in the edges of the patch and hem down. Finally turn in and hem down the edges of the hole to the patch.

'Topping and tailing' is a special variety

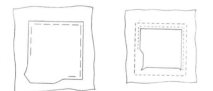

Fig. 75

of patching used to mend men's shirts when, as often happens, the edge of the collar rubs a little hole through in front while the rest of the shirt is in good condition. As the patch needed will show, it must be of the identical material and large enough for its edges not to be visible in wear. So from the shirt tails cut a piece large enough to extend right up to the shoulder seam and collar band, and far enough down for its join to be covered by the waistcoat.

The damaged tail can then be made good with pieces that don't match, cut from a shirt past repair.

Ordinary white tape is often useful for patching. On household linen, such as sheets, towels, and tea-cloths, you will have noticed that the corner by which they are pegged up on the line wears first, or (if they are sent to a laundry) the corner disfigured with marking ink. Patch such a worn corner with a strip of tape. Tape patches should merely be hemmed on.

A family of active children always make plenty of patching, and often time is wasted finding the particular left-over needed among a number of others. A good remedy is to have a net bag for each member of the family, placing all the pieces from that particular person's garments together in the bag. You can see in a moment through the net if the particular pattern you want is there.

MISCELLANEOUS MENDING

Replacing Buttons

This is, after darning and patching, probably the most frequent mending job, for laundries and washing machines are often cruelly hard on fastenings—and so are romping children.

For children's clothes it is wise to replace missing buttons by using crochet cottons instead of sewing cotton, for the crochet variety will stand far more tug and strain. For general hints on sewing on buttons and making other fastenings, *see Fastenings on page 127.*

Belts

These often detach themselves from their frocks after a certain amount of wear. When replacing them, make just a few joining stitches with darning silk and they will stay in place very much longer than if cotton were used.

Decorative Mending

This is the only kind possible if a hole or stain occurs in a conspicuous place where a darn or patch would spoil the look of the garment. When this happens you must exercise ingenuity, and think how the bad place can be covered with some form of trimming. No absolute rules can be given, as everything depends on the individual case, but here are some suggestions to choose from:

A matching or contrasting patch pocket.

An embroidered *broderie anglaise* spray incorporating a tiny hole. (*See Broderie Anglaise, page 48*.)

Appliqué embroidery to cover a small hole or stain.

Decorative panel down centre front.

Contrasting panel right across (for a cushion).

Frill or ruching.

Knitted Articles

For the repair of these, refer to the Knitting and Crochet Section.

Men's Soft Collars

If the tear or fray is where it will not show when worn, as near the right-hand button-hole, patch neatly with tape. (*See Patching, page 146*.) If in more or less visible spot, match the stripes very carefully with a piece of material cut from the tail of the matching shirt.

Sheets

These usually wear ominously thin in the centre while they are still good at each side. When this happens, cut the sheets in half lengthwise, and overlap and stitch the selvedge edges to make a new seamed centre. Keep this seam as flat as possible, stitching with rather a loose tension. To get rid of the worn portions, which are now along each edge, either cut the sheet smaller —use a double-bed size for a single bed, or single-bed size for a child's cot—or re-inforce the worn edge with a wide facing cut from the best parts of another old sheet.

Where a hole has been torn in a sheet too small for a patch it should be darned neatly. This may be done by machine using the darning attachment and working with the material held in a hoop frame. If darning by hand it is better to darn diagonally across the grain of the material as the new threads are less likely to pull in thin material.

Tablecloths

They are apt to get frayed at the edges. Cut off all the weak parts in even strips and re-hem, if it does not matter the cloth being a little smaller. If the size must be preserved, stitch the raw edge between a new double hem, white or coloured, or join it on with faggoting. (*See Seams on page 104*.) In the case of an afternoon tablecloth, lace may be added round the edges or insertion inlet into the cloth to enlarge it. Table napkins may be repaired in much the same way. If either of these items wears thin along its creases, cut a 2-inch strip off one side and end, and re-hem. This alteration will automatically cause the folds to come in fresh places and save further wear on the thin spots.

Towels

Bath towels usually wear at the long edges in time, though the centre remains in good condition. You can do one of two things with these towels. Either you can cut a large towel down to make a smaller one and perhaps a face cloth as well. Or you can merely narrow the towel. The simplest way to do this is simply to cut away the worn edge, turn in once and machine stitch using a rather large stitch and pushing the material through easily so that the stitch is not tight. If you prefer you can either bind or face the raw edges with cotton tape (which should be dipped in water to shrink it before use).

PATCHWORK
AND
RAGCRAFT

MOST of us from time to time have left-overs of materials we have used in dressmaking or upholstery; sometimes as well we have a dress which we cannot renovate or convert, but of which we love the pattern or the colour. All these scraps may be tidied away in a box and when there are enough can be used to make some attractive patchwork article or a solid and useful piece of ragcraft.

There are two main types of this thrift needlework—patchwork made by joining the pieces together into a flat surface; and various kinds of rug and cushion making in which the rags are set on a foundation so as to form a thick pile.

PATCHWORK

The Crusaders, going to Palestine in the eleventh century, brought patchwork home to England in the form of gay banners. For centuries it was very highly thought of at Court, and Queen Elizabeth I used it for some of her dresses. Right down to late Victorian times ladies pieced patchwork quilts and cushions from their oddments of material, and children learnt their plain sewing stitches by putting together innumerable squares or hexagons.

But some of the loveliest patchwork comes from the United States, where it has attained the rank of a folkcraft, constantly improving for several centuries. This is due to the fact that the early settlers in America had to get all their materials thousands of miles from England. In consequence they were so scarce and expensive that the women evolved all sorts of patterns and methods for using up even the smallest fragments from worn-out garments. As the winter nights were bitterly cold, quilts—patchwork on the top, warmly interlined, and the layers held together by quilting—were the things most often made.

There has been a revival of patchwork in recent years. Old designs have been rescued from attics, American patterns and methods have been introduced, and modern fadeless fabrics bring a new beauty into old or modern designs. Besides being an economical way of using up the small pieces of

Patchwork in hexagonal shapes are cleverly used in an applied pattern on a table mat

Plate 52

material which collect in every home where sewing is done, patchwork has a real fascination of its own, and offers wonderful opportunities for blending colours and evolving patterns.

Modern patchwork is used for a wide variety of things—not only quilts, but cushions, pram covers and tea-cosies, and as a panel or border trimming on runners, chairbacks and household linen.

There are four varieties of patchwork— crazy, in which the pieces are put together higgledy-piggledy, according to their shape, without any attempt at design; strip patchwork in which rectangles are joined into long strips to make a piece of fabric; all-over patchwork (the usual English kind); and American block patchwork, made in a series of small squares, each with the same design, and joined together.

CRAZY PATCHWORK

This is the real economy variety. The idea is not to waste even an inch or two of material by cutting it to shape, but to use each piece just as it is, fitting them together at random in the manner of a crazy pavement. Silk, velvet, linen or cotton patches

Plate 53

A traditional-looking patchwork cushion using plain and patterned fabrics. Hexagonal and diamond shapes are married together to form this star shape

Plate 53a

A strikingly modern interpretation of a patchwork cushion by R. Johnston, using tiny multi-patterned squares and coloured braiding

may be used. The first two mix quite well, so do linen and cotton, but in general it is best to keep to one type of material for each article.

Owing to the irregular shapes of the pieces, crazy patchwork is not pieced (directly seamed) together. Instead, a foundation of unbleached calico or some cheap material is used, and on this the patches are arranged, as prettily as possible, with the edges of one patch turned in and overlapped over the raw edges of another. See that the patches lie smooth, and secure them with careful tacking to the background. Afterwards hold them down permanently with feather stitch or chain stitch (*see pages 29 and 26 for these stitches*) worked in a contrasting colour or in black.

Crazy patchwork looks best if not more than one-third of the patches are patterned. It may form an entire cushion cover or other article, or be arranged as a panel or border on a plain article such as a tablecloth.

This is a good method of using up mere scraps of patterned fabric. When so many different designs are used some definite colour harmony is needed. For instance, if the cloth is pink, choose only patterns for the patchwork which have a touch of pink somewhere in them. Vary the width to get the crazy effect, and seam the patches together first in long strips, arranging them in 'steps' (each starting rather below the level of the preceding one) so that they can be placed round the cloth with seams well slanted—a much prettier effect than if they were straight. A line of couching in a deeper colour is an effective way of covering the inner hemmed-down edges of the patches.

Crazy Patchwork Dressing-gown

Patchwork can be used very colourfully for certain garments. Dressing-gowns of the housecoat type, can be made most successfully from a medley of silk or cotton patches or of woollen pieces all of one shape and size, rectangles or squares, but such a large garment takes a great number of patches and a considerable amount of patience.

But the work is basically simple and fascinating. Cut out the pieces of the pattern in butter-muslin, which will serve as a foundation for the crazywork with which you will cover it. Use all-woollen pieces— dressmaking left-overs, the best bits of old frocks or summer coats, scarves which are out-of-date or worn in places. From these build up your crazy patchwork on the muslin pieces, using patches as large as possible and all shapes and sizes. Here again, as with all crazywork, employ a majority of plain colours—usually an easy matter in woollens, which are less apt to be patterned than thin materials. Tack down the pieces, then work over them firmly with feather stitch or chain stitch, as already suggested under Crazy Patchwork.

Afterwards seam and make up the garment in the ordinary way, lining it, if possible, with a thin fabric which will hide the butter-muslin and the wrong side of the embroidery stitches.

STRIP PATCHWORK

One way of making up patchwork which can be used for garments, bedcovers or cushion covers, is to join the pieces into strips which are in turn joined to make a piece of cloth. This method is halfway between crazy patchwork and the geometrical kind where small shaped patches are used. It is a quick and useful way of making something gay at no cost whatever.

For successful patchwork of this kind all the pieces should be of the same fabric, either all cotton, all wool (tweeds of various kinds can be put together), all rayon and so on. Cut your patches into approximately the same size oblongs (about 2 inches wide by 3 inches deep is a good size). Now join them into long strips across their shorter sides using single seams. The length of strips will depend on what you are going to make of your patchwork; if you are making a bedcover you need the strips to be either the length or the width of the finished cover, if a cushion cover then probably about 20 inches would be long enough. Arrange the patches in a gay assortment of colours.

When you have enough strips join these together down their long sides alternating the strips so that the cross seams of one strip are in the centre of the patches of the adjoining strip. When all the strips are joined in this way you will have a piece of material made up of patchwork which you can use as any new fabric.

A housecoat for yourself or a dressing gown for a child can be made from gay strip patchwork. In this case it saves the 'material' if you join your long strips into large oblongs in the various sizes of the pattern pieces. When you cut out lay the pattern pieces on a relevant piece of patchwork fabric to cut to the correct shape. The garment will of course have to be lined to hide the joins of the patchwork.

ALL-OVER GEOMETRICAL PATCHWORK *(Pls. 52, 53 and 53a)*

This variety is typically English and most Victorian patchwork was of this type. Geometrical shapes were always used, because they are the only kind that will join endlessly to each other without leaving gaps or spoiling the pattern, and the joins are made by piecing. While the pattern is kept regular, usually plain and patterned patches of every colour are mixed together.

Appliqué and patchwork, by the way, shade into each other, and it is difficult to say where one ends and the other begins; but roughly speaking appliqué is made with embroidery stitches and patchwork with plain sewing ones.

It is easy and fascinating to build up simple all-over designs with squares, oblongs, hexagons, diamonds, and triangles. Metal templates of these shapes may be bought, which only need to be pencilled round on paper to provide a pattern for the patches—a pattern for EACH patch, strictly speaking. For, remember, the only way to keep geometrical patchwork absolutely uniform and unstretched, if there are any bias-cut edges (and there must be when using hexagons, diamonds, or triangles), is to make up each over a paper shape.

The method is very simple. Cut for each patch a pattern in brown or other stiff paper. Cut all the paper patterns from one template or model, not from each other, so that the size does not vary in the slightest. To cut a patch, pin a paper pattern on to material and cut round it with $\frac{1}{4}$ inch turnings. Fold these turnings back over the paper to the wrong side and tack securely all round through patch, paper, and turnings. When sufficient patches are thus prepared, arrange them according to the pattern and oversew their folded edges together from the wrong side. Do not remove the tackings and release the papers until the whole of the patchwork is done.

A quilt or other single-thickness item made in this way must be lined to cover the raw edges of the patches. Patchwork of this kind is very hardwearing and many painstaking samples of traditional British patchwork may be viewed in the Victoria and Albert Museum in London.

AMERICAN BLOCK PATCHWORK

The characteristics of this type are: it is made up from a series of squares of unbleached calico (called 'blocks') which are joined together, with or without intermediate strips and a border, to form a quilt. Each block is made up separately first with a definite pieced or appliqué patchwork design, and only one design is used throughout a quilt, though the colours may vary according to the pieces available. The 'top' as the set of joined-together blocks is called, is nearly always interlined, lined, and quilted finely in white. No embroidery stitches are used.

A quilt is a large piece of work (the old American examples still preserved are usually 8 feet square) and would be very cumbersome to handle if all in one piece. But divided up into 9-inch, 12-inch, or 18-inch blocks, each of which is patched separately, it becomes pleasant light work to pick up in odd moments. Old-time quilt-makers usually took a whole winter to piece a quilt top, making a block here and there, as opportunity (and patches) offered. And although a modern quilt can be made in a few days with the help of a sewing-machine, if an accommodating design is chosen, grandmother's method is still much the more interesting. It is such fun to watch the pile of blocks grow larger, and if the work is done a little at a time, it never becomes monotonous.

Block patchwork may be either pieced (all the patches seamed together) or laid (appliquéd). Frequently it is a mixture of both, the patches being first joined into a pattern and then appliquéd down to the background but piecing is more economical, as no background is required. Appliqué, however, has the advantage that complicated and curved outlines, which could not be joined together, may be used to give variety and charm to the design.

Pls. 54 and *55* show two beautiful examples of genuine American quilts in traditional patterns.

All these traditional patterns have names —often two or three, varying in different parts of the country. Old quilt-makers seem to have put all their innate poetry into the designing and christening of quilts, for all the names are fanciful and many very beautiful. Here are a few: Crosses and Losses; Delectable Mountains; The Lady of the Lake; Robbing Peter to Pay Paul; Dove-in-the-Window; Texas Rose; Queen Charlotte's Crown. The two seen in the photographs are called, respectively, Princess Feather and Christmas Bride.

Some patterns were pieced in the way already described for all-over geometrical quilts with large white spaces between the designs filled with quilting.

In the case of appliqué patterns, either cut out whole or pieced together from small patches, they are simply applied on their blocks with blind appliqué. Single 18-inch blocks of any pattern make pretty and easily washable cushion covers.

Silk is very seldom used for American block patchwork. The correct material is cotton printed in small all-over designs; pieces saved from summer cotton frocks, especially children's frocks, and from men's worn-out shirts, are exactly right. Plain coloured materials are not used, and white only for backgrounds. Contrary to the rule given for crazy patchwork, it does not matter how many different patterns are used together, especially in appliqué quilts, as the plain white background prevents them from becoming unsightly. Unbleached calico is a good and cheap background material.

For warmth's sake and for longer wear, the old patchwork tops were always quilted. Modern ones are often merely lined, as they are used as bedspreads and not to replace blankets. But if you have the energy to attempt quilting, it has two decided advantages. Firstly, it adds greatly to the wearing qualities of the work, and makes it practically uncrushable. Secondly, it doubles its

Plate 54

Princess Feather *is the name of this attractive early-American quilt pattern*

beauty, for quilting charmingly fills all the spaces in the patchwork and makes the wrong side as pretty, in its white way, as the right.

QUILTING PATCHWORK

Such large things as quilts should, properly, be quilted in a frame, though a modern substitute is to quilt each block separately and join them together afterwards. A quilt frame is merely four very long, stout pieces of wood, secured together at each corner by iron clamps. Each edge of the frame has nailed to it a narrow strip of heavy material such as ticking, extending about an inch into the interior of the frame. The various layers of the quilt are pinned or tacked to these strips to keep them stretched and immovable during quilting.

Carefully stretch and fix in the frame first the back or lining of unbleached calico or some other white cotton material; over it the padding, which may consist of one or two layers of wincey or flannelette or of an old blanket, worn very thin and smooth; over that again the patchwork top, with all its tiny seams carefully pressed out flat and its right side uppermost. Adjust the clamps tightly so that nothing can slip, and support the frame on the backs of four chairs of even height, so that you can sit at it comfortably for quilting.

The quilting pattern may be marked out on the top before it is put in the frame, or afterwards—a little at a time in the latter case. Suitable transfers can be bought, or a simple arrangement of ruled diagonal lines or of overlapping circles made round a teacup is easily marked out. This is in cases where plain squares, white or coloured, to be quilted, are alternated with patchwork blocks—a favourite modern plan to save work. If every block is patchworked, the best plan is usually to quilt along the lines of the patchwork pattern, thus saving all marking.

Quilting such a big item is, of course, a long job. In the old days in America quilting parties were given. Eight women sat all day at a frame, four along each side, finished the quilting by evening, and then ended with a festive supper; and this is a plan that could well be copied today. However, if you intend doing all the quilting yourself, either keep the frame in position in a spare room until the work is finished, or stand the frame in a corner.

As you work in towards the centre, you will find that you cannot stretch over far enough to reach the inner parts. When this occurs, loosen the clamps, roll the edges already quilted over the frames, and re-clamp them closer together.

Quilting may be accomplished in sections by using the panel of a large clothes-horse as a frame. This has the advantage of standing upright and not needing to be supported.

The actual process of quilting is described on *page 73*. Use white sewing cotton, not embroidery threads.

A lined quilt, whether quilted or not, should have its edges all enclosed together in a straight-cut binding of one of the materials used in the patchwork.

PILE CUSHIONS AND RUGS

Ragcraft does not make a pieced fabric, as patchwork does. It uses similar oddments of material but transforms them into a pile fabric which is thick, warm and surprisingly hard-wearing. This heavy pile lends itself only to simple, broadly planned designs and is suitable when finished for substantial cushion covers to make a wooden or rush stool or a cane-seated chair more comfortable, for little foot-mats to keep feet warm

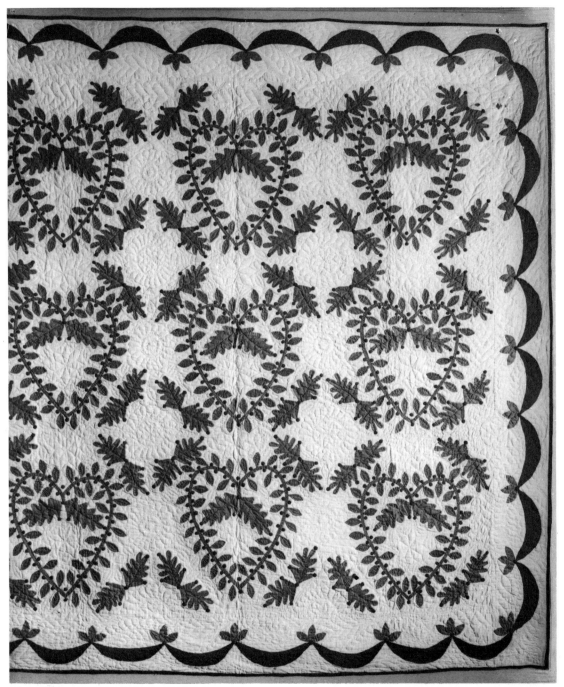

Plate 55

Romantic heart shapes are worked into this finely quilted coverlet in the Christmas Bride *pattern*

under desks, or for small silky-looking rugs.

Ragcraft costs practically nothing if you save and beg from your friends suitable rags or pieces for it. Your only expense will be a piece of hessian bought by the yard for foundation and, in some kinds of ragcraft, a few shillings for a rug tool to work with.

Suppose you decide to use rayon or other material of man-made fibres. Rayon material by the yard, as used for dresses, is unsuitable. What you want is the rayon or nylon jersey from which underwear, slips, sports shirts, and stockings are made. Save old stockings, worn out or laddered and the best portions of jersey garments, washing each piece, of course, before putting it away. To save storing space, cut off all worn portions, elastics, seams and hems.

Cushion covers or quite small mats or rugs are suggested because it takes a very long time to collect enough rags for a full-sized rug. A 16-inch square foot-mat or a cushion cover to fit the top of a square or oblong stool is a good item for a first attempt.

Cut the hessian the size required with an inch-turning all round. Fold in the raw edges singly an inch and tack them down. Use the side on which the raw edges are as the right side—thus you can conceal them entirely with the pile and no hemming is needed. With a ruler to help you, mark out your design on the hessian. A triangular design is effective and very simple to mark out. Find the middle of each side of your square or oblong and connect opposite middles with ruled lines. Rule across diagonally from each corner and the design is complete. Each triangle thus formed should be worked in one colour or shades of one colour. If your shades are too light for usefulness home-dye them darker or brighter before starting work.

The design should be marked first with tailor's chalk, then made permanent by going again over the lines with a water-colour paint-brush dipped in Indian ink.

There are several different methods of making pile. Here is one which requires no special tool—only a strong sewing needle. This is an American thrift method, hardly known in this country.

American Pleated Rag Rugs

Use a foundation of hessian the size for a small foot-mat or a cover for a stool-top. Turn in the edges as already described and mark on the hessian a simple design. Preferable, really, is a simple arrangement of 4-inch squares; or a dark border 3 inches wide all round, a ground of lighter colours used haphazard to give a pleasantly mottled effect, and, if there seems room enough, a bright diamond, all one colour, in the centre.

Cut all your left-overs of jersey into straight strips as long as possible, making each about 1 inch wide. This width is correct if they are of thick knitted fabric, such as is used for underwear and sports shirts. Stockings or other fine-knit fabrics should be cut twice as wide and used doubled lengthways, as they are so much thinner that more fabric is needed to give the same bulk. Before starting work, divide each strip up into pieces 2 inches long.

Thread a strong needle with No. 30 linen thread—failing that, with strong cotton used double. Take a cut piece and fold a tiny lengthwise pleat in it. Then stitch it down, across the pleat, in position on the hessian. The two ends now lie flat, but as you add more pieces, sewing each close to the last, the pile begins to stand up through sheer closeness. Work in rows, making the rows $\frac{3}{4}$ inch to 1 inch apart. The closer the rows are, of course, the higher the pile will be and the softer and warmer the result. Start a new thread whenever necessary, and change colours when the design you are making demands it.

When starting a new thread, do so with

the knot on the right side of the hessian. The pile will hide it entirely, whereas if left on the wrong side it may wear out through the friction of the floor and so loosen some of the pile. It is a good plan to line the finished work—if it is a foot-mat—with another piece of hessian. A stool cushion cover should be made up in the ordinary way, with a piece of thick material for its underside to give it body.

KNITTING AND CROCHET

THERE are not many women today who do not knit, though there are many who knit better than the average. Not only is their actual knitting more even but they have the confidence to attempt intricate patterns and make a success of them. Also, of course, they give the completed garment that professional finish which is so enviable.

Crochet too, is a simple pastime occupation which is now again very much in fashion. It has the advantage of being something you can take up in odd moments.

Knitting and crochet can give plenty of variety to one's wardrobe. Tired of a jumper or cardigan? Then you can unravel it and re-knit it in a different style and stitch and feel you have got an entirely new garment. Children's garments can often be made from the yarn of an adult's unravelled jumper.

EQUIPMENT

This is of the simplest and most inexpensive as very few accessories are wanted. The cost of the work is in the yarn—wool, cotton or synthetic—that you choose for the article you wish to make. There are so many varieties at the present day that there should be no difficulty whatever in making a choice to suit your taste. It is well to remember that very cheap yarns should be avoided. They are often more difficult to deal with when actually working and do not give nearly such satisfactory results in the finished article.

Knitting Needles

These are now nearly all made of a light alloy. They are available in pairs at 10, 12 or 14 inch lengths, also in sets of four, double pointed, for socks and other knitting on four needles. For quick, loose knitting with thick wool there are wooden needles and also some slightly less large in composition.

The range of numbers in needles is from 000, 00 and 0 for wooden needles and up to size 16 in the alloy. Double pointed needles range from sizes 1 to 14 (the larger the number the finer the needle). Circular knitting needles are also available in different lengths and sizes for tubular knitting.

After a great deal of use or if roughly used the tips of the needles may become worn. When this happens the needles should be discarded and a new pair bought or they will spoil the wool.

Table linen can be given a touch of distinction by embroidery as in this small plate mat with an attractive wheat-ear pattern

The stylised sunflower is in simple surface stitches on a pure linen background. The fringed edging gives a simple finish

Cutwork is a favourite form of embroidery, and though more often seen on a cream or white background, it makes a modern impact when worked on a colour such as a rich blue, a warm red or vivid emerald green

Tired furniture can be restored with new covers chosen from a wonderful range of furnishing materials in the shops today

Crochet Hooks

For fine crochet with cotton as for lace a steel hook is necessary. These come in sizes ooo to 6 and also in half sizes. Alloy hooks for wool crochet range in sizes from 2 to 14.

Wool Winders

Though most wool is available ready wound in balls some of the cheaper varieties may be bought in skeins. Wool that has been unravelled and is to be re-knitted will be in skeins to be pressed out (*see page 195*) before being wound into balls. Using a wool winder simplifies this process and is worth having if you are likely to do a lot of re-knitting.

Stitch Holders

These consist of very large safety pins from 3 to 6 inches long, with blunt points. Stitches can be transferred to a holder of this description and the pin fastened while another portion of the work is proceeded with. This is useful when two sides of a garment have to be divided for the neck.

HOW TO KNIT

Casting On

There are two methods of casting on. It consists of making a series of loops one after the other on one needle, until the required number is made up.

First method: Start with a slip-knot which should not be pulled too tightly, placing the second needle upwards through the loop. Now pass the wool behind the two needles, bring the point of the right-hand needle, carrying with it the wool, through the loop on the left-hand needle, so making a second loop, which is then placed on the left-hand needle. Repeat as often as necessary. As casting on in this method is often fairly loose it is often better to knit the first row into the backs of the stitches.

Second method: This is known as the corded method of casting on and is often preferred. Begin as above and when there are two stitches on the left-hand needle, insert the right-hand needle between the two stitches, pulling the wool through and thus making a loop. Continue in this manner until you have the required number of stitches. As this gives an even edge it is not necessary to knit into the backs of the stitches of the first row.

Casting Off

To finish off your garment and get rid of all the stitches, the following method is employed. Knit the first two stitches of the row, and with the left-hand needle pass the first stitch over the second one, allowing it to drop under the right-hand needle. Knit another stitch, and pass the first over the second, as before, and continue in this way until one loop is left. Remove this from the needle, break off the wool, and pass the end of it through the loop, pulling it tightly. The end of wool is afterwards darned into the work.

Plain Knitting

Cast on the necessary number of stitches on to a needle, which should be held in the left hand. Place the right-hand needle through the first loop, pass the wool, which should be at the back of the work, over the point of the right-hand needle, make a loop, as you would for casting-on, and slip the first loop off the left-hand needle. Continue working the stitches in this way to the end of the row. On all subsequent rows, slip the first stitch—that is, pass it from one needle to the other without knitting it.

Purling

Cast on as usual, and hold the cast-on stitches in the left hand. Slip the first stitch, then bring the wool forward between the needles. Put the right-hand needle through the front of the first loop, the needle being tilted downwards a bit, pass the wool round the point of the right-hand needle, drawing it through the loop to make a new stitch, while the old one is slipped off the needle. Work each loop in this manner.

Plain knitting and purling are the foundations of all patterns in knitting; once you have learnt these two and had a little practice in working them, you will be able to follow out any instructions in a book, and will probably before long be filled with the desire to make your own designs.

Increasing

When it is necessary to add to the number of stitches, knit into a stitch in the ordinary way, but before slipping it off the needle, knit also into the back of the loop. Increasing is usually carried out at the beginning or end of a row, when the second stitch and the one before the last are the ones to be knitted twice, not the first and the last, as this would make an uneven edge. Adding to the number of stitches may be done at almost any point, if required.

Decreasing

To narrow a garment, or when finishing off, decreasing must be done. There are two ways of doing this:

1. Knit two stitches together, or if it is a purl row, purl them together.

2. Slip a stitch, knit the next, then pass the slipped over the knitted one, letting it drop off the needle. A slipped stitch should always be transferred from one needle to another, with the needle in position, as for knitting, not purling.

Tension

It is most important to have the same tension to your knitting as there is in the pattern you are copying. This is regulated by the number of stitches to the inch, and the size of the finished garment depends entirely on getting the right tension. The best way to ensure this is to knit a sample about 4 inches square, press it with a hot iron and a damp cloth, then measure how many stitches there are to the inch. If this does not agree with the pattern, you will have to alter the size of the needles accordingly; if your knitting shows too few stitches to the inch, you must use finer needles, but if too many, coarser ones must be employed.

If you are either a loose or a tight knitter, you will have to make allowance for the fact, even if you use the exact thickness of wool and the same sized needles that are recommended, as patterns are given for medium tension.

Joining Wool

When the thread has to be joined, it is always better to do it, if possible, at the beginning of a row. Lay the two ends of wool, the new and the old, parallel with one another, overlapping about 3 inches, and knit five or six stitches with the double thread. The loose ends can afterwards be threaded into the garment on the wrong side and will be completely hidden.

Grafting

This method is used for joining together stitches on two separate needles, as in the toe of a sock, or stocking, or sometimes the shoulder seams of a sweater or jumper. In such places it is important not to have a ridge such as would be formed if the stitches on the two needles were cast off simultaneously.

Have the same number of stitches on each needle, with the right side of the work towards you. Break off the wool, leaving a foot or so of length, and thread it with a darning needle. Place the two knitting needles parallel with one another, thread the darning needle through the first stitch on the front needle knitways and pass it off the needle, then thread the darning needle through the second stitch of the front needle, purlways, but leave it on the needle. Bring the thread round under the front needle to the back one and insert it in the first stitch purlways, slipping the stitch off, then in the next stitch knitways, leaving the stitch on the needle. Repeat this process until all the stitches are worked off, fastening the thread securely at the end.

You will find that the grafting has left the work looking exactly as if there were no join at all, if you have pulled the thread evenly throughout.

This is the method used when working in stocking stitch (*see this heading*), but if the garment is in garter stitch you must work in the same way as described above on the front needle; but instead of reversing the directions for the back needle, repeat the instructions for the front needle. In other words, both the front and back needles are worked the same.

STITCHES AND PATTERNS

The only two actual stitches ever used in knitting are plain, which is generally referred to as 'knitting', and purl, which is always called thus. Every fancy pattern is made up of these stitches worked in different ways. You often find that groups of stitches are given the name of a certain stitch, when really they would be more correctly called patterns, for example, moss stitch is simply a certain way of grouping plain and purl, and does not involve any new stitch. The same may be said for most of the so-called stitches mentioned below, but the most commonly understood meaning of the terms has been retained in each case to avoid any confusion.

When trying a stitch for the first time, practise for a bit on an odd piece of wool, so as to get the general effect and to avoid making mistakes on the garment itself. It is

well worth while to spend an hour or so doing this, as it often prevents your having to undo your work and so spoil the wool for re-knitting.

In the following pages, abbreviations as under are used:

K. = knit plain; p. = purl; st. = stitch; tog. = together; w.fwd. = wool forward; t.b.l. = through back loops.

For a fuller list of abbreviations *see page 196.*

GARTER STITCH *(Pl. 56)*

This is the easiest of all stitches, and can very suitably be used for babies' bonnets, coats and socks, while a number of people like it also for children's jumpers, berets of all sorts, and collars and cuffs. Its finished effect is not as smooth as stocking stitch (*see overleaf*), but its somewhat raised surface has an attraction of its own.

Any number of stitches, odd or even, may be used.

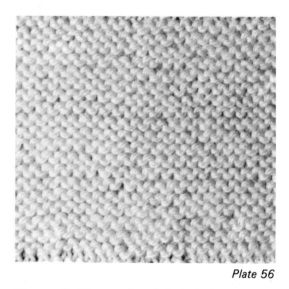

Plate 56

To work Simply do plain knitting on two needles.

STOCKING STITCH *(Pl. 57)*

This stitch has the smooth effect which is necessary for a stocking or sock. It is also very suitable for almost any other garment where a flat surface is desirable.

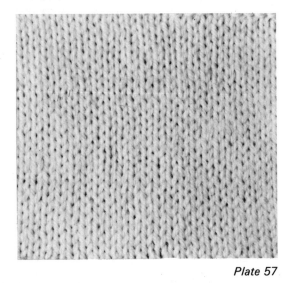

Plate 57

To work On two needles this stitch is made by knitting one row and purling the next. Continue alternately in this manner. On four needles, continuous knitting without any purling will produce stocking stitch.

RIBBING *(Pl. 58)*

This is employed where the material will receive a certain amount of stretching, as it forms an elastic piece of knitting which retains its shape in spite of a good deal of tension. It is used at the tops of stockings and socks, where the wool is required to grip tightly, at the lower edge of jumpers, and for the cuffs of sweaters.

To work Take care in casting on that the number of stitches is some multiple of the total number in the part which is to be

Plate 58

repeated. For example, if you are using knit 2, purl 2, there are 4 stitches in the repeated portion. Therefore your full number of stitches must be divisible by 4. Knit 2 stitches, purl 2, and repeat this to the end of the row. A variation of this is to knit 1, purl 1, when a smaller rib is produced, or knit 4, purl 4, giving a somewhat coarse effect.

MOSS STITCH *(Pl. 59)*

This very decorative stitch is suitable for an entire jumper, as well as for borders to various garments. It makes a suitable neck edging for a pullover or child's suit.

To work An odd number of stitches is best. Knit 1, purl 1, to the end of the first row. On the return row, you will be knitting every stitch knitted in the first row, and purling each purled one, which is just the opposite to ribbing. If the number of stitches is even (and sometimes it cannot be avoided), start the return row with a purl stitch.

A variation can be made by forming double moss stitch. In the first row, knit 2,

Plate 59

Plate 60

purl 2, to the end. In the second row, knit 2 (if you finished with knit 2 in the previous row), purl 2, and so on, but if you finished with purl, start also with purl.

BASKET STITCH *(Pl. 60)*

A fancy pattern suitable for a jumper, child's coat and various other garments. It produces a raised effect and has somewhat the appearance of plaiting. Each block may be of almost any size, from about 2 inches square to 9 or 10 inches square, the larger pattern being more suitable for such things as pram covers and sports sweaters.

To work Start with a number of stitches which is a multiple of 8, plus 1 stitch.

1st row—P.3, * K.3, P.5, rep. from * to last 6 sts., K.3, P.3.

2nd row—K.3, * P.3, K.5, rep. from * to last 6 sts., P.3, K.3.

3rd row—As 1st row.

4th row—P.2, * K.5, P.3, rep. from * to last 7 sts., K.5, P.2.

5th row—K.2, * P.5, K.3, rep. from * to last 7 sts., P.5, K.2.

6th row—As 4th row.

These 6 rows form the pattern.

FISHERMAN'S RIB PATTERN
(Pl. 61)

Cast on a multiple of 2 stitches.

1st and every row—Sl.1 knitwise, * K.B.1, P. into next stitch 1 row below, at the

Plate 61

same time slipping off sts. above, rep. from * to last st., K.1. Continue in this manner.

CABLE STITCH *(Pl. 62)*

This stitch is used a great deal for men's sweaters and pullovers. It produces the effect of a twisted rope at intervals in the pattern, and makes a strong, hard-wearing garment. It is a more elaborate pattern than some here described, but once you have memorized the 4 rows which make up the design, you will find you can work it very quickly. An extra needle of the same size is needed; 'C.' indicates when this should be used.

Plate 62

To work Cast on a multiple of 13 sts. plus 1.
1st row—* K.1, P.2, K.8, P.2, rep. from * to last st., K.1.
2nd row—* K.3, P.8, K.2, rep. from * to last st., K.1.
3rd row—* K.1, P.2, C.2B., C.2F., P.2, rep. from * to last st., K.1.
4th row—As 2nd row.
These 4 rows form the pattern.

LACE STITCH

There are numerous varieties of lace stitches, but they all give the open effect of lace work and are most useful as a decoration for jumpers, children's frocks and shawls, not to mention the ever-popular beret. The whole garment may be worked in this stitch, if desired, though the beginner in knitting will find it simpler to confine herself to a border only, as a start. Lace stitches require rather close attention until the pattern is well known. Abbreviations on page 196.

Simple Lace Stitch *(Pl. 63)*
With No. 11 needles cast on a multiple of 7 +4 sts.
1st row—* K.2, w.fwd., K.2 tog., t.b.l., w.fwd., sl.1, K.2 tog., p.s.s.o., w.fwd., rep. from * to last 4 sts., K.2, w.fwd., K.2 tog. t.b.l.
2nd row—* P.2, w.r.n., P.2 tog., P.3, rep. from * to last 4 sts., P.2, w.r.n., P.2 tog.
3rd row—* K.2, w.fwd., K.2 tog. t.b.l., K.3, rep. from * to last 4 sts., K.2, w.fwd.,

Plate 63

K.2 tog. t.b.l.

4th row—* P.2, w.r.n., P.2 tog., P.3, rep. from * to last 4 sts., P.2, w.r.n., P.2 tog.

These 4 rows form the pattern.

KNITTING IN DIFFERENT COLOURS

This form of work is particularly suitable for stocking tops and as a decoration to sweaters and jumpers, and produces a delightful effect if the colours are well blended. A flat, even surface must be made. Herein lies the chief difficulty, as the beginner often finds some trouble in keeping the wool from pulling too tightly, or again from being altogether too slack. The great secret of success in this particular form of knitting is to keep your balls of wool in a definite order, by twisting the colour which is being worked under and over the colour or colours not in use. The latter must be left at a fairly slack tension, or enough wool will not be allowed for stretching when the garment is in use.

On the wrong side the strands of wool should lie flat without being in loops, but they should not be so tight that a little stretching will result in the work being unduly dragged.

Coloured pattern work always looks best when done in stocking stitch, as the smooth nature of the surface shows the variation to its full advantage; but sometimes it is advisable to place a stripe of a different colour on a cuff which is worked in ribbing. In that case only one colour should be introduced.

Fair Isle jumpers show an elaboration of this pattern work; they may be worked in design throughout, or merely have a border collar and cuffs of the coloured part. Before starting on knitting of this sort, try a small sample in different colours, so as to get used to the manipulation of the wool.

EMBROIDERY ON KNITTING

It is often a simple matter to embroider a little stitching on a garment than to work in different colours while the making is actually in progress. The result is somewhat the same, though the application of stitching afterwards produces rather a raised look, which one does not find when the wool is knitted in several shades.

A pleasing effect can be produced by working on stocking stitch as on the gloves in *Pl. 66*. But it is not advisable to try it in garter stitch or ribbing, as these stitches tend to hide the embroidered pattern.

Decoration need not be confined to cross stitch; almost any simple embroidery stitch described in the Embroidery Section is suitable. It is really better to use wool on wool and cotton on cotton, as then there is no difficulty about the tension except to see that you do not pull the embroidery stitch too tightly, which there is always a slight danger of doing, thereby destroying the smooth effect of the finished work.

Children love a few bright colours worked into their frocks and coats, so try this suggestion next time you are finishing off something for one of them, and just see how they appreciate your originality.

One of the beauties of this sort of work is that when you get tired of one design you can unpick the whole thing and substitute another one, and there is no reason why the garment should look any the worse for it if you press the affected part under a damp cloth before starting the new pattern.

SLOTS

Slots are needed in many different sorts of garments for making a hole such as is required to thread a draw string through, both in knitting and crochet.

Knitting

To make a row of slots, work as follows:

1st row—* Knit 2, wool forward, knit 2 together, knit 2. Repeat from * to the end of the row.

2nd row—Purl, using each extra loop made by bringing the wool forward in the previous row. You will thus keep the same number of stitches.

For this particular form of slotting, the number of stitches must be a multiple of 6, but if the holes are wanted farther apart, knit 4 instead of 2, after knitting 2 together, to gain this effect.

Crochet

It is simpler to thread a string through in crochet than in knitting, as the work is of a more open type, so that often special holes need not be made.

The following will give you plenty of scope for slotting:

1st row—4 chain, a double crochet into every fourth loop of previous row.

2nd row—Revert to original pattern of garment.

There will be a danger of either drawing your slotting row too tightly, by choosing loops from the previous row which are too far apart; or of making it too loose, by taking up stitches too close together. You will have to make sure that neither of these happens, by noticing the effect of the first few stitches, and altering your work accordingly.

BUTTONHOLES

It is all-important to have a buttonhole which will not stretch and pull out of shape after a few weeks' use, and those made in wool are apt to do so if they are not carefully formed in the first place, and duly strengthened afterwards with embroidery or wool.

The simplest method of making the hole is to cast off a certain number of stitches, according to the size required, in one row, and cast them on again in the next row, but both operations should be done tightly. Even then you will very likely find that the hole is too big, and the remedy, in that case, is to run several threads of wool round the opening, on the wrong side, to reinforce it and pull it together a bit. If necessary, a line of buttonhole stitch may be worked as well.

For babies' garments crocheted loops are frequently used. They are more quickly made, and simply consist of a line of chain worked on a fine hook.

With crocheted garments, use can often be made of holes in the pattern, which should be buttonholed round to prevent their stretching and pulling out of shape.

When buttons are sewn on knitted or crocheted clothes, make sure that they have a good foundation by placing, on the underside, a small piece of material of the same colour and sewing through on to that. This is particularly recommended for children's cardigans or coats.

MAKING POCKETS

Knitting

There are two recognized ways of doing this; you may simply make a patch pocket, which is on the whole the easier method, or you may knit the pocket into your garment, so that it is part of it and not merely a piece added afterwards.

One of the great dangers in making pockets is that they become too loose with the continual stretching. Care must be taken, therefore, to guard against this by finishing off the top of the pocket with several rows of ribbing. Moss stitch is often used, and is very effective as a border, though more liable to stretch. When using moss stitch it is as well to change to a size smaller needles for the top of the pocket, so that the loose appearance will be avoided.

Patch Pocket

The directions given are suitable for an adult's coat or jumper.

Cast on 32 sts. (this is assuming the needles and wool to be of average thickness).

1st row— K. into back sts., then k. and p. alternate rows until 4 inches have been worked, slipping the first st. of every row.

Now work ribbing in k.2, p.2, for 1 inch. Cast off tightly, with the wrong side of work facing you.

Sew this pocket neatly on to the garment with the same coloured wool.

Set-in Pocket

Suppose you are working the right front of a coat of 66 sts. Beginning at centre front, k.20, p.2, k.2, for 26 sts., k. to the end of the row. Continue the ribbing on the 26 sts. until you have 1 inch of it, ending on a knit row. Now on the next row, purl 20 on to a spare needle, cast off 26, purl to the end of the row. Slip the last lot of sts. on to a stitch-holder or another spare needle.

Now make a pocket lining as follows:

Cast on 26 sts. Knit and purl alternate rows until you have 6 inches of work. Do not cast off, but leave stitches on needle. Now go on working the front.

Knit 20, then instead of casting on 26 to make up for pocket opening, knit the 26 sts. from the lining on to needle, then continue to end of row. Now go on with the front.

Sew the pocket lining neatly down to the underside of the front, taking care that the stitches do not show through to the front.

HOW TO KNIT A SOCK

Socks are knitted on four short needles. The effect produced is that of stocking stitch, but actually it is ordinary knitting, without any purling, except in the ribbing. This makes it very simple to do as, unless a fancy pattern is introduced, there is little change throughout the sock.

For men's socks and stockings use 4-ply Fingering or a nylon sock yarn, but for children's and especially babies' garments, 2- or 3-ply, with No. 15 or No. 16 needles.

When dividing the stitches between the three needles, you should see that two have the same number, and the third a different number. This last will form the 'heel' needle, and will be treated rather specially in several ways, so it is as well to be able to recognize it easily.

You will have to decide whether the ribbing at the top of the sock is to be fine or coarse, and regulate your number of stitches accordingly. The total should be a multiple of the number in each complete rib—that is, if you are working 2 plain, 2 purl, the number must be divisible by 4.

When changing from one sort of knitting to another during the working of a sock, always finish the round, the beginning of which can always be seen if an end of wool is left when making the first stitch in casting on.

The first few stitches on each needle are apt to be looser than the others, so special care must be taken to knit them tightly, otherwise an unintentional seam is produced, giving the appearance of a 'ladder'.

Turning the Heel

There are several methods of doing this. Two methods are given in the sock patterns which follow.

Shaping the Toe

One common and simple method is given in the directions for making a sock, but another way can be employed and is given below.

Square Toe

This produces a square effect at the end of the toe, and is worked as follows:

Divide the sts. so that there are half the total number on the instep needle, a quarter on the second, and a quarter on the third needle.

* K. to the last 3 sts. of the first needle, then k.2 tog., k.1. On the second needle, k.1, k.2 tog., k. to the last 3 sts., then k.2 tog., k.1. On the third needle, k.1, k.2 tog., then k. to the end of the needle. K.2 rounds without decreasing. Repeat from * until 24 sts. are left. Now k. the sts. from the first needle on to the third needle. Place the two needles parallel and graft off the sts. (*See Grafting on page 162.*)

This type of toe is particularly suitable for children's footwear, as it fits more naturally into the shape of their feet but it can be used with advantage for broad-toed people, for whom the round toe (*described opposite*) might act as a slight restriction to free movement of the feet.

STRENGTHENING FOOTWEAR

In children's footwear, both heels and toes often need a certain amount of strengthening, to resist the heavy wear inflicted on them. This can be done in several ways.

1. Slip every other stitch on the plain rows of the back of the heel, purling back as usual.

2. Slip a stitch and purl a stitch on each of the plain rows.

3. Using a second ball, and holding the thread over the fingers of the left hand, knit under the second thread, then over, so as to weave it in to form a 'double heel'. When purling back, the thread should be kept in front of the work.

All these three ways will give you a much more durable piece of knitting.

As the toe opposite is worked only in plain knitting, the strengthening instructions for the purl rows may be neglected, as every row consists of the same stitch.

The best way to deal with the toe is to use the third method described above, starting the extra thread when decreasing begins, and keeping it on until you are ready to start the casting off.

MAN'S PLAIN SOCKS (*Pl. 64*)

French heel and flat toe.

Materials: 3 oz. Patons Nylox 3-ply Patonized. Set of four No. 13 needles with points at both ends.

Measurements: Length of foot, 10½ (11, 11½) ins.

Tension: 9 sts. and 11 rows to one square inch on No. 13 needles, measured over stocking stitch.

Abbreviations—*see page 196 for complete list.*

Cast on 80 sts., 28 on each of 1st and 2nd needles, 24 on 3rd needle. Work in rounds of K.2, P.2 rib for 4 ins. Work in stocking stitch (every round K.) for 4 ins.

Shape leg as follows: 1st round—K.2 tog., K. to last 2 sts., K.2 tog. t.b.l. Work 6 rounds without shaping. Rep. last 7 rounds until 70 sts. remain. Continue without shaping until work measures 12 ins. from beginning.

Divide sts. for heel as follows: K. first 18 sts. of round on to one needle, slip last 18 sts. of round on to other end of same needle (these 36 sts. are for heel). Divide remaining sts. on to two needles and leave for instep.

Commence heel as follows: 1st row—Sl.1, P. to last st., K.1. 2nd row—Sl.1. K. to end. Repeat these 2 rows 17 times more, then 1st row once.

Turn heel as follows: 1st row—K.22, K.2 tog., turn. 2nd row—P.9, P.2 tog., turn. 3rd row—K.10, K.2 tog., turn. 4th row—P.11, P.2 tog., turn. 5th row—K.12, K.2 tog., turn. Continue in this manner until all sts. are worked on to one needle again. Next row—K.11 (thus completing heel). Slip all instep sts. on to one needle. Using spare needle K.11 heel sts., knit up 20 sts. along side of heel, using 2nd needle K. across 34 instep sts., using 3rd needle knit up 20 sts. along other side of heel, K. across 11 heel sts. (96 sts.).

Shape instep as follows: K.1 round. Next round—1st needle: K. to last 4 sts., K.2 tog., K.2. 2nd needle: K.; 3rd needle: K.2. K.2 tog. t.b.l., K. to end. Rep. these 2 rounds until 76 sts. remain. Continue without shaping for 6½ (7, 7½) ins. Slip last 2 sts. of 1st needle on to beg. of 2nd needle, and first 2 sts. of 3rd needle on to end of same needle.

Shape toe as follows: 1st round—1st needle: K. to last 3 sts., K.2 tog., K.1; 2nd needle: K.1. K.2 tog. t.b.l., K. to last 3 sts., K.2 tog., K.1. 3rd needle: K.1, K.2 tog. t.b.l., K. to end. 2nd round—K. to end of round. Rep. these 2 rounds until 28 sts. remain. K. sts. of first needle on to end of 3rd needle.

Graft sts. or cast off sts. from two needles tog. Press with warm iron and damp cloth.

RIBBED TURNOVER-TOP SOCKS
(Pl. 65)

Dutch heel and flat toe.

Materials : 3oz. Patons Nylox 3-ply, Paton-ized. Set of four No. 13 needles with points at both ends.

Measurements : Length from top to base of heel with top turned over, 12 ins. Length of foot, 8 ins. (adjustable).

Tension : 9 sts. and 11 rows to one square inch on No. 13 needles, measured over stocking stitch.

Abbreviations—*see page 196 for complete list.*

Plate 64

Men's socks with French heel and flat toe

Ribbed turnover-top socks with Dutch heel

Plate 65

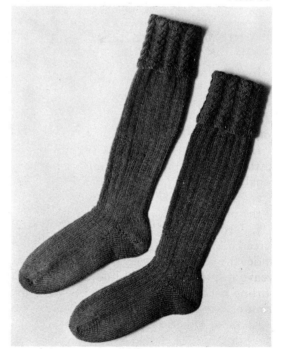

Cast on 72 sts., 24 on each of 3 needles. Work 4½ ins. in rounds of K.1, P.1 rib. Next round—* K.3, P.1, rep. from * to end of round. Rep. this round for 2½ ins.

Shape leg as follows: ** Next round—Work 2 tog., rib to last 7 sts., work 2 tog. t.b.l., rib 5. Work 6 rounds without shaping.** Work from ** to ** 3 times (64 sts.). Continue without further shaping until work measures 12 ins. from beg.

Divide sts. for heel as follows: Rib 13, slip last 18 sts. of round on to other end of same needle (these 31 sts. are for heel). Divide remaining sts. on to two needles and leave for instep.

Commence heel as follows: 1st row—Sl.1, P. to last st., K.1. 2nd row—Sl.1, K. to end. Rep. these 2 rows 9 times more, then 1st row once.

Turn heel as follows: 1st row—K.19, sl.1, K.1, p.s.s.o., turn. 2nd row—P.8, P.2 tog., turn. 3rd row—K.8, sl.1, K.1, p.s.s.o., turn. 4th row—P.8, P.2 tog., turn. Rep. 3rd and 4th rows until all sts. are worked on to one needle again. Next row—K.5 sts. (thus completing heel). Slip all instep sts. on to one needle. Using spare needle K.4 heel sts., knit up 17 sts. along side of heel, using 2nd needle rib across 33 instep sts., using 3rd needle knit up 17 sts. along other side of heel, K.5 heel sts. (76 sts.).

Shape instep as follows: 1st round—1st needle: K.; 2nd needle: rib all across; 3rd needle: K. 2nd round—1st needle: K. to last 3 sts., K.2 tog., K.1; 2nd needle: rib all across; 3rd needle: K.1, K.2 tog. t.b.l., K. to end. Rep. these 2 rounds until 66 sts. remain. Work 3 ins. without shaping (adjust length at this point).

Shape toe as follows: 1st round—1st needle: K. to last 3 sts., K.2 tog., K.1; 2nd needle: K.1, K.2 tog. t.b.l., K. to last 3 sts., K.2 tog., K.1; 3rd needle: K.1, K.2 tog. t.b.l., K. to end. K.2 rounds. Rep. these 3 rounds until 26 sts. remain. K. sts.

from first needle on to end of 3rd needle. Graft sts. or cast off sts. from two needles together.

Press using a warm iron and damp cloth.

JUMPERS, COATS AND CARDIGANS

For this type of garment two needles only are used. Alternate rows of plain and purl produce the familiar stocking stitch when the knitting is worked first on one side and then on the other, as it is when two needles are employed. Every row plain results in garter stitch, which is frequently used for children's wear, but is not so effective for grown-ups. Moss stitch can be used for an all-over pattern, if preferred.

If a garment of this description has sleeves, it is usual to make it in five pieces (this does not generally apply to a jumper in which the front is all in one)—the back, the right front, the left front and the two sleeves. The back and the two fronts, may, if desired, be knitted in one piece, but the drawback to this, with any but small garments, is that the work becomes heavy and tiresome to hold with so much weight on the needles.

Work is started at the lower edge of the article in all cases; that is particularly important with sleeves, which usually have at the cuff a few inches of ribbing to grip the wrist. If this is the point at which the work is finished off, you will find that it is not very easy to cast off at just the right tension to give the ribbing the amount of elasticity it should have.

All seams joining the pieces together must be neatly sewn with the same wool and not stretched in any way in the process. To a certain extent a knitted coat or jumper adapts itself to the figure, and so does not need to be shaped in the same way as one made of material.

CHILD'S CARDIGAN
(Colour plate)

Materials : 4 oz. Dark, 1 oz. Light, Paton's Brilliante 3-ply 100% Bri-Nylon. Four buttons. Two No. 13 and two No. 11 needles.

Measurements : To fit 21, 22 inch chest. Length, 11¼, 12¼ ins. Sleeve seam 7¼, 8 ins. (adjustable). The figures in square brackets refer to the large size.

Tension : 8 sts. and 10 rows to one square inch on No. 11 needles, measured over stocking stitch.

Abbreviations—*see page 196 for complete list.*

Back Using No. 13 needles and Dark, cast on 88 [92] sts. Work in K.1, P.1 rib for 1½ ins.

Change to No. 11 needles and proceed as follows: Next row—K.3 [5], (inc. in next st., K.4) 16 times, inc. in next st., K. to end (105 [109] sts.). Next row—P.

Continue in stocking stitch working rows 1 to 11 from Chart A (*Fig. 76a*) reading chart from right to left on K. rows and left to right on P. rows placing the first 2 rows as follows: 1st row—Work first 4 [6] sts. as marked on chart, then work 12 st. repeat to last 5 [7] sts., work last 5 [7] sts. as marked on chart. 2nd row—Work first 5 [7] sts. as marked on chart, then work 12 st. repeat to last 4 [6] sts., work last 4 [6] sts. as marked on chart.

Using Dark next row—P. Next row—K.3 [5], (K.2 tog., K.4) 16 times, K.2 tog., K. to end (88 [92] sts.). Commencing with a P. row work 7 rows in stocking stitch. Next row—K.3 [5], (inc. in next st., K.4) 16 times, inc. in next st., K. to end (105 [109] sts.). Next row—P. Work rows 1 to 11 from chart as before. Break off Light.

Using Dark next row—P. Next row—K.3 [5], (K.2 tog., K.4) 16 times, K.2 tog., K. to end (88 [92] sts.). Commencing with a P. row continue in stocking stitch until work measures 6 [6¾] ins. from beg., finishing at end of a P. row.

Shape raglan armholes as follows: 1st and 2nd rows—Cast off 4 [5], work to end. 3rd row—K.1, K.2 tog. t.b.l., K. to last 3 sts., K.2 tog., K.1. 4th row—K.1, P. to last st., K.1. Rep. 3rd and 4th rows 24 [25] times more, then 3rd row once (28 [28] sts.). Cast off.

Right Front Using No. 13 needles and Dark, cast on 44 [46] sts. Work in K.1, P.1 rib for 1½ ins.

Change to No. 11 needles and proceed as follows: Next row—K.1 [2], (inc. in next st., K.4) 8 times, inc. in next st., K. to end (53 [55] sts.). Next row—P. Continue in stocking stitch, working rows 1 to 11 from Chart B (*Fig. 76b*) reading chart from right to left on K. rows and left to right on P. rows, placing the first 2 rows as follows: 1st row—Work 12 st. repeat to last 5 [7] sts., work last 5 [7] sts. as marked on Chart. 2nd row—Work first 5 [7] sts. as marked on chart, then work 12 st. repeat to end.

Using Dark. Next row—P. Next row—K.1 [2], (K.2 tog., K.4) 8 times, K.2 tog., K. to end (44 [46] sts.). Commencing with a P. row, work 7 rows in stocking stitch. Next row—K.1 [2], (inc. in next st., K.4) 8 times, inc. in next st., K. to end (53 [55] sts.). Next row—P. Work rows 1 to 11 from chart as before. Break off Light.

Using Dark. Next row—P. Next row—K.1 [2], (K.2 tog., K.4) 8 times, K.2 tog., K. to end (44 [46] sts.). Commencing with a P. row continue in stocking stitch until work measures same as Back to armhole shaping, finishing at end of a P. row.

Shape front slope and raglan armhole as follows: 1st row—K.2 tog., K. to end. 2nd row—Cast off 4 [5], P. to end. 3rd row—K. to last 3 sts., K.2 tog., K.1. 4th row—K.1, P. to end. Continue dec. at armhole edge on next and every alt. row as before, at the same

173

time dec. 1 st. at front edge on next and every following 4th row until 3 [4] sts. remain. Continue dec. at armhole edge only until 1st. remains. Fasten off.

Left Front Work to match Right Front reversing chart and all shapings, noting that tog. t.b.l. in place of tog. will be worked at armhole edge and that chart will be read from left to right on K. rows and right to left on P. rows placing the first 2 rows as follows: 1st row—Work first 5 [7] sts. as marked on chart, then work 12 st. repeat to end. 2nd row—Work 12 st. repeat to last 5 [7] sts., work last 5 [7] sts. as marked on chart.

Sleeves Using No. 13 needles and Dark, cast on 42 [44] sts. Work in K.1, P.1 rib for 1½ ins. Next row—Rib 2 [3], (inc. in next st., rib 3) 9 times, inc. in next st., rib to end (52 [54] sts.). Change to No. 11 needles and proceed in stocking stitch, inc. 1st at both ends of next and every following 7th [7th] row until there are 68 [72] sts. Continue on these sts. until work measures 7¼ [8] ins. from beg., finishing at end of a P. row (adjust length at this point). Shape top as on Back from ** to ** (8 [8] sts.). Cast off.

Front Band Using No. 13 needles and Dark, cast on 9 sts. 1st row—K.2, (P.1, K.1) 3 times, K.1. 2nd row—(K.1, P.1) 4 times, K.1.

21 Inch Size only Rep. 1st and 2nd rows once more.

Both sizes. Next row—Rib 3, cast off 3, rib to end. Next row—Rib 3, cast on 3, rib to end. Continue in rib working a buttonhole as on last 2 rows on every 23rd and 24th [27th and 28th] rows from previous buttonhole until 4 buttonholes in all have been worked. Continue in rib without further buttonholes until work measures 28 [30] ins. from beg. Cast off in rib.

To Make Up Omitting ribbing, with wrong side of work facing, block each piece by pinning out round edges. Omitting ribbing, press each piece using a warm iron and damp cloth. Using a flat seam for ribbing and a fine back-stitch seam for remainder, join side and sleeve seams. Using a flat seam stitch sleeves into position. Stitch on front band. Attach buttons. Press seams.

FLOWER MOTIF GLOVES (Pl. 66)

Materials: 2 oz. Patons Beehive 4-ply, Patonized, or Patons Nylox Knitting 4-ply, Patonized. Oddments of 1st and 2nd Contrast for motif embroidery. Two No. 12 needles.

Measurements: Width all round above Thumb, 7 ins. Length from lower edge to top of middle finger, 9 ins.

Tension: 8 sts. and 10 rows to one square inch on No. 12 needles, measured over stocking stitch.

Abbreviations—*see page 196 for complete list.*

Right Glove Cast on 56 sts. Work in K.1, P.1 rib for 2 ins. Proceed in stocking stitch with thumb gusset as follows: 1st row—K.28, P.1, K.2, P.1, K to end. 2nd row—K.1, P.23, K.1, P.2, K.1, P., to last st., K.1. 3rd row—K.28, P.1, M.1K., K.2, M.1K., P.1, K. to end. 4th row—K.1, P.23, K.1, P.4, K.1, P. to last st., K.1. 5th row—K.28, P.1, K.4, P.1, K. to end. 6th row—K.1, P.23, K.1, M.1P., P.4, M.1P., K.1, P. to last st., K.1. 7th row—K.28, P.1, K.6, P.1, K. to end. 8th row—K.1, P.23, K.1, P.6, K.1, P. to last st., K.1. 9th row—K.28, P.1, M.1K., K.6, M.1K., P.1, K. to end.

Continue in this manner, inc. 1st. at each side of thumb gusset on every 3rd row until there are 18 sts. between the 2 purl sts. (72 sts.) Work 2 rows.

Work thumb as follows: 1st row—K.28, P.1, K.18, turn. 2nd row—K.1, P.17, cast on 2. **Knitting st. at both ends of every row, work 20 rows in stocking stitch.

Shape top: 1st row—(K.2 tog.) 10 times.

174

Plate 66   *Gloves in stocking stitch with embroidered motif*

2nd row—K.1, P. to last st., K.1. 3rd row—
(K.2 tog.) 5 times. Break off wool. Thread
wool through remaining sts., draw up and
fasten off securely. With right side facing,
rejoin wool and knit up 2 sts. from base of
thumb, K. to end (56 sts.). Knitting st. at
both ends of every row, work 9 rows in
stocking stitch.**

First Finger: 1st row—K.36, turn. 2nd
row—K.1, P.15, cast on 2, turn. Knitting
st. at both ends of every row, work 24 rows
in stocking stitch. Shape top: 1st row—
(K.2 tog.) 9 times. 2nd row—K.1, P. to last
last st., K.1. 3rd row—(K.2 tog.) 4 times,
K.1. Break off wool. Thread wool through
remaining sts., draw up and fasten off
securely.

Second Finger: With right side facing,
rejoin wool and knit up 2 sts. from the 2
cast-on sts. at base of First Finger, K.7
turn. Next row—K.1, P.15, cast on 2, turn.
Knitting st. at both ends of every row, work
28 rows in stocking stitch. Shape top and
complete as First Finger.

Third Finger: With right side facing rejoin wool and knit up 2 sts. from the 2
cast-on sts. at base of Second Finger, K.7
turn. Next row—K.1, P.15, cast on 2, turn.
Complete as First Finger.

Fourth Finger: With right side facing,
rejoin wool and knit up 2 sts. from the 2
cast-on sts. at base of Third Finger, K.6,
turn. Next row—K.1, P.12, K.1 turn.
Knitting st. at both ends of every row, work

20 rows in stocking stitch. Shape top: 1st row—(K.2 tog.) 7 times. 2nd row—K.1, P. to last st., K.1. 3rd row—(K.2 tog.) 3 times, K.1. Break off wool. Thread wool through remaining sts., draw up and fasten off securely.

Left Glove Cast on 56 sts. Work in K.1, P.1 rib for 2 ins. Proceed in stocking stitch with Thumb gusset as follows: 1st row—K.24, P.1, K.2, P.1, K. to end. 2nd row—K.1, P.27, K.1, P.2, K.1, P. to last st., K.1. 3rd row—K.24, P.1, M.1K., K.2, M.1K, P.1, K. to end. 4th row—K.1, P.27, K.1, P.4, K.1, P. to last st., K.1. 5th row—K.24, P.1, K.4, P.1, K. to end. 6th row—K.1, P.27, K.1, M.1P., P.4, M.1P., K.1, P. to last st., K.1. 7th row—K.24, P.1, K.6, P.1, K. to end. 8th row—K.1, P.27, K.1, P.6, K.1, P. to last st., K.1. 9th row—K.24, P.1, M.1K, K.6, M.1K., P.1. K. to end. Continue in this manner, inc. 1 st. at each side of thumb gusset on every 3rd row until there are 18 sts. between the 2 purl sts. (72 sts.) Work 2 rows.

Work Thumb as follows: 1st row—K.24, P.1, K.18, cast on 2, turn. 2nd row—K.1, P.18, K.1, turn. Work as right glove from ** to **.

First Finger: 1st row—K.36, cast on 2, turn. 2nd row—K.1. P.16, K.1. Complete as first finger of right glove.

Second Finger: With right side facing, rejoin wool and knit up 2 sts. from base of first finger, K.7, cast on 2, turn. Complete as second finger of right glove.

Third Finger: With right side facing, rejoin wool and knit up 2 sts. from base of second finger, K.7, cast on 2, turn. Next row—K.1, P.16, K.1, turn. Complete as third finger of right glove.

Fourth Finger: As fourth finger of right glove.

To make up and embroider (*Fig.* 77) Omitting ribbing, press on wrong side using a warm iron and damp cloth. Using odd-ment of 1st contrast work motif in Swiss darning from chart, on back of gloves. Using oddment of 2nd contrast, work 4 lazy daisy stitches in between flower motif, then using 1st contrast, work a French knot inside each lazy daisy. Using a flat seam, join side, thumb and finger seams. Press seams.

TOY RABBIT *(Colour Plate)*

Materials: Of Patons Double Knitting, 2 ozs. white, 1 oz. pink, small ball (less than $\frac{1}{2}$ oz.) red for scarf; scraps of black and blue wool for features. Pair No. 11 needles. Kapok for stuffing.

Measurements: Height to top of head, 11 ins. Abbreviations—*see page 196 for complete list.*

Knit in garter stitch, i.e. every row knit, unless otherwise stated. When making up, oversew all seams on right side.

Body and Legs With P. wool, cast on 12 sts. and knit 1 row. Change to K.1, P.1 rib and work 5 rows. Change to garter st. Next row—Knit. Next row—Knit, inc. 1st at each end. Knit 18 rows. Next row—Knit, inc. 1st at each end: 16 sts. Knit 9 rows.

Break wool and push sts. to end of needle, then cast on another 12 sts. and work another leg the same. Work across both sets of sts., and knit 2 rows. Next row—K.2 tog., K.5, K.2 tog., K.4, K.2 tog., K.2, K.2 tog., K.4, K.2 tog., K.5, K.2 tog.; 26 sts. Next row—K.2 tog., K. to last 2 sts., K.2 tog. Next row—K.6, K.2 tog., K.2, (K.2 tog.) twice, K.2, K.2 tog., K.6. Change to K.1, P.1 rib and work 5 rows. Change to garter-st. and knit 14 rows. Cast off 2 sts. at beg. of next 2 rows and 3 sts. at beg. of foll. 2 rows. Cast off.

Make another piece the same. Join halves together leaving neck open for stuffing. Stuff firmly.

Feet With W. wool, cast on 9 sts. and

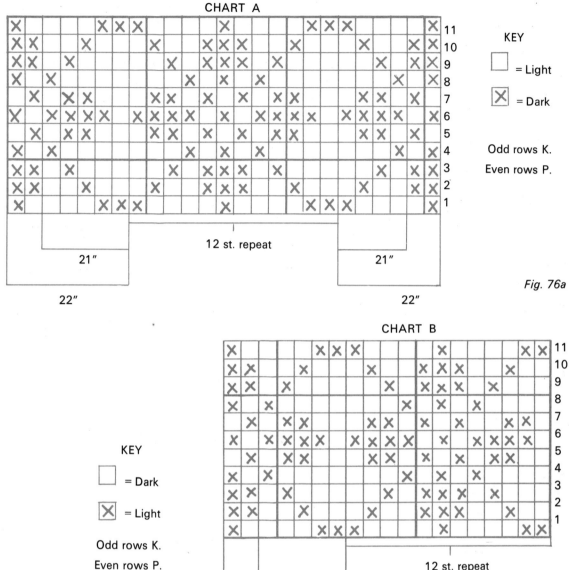

CHART A

11 10 9 8 7 6 5 4 3 2 1

12 st. repeat

21" 21"

22" 22"

KEY

☐ = Light

☒ = Dark

Odd rows K.
Even rows P.

Fig. 76a

CHART B

11 10 9 8 7 6 5 4 3 2 1

12 st. repeat

21"

22"

KEY

☐ = Dark

☒ = Light

Odd rows K.
Even rows P.

Fig. 76b

Swiss Darning

Fig. 77

☒ = 1st Contrast

knit 1 row. Incr. 1st. at each end of next 2 rows. Knit 13 rows. Decr. 1 st. at each end of next 2 rows. Cast off. Make 3 more the same. Sew each pair together leaving an opening for stuffing. Stuff and sew up opening. Sew feet to legs.

Tail With W. wool, cast on 9 sts. and knit 1 row. Incr. 1st. at each end of next 3 rows. Knit 12 rows. Decr. 1 st. at each end of next 3 rows. Knit 1 row. Cast off. Make another piece the same. Join halves together leaving an opening for stuffing. Stuff firmly and sew up opening. Sew tail to body.

Head Start at neck. With W. wool, cast on 12 sts. Knit 3 rows. Next row—K. to last st., incr. in last st. Next row—Incr. in 1st st., K. to end. Next row—K. to last st., incr. in last st. Next row—Knit, incr. 1 st. at each end. Rep. the last 4 rows once more: 22 sts. Next row—Knit. Next row—K.7, (incr. in next st.) 4 times, K.11: 26 sts. Knit 5 rows. Next row—K.2 tog., K. to end. Next row—K. to last 2 sts., K.2 tog. Next row—K.2 tog., K.5, (K.2 tog.) 4 times, K.7, K.2 tog. Next row—K. to last 2 sts., K.2 tog. Next row—K.2 tog., K. to end. Rep. the last 2 rows 3 times more. Next row —K.2 tog., K. to last 2 sts., K.2 tog. Cast off.

Work another piece the same. Sew halves together leaving cast-on edges open for stuffing. Stuff firmly, pushing head out to shape.

Features Eyes: Half blue buttonhole-st., half black satin-st. separated by 2 straight-sts. in W. with straight-st. in W. on black. Eyebrows: Black straight-sts. Nose and mouth: Black satin spot for nose, 3 black straight-sts. for mouth. Whiskers: Straight-sts. in black cotton.

Neck With W. wool, cast on 24 sts. and knit 3 rows. Then work 3 rows K.1, P.1 rib. Next row—Knit. Cast off. Join short ends to form circle and sew one end round open end of head. Stuff firmly, then sew other end round open end of body.

Ears With W. wool, cast on 3 sts. and knit 1 row. Next row—Knit, incr. 1 st. at each end. Next 3 rows—Knit. Rep. the last 4 rows 7 times more: 19 sts. Next row— K.8, K.3 tog., K.8. Next row—K.7, K.3 tog., K.7. Next row—K.6, K.3 tog., K.6. Next row—K.2 tog., K. to last 2 sts., K.2 tog. Cast off. Make 3 more pieces the same. Sew each pair together. Sew ears to head folding wide end in half so that they curl forward.

Arms With W. wool, cast on 9 sts. and knit 1 row. Incr. at each end of next 2 rows. Knit 14 rows. Decr. at each end of next 2 rows. Knit 1 row. Break wool. Push sts. to end of needle, then cast on another 9 sts. in W. and make another piece the same. Break W.

Join in P. and knit across both sets of sts. thus: Next row—Knit. Work 5 rows K.1, P.1 rib. Next 3 rows—Knit. Next row— Knit, incr. 1st. at each end: 20 sts. Next 6 rows—Knit. Next row—K.9, (K. twice in next st.) twice, K.9. Next row—Knit. Cast off.

Make another piece the same. Fold in half and join leaving cast-off edges open. Stuff firmly, then sew open end of arms to body.

Tie With red wool, cast on 2 sts. and knit 1 row. Next row—K. to last st., incr. in last st. Next row—Incr. in 1st st., K. to end. Rep. the last 2 rows once more. Knit 123 rows. Next row—K. to last 2 sts., K.2 tog. Next row—K.2 tog., K. to end. Rep. last 2 rows once. Cast off. Tie round neck. Brush up hands, ears, feet and tail to give furry effect.

CHICK EGG COSIES *(Pl. 67)*

Quick to make in stocking stitch with a garter stitch border these fluffy egg cosies need only a ½ oz. ball of angora wool for three little chicks.

Materials: ½ oz. ball of Patons *Fuzzy-Wuzzy*, a little cotton wool for padding, black darning wool for eyes, scraps of orange and yellow felt and 1 pair of No. 10 knitting needles.

Tension: 7½ stitches to 1 inch.

Abbreviations—see page 196 for complete list.

To make Cast on 40 sts. K. 2 rows. Proceed in st.-st. until work measures 1½ inches, after a p. row. Next row (K.6, K.2 tog.) 5 times. P.1 row. Next row (K.5, K.2 tog.) 5 times (30 sts.). Proceed until work measures 2½ inches, after a p. row. Next row (K.5, inc. in next st.) 5 times (35 sts.). Proceed until 4 inches, after a p. row. Dec. in next and every alternate row thus: 1st row (K.3, K.2 tog.) 7 times. 3rd row (K.2, K.2 tog.) 7 times. 5th row (K.1, K.2 tog.) 7 times. Break wool, thread end through remaining stitches, draw up and fasten off neatly.

Join seam. Pad head, run a thread through knitting at neck level and draw up slightly. Embroider eyes. Cut out beak in orange felt and stitch across centre. Cut out wings in yellow felt and attach each side with a few light stitches.

___

HOW TO CROCHET

Crocheting is one of the easiest forms of handicraft to learn, so it is well worth your while to master the few simple stitches which are the foundations of this work. The equipment is of the simplest, as the only tool required is a crochet hook.

If you are a beginner it is a good idea to buy a fairly coarse hook to practise the stitches with, and do these again and again until you are quite familiar with them, and have attained a fair speed. Then you will be able to follow any pattern given you in a book.

Plate 67

The knitted chick egg cosies are in angora wool

___

CHAIN STITCH
(Figs. 78a and 78b)

___

The basis of all crochet is the chain stitch. This is made by forming a loop on the hook, which is held in the right hand in the

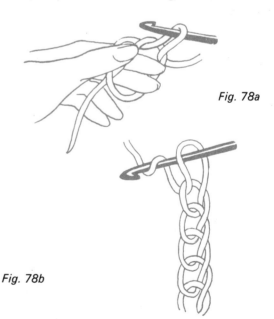

Fig. 78a

Fig. 78b

same way as you would hold a pencil. Hold the thread between the thumb and first finger, so that it is passed over the second finger, under the third, and over the fourth. If this arrangement is used, the thread will slip easily through the fingers and not get caught or 'stick'. Other methods of holding the thread may suggest themselves to you, and whatever makes for smooth working is, of course, to be recommended. With your first stitch on the hook, place the hook under the thread from left to right and draw the thread through the loop already on the hook. Repeat this action until a succession of stitches is formed. Do not pull the thread too tightly, and try to keep the stitches as uniform in size as possible.

SINGLE CROCHET OR SLIP STITCH
(Figs. 79a and 79b)

This makes a small stitch, and is used principally for joining and fastening.

Fig. 79a

Fig. 79b

Place hook through two top threads of the stitch below; draw the loop through the stitch and through the loop on the needle at the same time.

DOUBLE CROCHET STITCH
(Fig. 80)

Place hook through two top threads of stitch below, draw the loop through, place the hook under the thread and draw up a loop, which must be pulled through the two on the hook.

Double crochet may be made in two ways, which give slightly different effects. In one case a flat surface is produced, and in

Fig. 80

the other case a ridged surface. It depends entirely on the taste of the worker which is chosen. It is as well to try both ways before deciding which method is best for the piece of work in hand.

TREBLE STITCH *(Fig. 81a)*

There are several variations of this stitch, which are given below.

Fig. 81a

Half Treble

Place the hook under the thread and insert it through the top of the stitch below and draw a loop, turn the thread again over the hook, and draw this loop through the three on the hook.

Ordinary Treble *(See Fig. 81b)*

When treble is mentioned, it is this stitch which is meant. As in the last stitch, place the hook under the thread and insert it through the top of the stitch below. Draw the loop through, place hook under thread

Fig. 81b

and through two loops on the hook, then place hook under thread once more and draw it through the remaining two loops on the needle.

Long Treble or Double Treble
(See Fig. 82a)

In this variety, you wind the thread twice round the hook (or in other words, place hook under thread twice before inserting

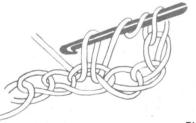

Fig. 82a

it in the stitch below), then draw the loops through just as in the ordinary treble.

Triple Treble *(See Fig. 82b)*

This is made by placing the hook under the thread three times in succession before inserting in the stitch below, then working off the loops, as before.

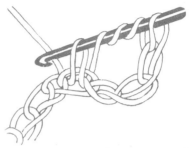

Fig. 82b

It is possible to have Quadruple Treble or even Treble of a larger number, by increasing the number of times the hook is placed under the thread at the beginning of the stitch.

INCREASING

This is quite a simple matter, and consists merely of working two stitches into one loop, instead of one. It can be carried out in almost any part of the work, but is done, preferably, at the beginning or end of a row, if the work is being crocheted in rows.

DECREASING

The usual method is to miss a stitch of the previous row, thus shortening the length of the work. Again this should be done as near the beginning or end of the row as possible, so as not to be too obvious.

TENSION

As in knitting, it is important to know at what tension you are working, and the best way to check your tension with that of your pattern is to measure how many stitches and rows you are crocheting to a square inch. Compare it with your pattern. It is easy to work too loosely or too tightly when beginning, but if you are careful to use the size of hook recommended, a little practice should give you the required tension.

JOINING THREAD

The same general instructions apply as are given under this heading in the knitting section. Avoid making a join in the middle of a pattern if it is anyway possible.

STITCHES AND PATTERNS

When once the simple stitches have been learnt, there is no end to the variety of patterns which can be made up. A description will be given of some of the easiest and most commonly used ones, but the ingenious worker will soon learn ways of making variations to suit her requirements.

DOUBLE CROCHET PATTERN *(Pl. 68)*

This can be used for making bedroom slippers, children's bodices, shawls, etc.,

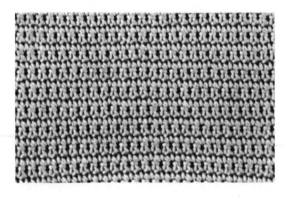

Plate 68

and consists of rows of double crochet worked to and fro, the hook being placed each time under both loops of the previous row of stitches. It is very simple to do and

produces a fairly compact piece of work.

RIBBED DOUBLE CROCHET PATTERN
(Pl. 68a)

This can also be used for any of the purposes mentioned above, and differs

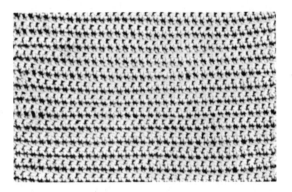

Plate 68a

from the previous stitch only in the hook being placed under the back loop alone of the stitch of the row below.

BLANKET PATTERN (PUFF STITCH)
(Pl. 69)

This stitch is an excellent one for any type of blanket and if worked on rather a small hook, will form a compact piece of work, which will be very warm.

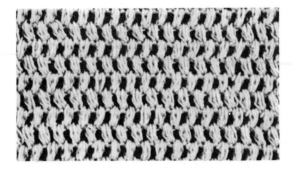

Plate 69

To work Commence with desired length of chain, having a multiple of 2 ch.

1st row: Draw loop on hook up ⅜ in., thread over hook, insert hook into 4th chain from hook and draw loop up ⅜ in., (thread over hook, insert hook into same stitch and draw loop up as before) twice, thread over and draw through all loops on hook, 1 ch. to fasten (a puff stitch made), * 1 ch., miss 1 ch., thread over hook, insert hook into next ch. and draw thread up ⅜ in., (thread over hook, insert hook into same place and draw thread through as before) twice, thread over and draw through all loops on hook, 1 ch. to fasten (another puff stitch made); repeat from * omitting a puff stitch at end of last repeat, 1 tr. into last ch., 3 ch., turn.

2nd row: *Puff stitch into next sp., 1 ch., repeat from * ending with 1 tr. into 3rd of 3 ch., 3 ch., turn. Repeat 2nd row for length required.

TRICOT CROCHET (Pl. 70)

This is so called because you are working most of the time with a number of stitches on the hook as in knitting. It produces a plain smooth effect, and, if desired, may be done in narrow strips, which can afterwards be joined. It is suitable for almost any plain garment.

To work Make a length of chain.

Plate 70

1st row: Missing the first chain, draw a loop through each of the remaining chains, leaving all the loops on the hook. At the end, work back by placing thread over hook and drawing through two loops every time until all the stitches are finished.

2nd row: Draw a loop through each stitch of the previous row, leaving them on the hook, and working back the same as before. Repeat the 2nd row as long as necessary.

TREBLE PATTERNS (Pls. 71a, 71b and 71c)

In the illustrations of Trebles (*Pl. 71*) you can see the effect produced by this stitch in its different forms—single, double and triple. All the varieties of treble patterns are very commonly used in insertion and lace, but they are also most useful for berets and as a decoration for jumpers and children's garments. As you can see, the effect of treble is to form columns or bars, which can be increased in height almost indefinitely by adding to the number of times the thread is wound round the hook at the beginning of the stitch.

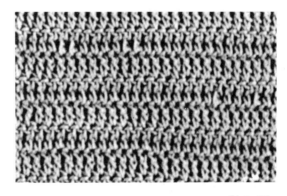

Plate 71a

It is, however, a good deal more difficult to maintain evenness in the work if you have too many loops to be pulled through by the hook, and a fair amount of practice is

Plate 71b

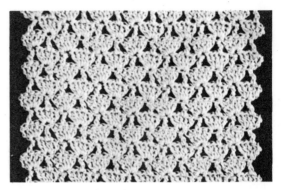

Plate 72

Plate 71c

required to work satisfactorily anything greater than triple treble.

When working trebles to and fro, and not just an odd stitch or two in a pattern, remember to make some chain stitches at the beginning of each row, and pass over the first treble below, which is replaced by the chain.

SHELL PATTERN *(Pl. 72)*

This forms an effective design which can be used for almost any purpose, but is particularly suitable for shawls and any type of children's garment. It may produce a very closely woven surface if worked on a small hook, and can just as easily be used as a border for a pram cover or counterpane.

To work Make a length of chain.

1st row: Into the 4th chain from hook make 4 treble, miss 2 chain, 1 treble stitch into next chain, * miss 2 chain, 5 treble in next chain, miss 2 chain, 1 treble stitch in next chain. Repeat from * to the end of the row.

2nd row—Make 3 chain, then on the first treble stitch make 4 treble, but on subsequent ones 5, and in centre of each group of trebles of the previous row, make 1 treble stitch.

Repeat the 2nd row as long as required.

CROCHET LACE *(Pl. 74a and 74b)*

Lace work is more suitably done in crochet than in knitting, and the possible varieties are much greater. It is also, on the whole, easier to work with a fine crochet hook than it is with fine knitting needles.

The most useful purpose lace serves nowadays is for household linen, such as afternoon tablecloths, doilies, and towels. But it is also suitable for lace collars and cuffs.

The instructions for two simple edgings are given below, both suitable to be worked as an ornamentation for a dainty handkerchief, tea napkin, or table mat. Both can be worked on the material, but if that is not desired, it is equally possible to make a length of chain as a foundation as in starting any other piece of crochet.

Abbreviations :   ch. = chain;   s.s. = slip stitch; d.c. = double crochet; tr. = treble; dbl. tr. = double treble.

The Open Border *(Pl. 74a)*

1st row: Cut fabric ¼ in. larger than required. Withdraw a thread ¼ in. from edge all round and turn back a small hem. Work a row of d.c. over hem and into space of thread. Attach thread to corner, 3 d.c. into same place, *d.c. closely along side having a multiple of 4 d.c. plus 3, 3 d.c. into next corner; repeat from * omitting 3 d.c. at end of last repeat, 1 s.s. into first d.c.

2nd row: 1 d.c. into same place as s.s., ** 5 ch., miss 1 d.c., 1 d.c. into next d.c., * 5 ch., miss 3 d.c., 1 d.c. into next d.c.; repeat from * to next corner; repeat from ** omitting 5 ch. and 1 d.c. at end of last repeat, 2 ch.,

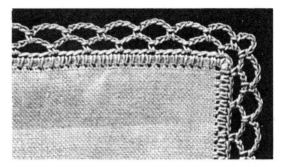

Plate 74a

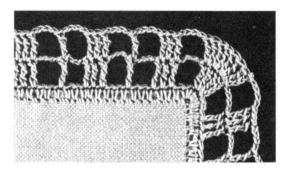

Plate 74b

Plate 73

1 tr. into first d.c.

3rd row: 1 d.c. into loop just formed, ** 5 ch., into next loop work 1 d.c. 5 ch. and 1 d.c. (corner), * 5 ch., 1 d.c. into next loop; repeat from * along side; repeat from ** omitting 5 ch. and 1 d.c. at end of last repeat, 2 ch., 1 tr. into first d.c.

Repeat as 3rd row for depth required having one loop more before corner at beginning of each row, ending last row with 5 ch., 1 s.s. into first d.c. Fasten off.

A Lattice Border *(Pl. 74b)*

1st row: Work 1st row as 1st row of Open Border but having a multiple of 8 d.c. plus 5.

2nd row: 1 s.s. into next d.c., 4 ch., 3 dbl. tr. into same place as last s.s., *4 ch., miss 2 d.c., 1 dbl. tr. into each of next 3 d.c., 4 ch.,

Fine crochet is often used for church work

Plate 75

An easy crochet edging for a guest towel

miss 2 d.c., 1 dbl. tr. into next d.c.; repeat from * along side ending with 4 ch., miss 2 d.c., 1 dbl. tr. into each of next 3 d.c., 4 ch., miss 2 d.c., 4 dbl. tr. into next d.c. (corner); repeat from first * omitting corner at end of last repeat, 1 s.s. into 4th of 4 ch.

3rd row: 4 ch., 1 dbl. tr. into same place as s.s., 2 dbl. tr. into each of next 3 dbl. tr., *4 ch., 1 dbl. tr. into each of next 3 dbl. tr., 4 ch., 1 dbl. tr. into next dbl. tr.; repeat from * along side ending with 4 ch., 1 dbl. tr. into each of next 3 dbl. tr., 4 ch., 2 dbl. tr. into each of next 4 dbl. tr. (corner); repeat from first * omitting corner at end of last repeat, 1 s.s. into 4th of 4 ch.

Repeat 3rd row for depth required working 2 dbl. tr. into each dbl. tr. at corners. Fasten off.

LACE EDGING FOR TOWEL (Pl. 75)

This lace edging is 2 inches in depth. It makes a handsome edging for a guest towel and can also be used to edge a cloth or a runner.

Materials : Coats Mercer-Crochet No. 10, crochet hook No. 2½. (1 ball is sufficient for a towel edging.)

Tension : Approximately 2 repeats of the pattern measure 1½ inches.

Abbreviations : ch. = chain; d.c. = double crochet; tr. = treble; d.tr. = double treble, which is cotton twice over the hook working the loops off in twos as for treble; t.tr. = triple treble; lp. = loop. *For fuller list of abbreviations see page 196.*

To work Begin with a length of chain having a multiple of 6 ch. plus 2.

1st row: 1 d.c. into 2nd ch. from hook, then 1 d.c. into each ch. all along row, 6 ch., turn.

2nd row: Miss first 3 d.c., * 1 tr. into next d.c., 3 ch., miss 2 d.c., rep. from * ending with 1 tr. into last d.c., 1 tr. into last d.c., 4 ch., turn.

3rd row: Miss 1st tr. * work (1 d.tr., 2 ch.) 3 times and 1 d.tr. into next tr., 1 d.tr. into next tr.; repeat from * working last d.tr. into 3rd of 6 ch., 7 ch., turn.

4th row: Miss first d.tr., * (leaving last lp. of each d.tr. on hook), work 1 d.tr. into next d.tr. 4 times, thread over hook and draw through all lps. on hook (4 d.tr. cluster made) 3 ch., 1 d.tr. into next d.tr., 3 ch.; repeat from * omitting 3 ch. at end of last rep. and working last d.tr. into 4th of 4 ch., 6 ch., turn.

5th row: Miss 1st d.tr., * 1 tr. into top of cluster, 3 ch., 1 tr. into next d.tr., 3 ch.; repeat from * ending with 1 tr. into 4th of 7th turning ch., 4 ch., turn.

6th row: As 3rd row, omitting turning ch. at end of row. Fasten off.

CROCHET MOTIFS (Pls. 76–77)

These lacy motifs may be joined to form table mats, tray cloths or a table runner. A simple filling is worked between them.

Materials : Coats Mercer Crochet No. 20
(20 grm.); Milwards crochet hook
No. 3.

Size of Motif : Each circle measures 3¾
inches in diameter.

Abbreviations : dbl. tr. = double treble; trip.
tr. = triple treble; lp. = loop; cl. =
cluster; rep. = repeat; sp.(s) = space(s);
p. = picot; st.(s) = stitches. *For fuller
list of abbreviations see page 196.*

First Motif

Commence with 9 ch., join with a s.s. to
form a ring.

1st row: 16 d.c. into ring, 1 s.s. into first
d.c.

2nd row: 3 ch., 1 tr. into same place as
s.s., *6 ch., 1 d.c. into top of last tr. (picot
made), 2 tr. into each of next 2 d.c.; repeat
from * omitting 2 tr. at end of last rep., 1 s.s.
into 3rd of 3 ch.

3rd row: s.s. into next tr. and to centre of
next p., 4 ch., leaving last lp. of each on
hook work 4 dbl. tr. into same p., thread
over and draw through all lps. on hook (4
dbl. tr. cluster made), * 9 ch., 5 dbl. tr. cl.
into next p.; rep. from * ending with 9 ch.,
1 s.s. into top of first cl.

4th row: 1 d.c. into same place as s.s., *
11 d.c. into next lp., 1 d.c. into next cl.; rep.
from * ending with 11 d.c. into next lp., 1
s.s. into first d.c.

5th row: 1 d.c. into same place as s.s., *
7 ch., miss 5 d.c., 1 d.c. into next d.c.; rep.

from * ending with 7 ch., 1 s.s. into first d.c.

6th row: 1 s.s. into next lp., 9 d.c. into
each lp., 1 s.s. into first d.c.

7th row: 1 s.s. into each of next 4 sts., 1
d.c. into same place as last s.s., * 7 ch., miss 8
d.c., 1 d.c. into next d.c.; rep. from * ending
with 7 ch., 1 s.s. into first d.c.

8th row: 1 d.c. into same place as s.s.,*
9 d.c. into next lp., 1 d.c. into next d.c.; rep.
from * ending with 9 d.c. into next lp., 1 s.s.
into first d.c.

9th row: 1 d.c. into same place as s.s., 1
d.c. into each of next 5 d.c.,* 6 ch., 1 d.c.
into top of last d.c. (p. made), 1 d.c. into

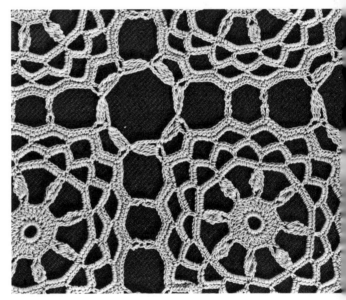

Plate 77

*Any size mat or cloth may be
made of these crochet motifs.
The detail shows how they are
joined*

Plate 76

Plate 78

Traycloth with crochet braid edging and detail of one corner

each of next 10 d.c., rep. from * omitting 6 d.c. at end of last rep., 1 s.s. into first d.c. Fasten off.

Second Motif

Work as first motif for 8 rows. To join the first motif:

9th row: 1 d.c. into same place as s.s., 1 d.c. into each of next 5 d.c., (3 c h., 1 s.s. into corresponding p. on first motif, 3 ch., 1 d.c. into top of last d.c. on second motif, 1 d.c. into each of next 10 d.c.) twice and complete as for first motif.

A filling may be worked as follows: attach thread to any free p. between motifs, 1 d.c. into same p., * 5 ch., 3 trip. tr. cl. into same p., 1 d.c. into next free p.; rep. from * omitting 1 d.c. at end of last rep., 1 s.s. into first d.c. Fasten off.

BRAID EDGING

A crochet braid has many uses and is extremely simple to work. It may be linked to make an edging for a tray cloth as in *Pls. 78 and 79*, or used for a set of table mats, or as a finish to a scarf or crochet lace jacket.

Materials : Coats Mercer-Crochet No. 10 (20 grm.). (For edging one traycloth of finished dimensions $12\frac{1}{2}$ in. by $20\frac{1}{4}$ in. you will need 3 balls) also a piece of linen $8\frac{1}{2}$ in. by 16 in. and a piece of stiff muslin 14 in. by 22 in.

Tension : 5 stitches to $\frac{1}{2}$ inch.

Abbreviations : ch. = chain; lp.(s) = loop(s);

Plate 79

rep. = repeat. *See page 196 for complete list.*

To work the braid commence with 7 ch.

1st row: Insert hook into 2nd ch. from hook and draw thread through,*insert hook into next ch. and draw thread through; rep. from * 4 times more. (7 lps. on hook.)

2nd row: *Thread over hook and draw through 2 lps. on hook; rep. from * 5 times more, 1 ch.

3rd row: *Insert hook into next vertical lp. of row before last and draw thread through; rep. from * 4 times more, insert hook into next 2 vertical lps. and draw thread through.

Rep. 2nd and 3rd rows for length required, ending with 2nd row. Fasten off.

For the Traycloth *(Pls. 78 and 79)*

Work 4 lengths of braid the required length. Baste in position on muslin and secure where braid overlaps and where curves join straight edges, without picking up any of the muslin. Remove all basting stitches and slipstitch inner edge of braid edging in position to outer edge of fabric. Press on wrong side, using a damp cloth.

BEDROOM SLIPPERS

This is a delightfully easy pattern, which the beginner can tackle without any fear of going wrong. Each slipper is crocheted in one piece, and the ribbed stitch of double crochet is used throughout. It is made for a medium-sized foot, but as the work is very elastic, it can be stretched or contracted to fit a slightly different sized slipper sole. The wool cord round the ankle ensures the fit of the slipper and prevents that loose feeling which so often occurs in a shoe of this type.

Materials : 4 oz. of 4-ply Fingering, a No. 10 crochet hook, a pair of slipper soles of the desired size.

Tension : 6 d.c. to the inch in length.

Abbreviations used : Ch. = chain, d.c. = double crochet, st. = stitch. *See page 196 for complete list.*

To work The work is begun at the toe, by making 9 ch.

1st row: D.c. in every ch.

2nd row: D.c. into every st., except first and last, which have 2 d.c. Repeat this 2nd row 12 times, then work without increasing till crochet measures 4½ inches from the toe.

Next rows: Make 22 ch., turn, d.c. to

middle, turn with 1 ch., and d.c. back. Continue with this side of the slipper until you have 3 inches from where the sts. were divided. Now work the other side the same.

Sew up the back seam with the same wool, and then neatly attach the crochet to the slipper sole with strong thread of a matching colour. Turn back the flaps and sew them down with small pompons of wool, and run a cord made of a chain of crochet round the ankle.

This will make rather a narrow string. If a stronger one is required, plait either three or six strands of wool together and finish off the ends with tassels. (*See page 191, Fig. 83.*)

An even simpler method of making this slipper is to crochet it as above until you get to the place where the stitches are divided, then continue working one half without any increase for 5 inches, and do the same with the other side. Join up the seam at the back of the heel and sew on to the slipper sole. Finish off the ankle edge with a row of shell pattern or any fancy stitch, working it rather tightly, as this part of the slipper is apt to stretch.

This will give you a slipper with less fullness in it than the one previously described, but, on the whole, it will cling to the foot better and therefore be warmer.

HOW TO USE UP ODDMENTS OF WOOL

After one has been knitting or crocheting for some time, a number of oddments of wool accumulate, and these are usually not enough in themselves to use for any complete garment.

There are quite a number of different ways in which they may be made use of, and one of the most effective is to collect as many varieties as possible of the same type of wool and try your hand at patchwork

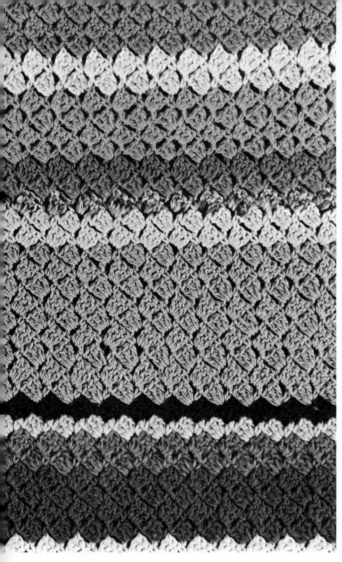

Cot blanket of rainbow crochet   Plate 80

RUG OR PRAM BLANKETS
(Pl. 80)

For pram blankets, rugs, and even for heavy scarves, select your thick double-knitting wool, but for lighter scarves, hot water bottle covers and workbags a thinner variety should be used.

The joining of the patches may be carried out with suitable wool, or by feather-stitching or other fancy stitching in embroidery cotton. A neat border can be made by a row or two of crochet round the edge. This has the effect of preventing the patches curling up, if they are made in stocking stitch; if garter stitch is used, there is not so much need for an edging, as the work will keep flat of its own accord.

A cosy rug can be made by knitting patches in garter stitch of several different colours. Each patch is made by casting on 30 stitches and working 30 rows plain.

This makes each section rather more oblong than square, but if an absolute square is desired, you will have to knit about 35 rows instead of 30. Work in strips, each strip containing a number of different coloured patches. These strips are light and easy to handle. When a number are made, sew them together, arranging the patches as effectively as possible. A similar rug can be made in treble crochet. Another good use for wool oddments is a pram rug crocheted in rainbow stripes.

FRINGES, TASSELS AND POMPONS

It is often very effective to finish off a scarf by adding a fringe of a contrasting colour. Here your bag of odd balls of wool, cotton or other yarn will be useful again. To make a simple fringe, cut the wool into lengths of 6 inches, thread each through a loop at the end of the scarf, knot it securely, seeing that the two ends are of equal size.

knitting. For this you will only need quite small lengths of wool, so that practically any remnants come in handy.

You will find it easier to have all the patches of the same size, as the appearance is then more uniform, and the sewing together of the pieces becomes much simpler; so the first thing is to decide the dimensions of each patch. Some sort of colour scheme is advisable, if the amounts of wool will permit it, but of course it is always possible to have a riot of colour, especially in a cushion cover or a child's cot rug.

If a thick fringe is required, as in a rug, use each piece double.

Tassels are very decorative, and on such articles as cushions and berets, add a nice finish at next to no cost. Use a piece of cardboard 5 inches long, and wind the wool round about a dozen times, or more if a thicker tassel is wanted (*see Fig. 83a*); slip a piece of wool through the strands at one end and tie them together, removing them from the card. Now bind the top of the tassel by twisting wool round about 10 times (*see Fig. 83b*), and secure the end, and pull it out of sight. Cut the other ends of the tassel evenly when this is finished.

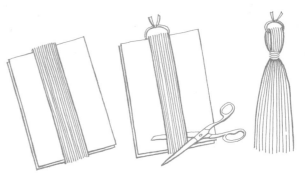

Fig. 83a   *Fig. 83b*

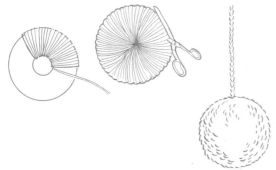

Fig. 84

Pompons are ideal for babies' and small children's clothing, either on little caps or to make the ending to a crochet chain used for a neck or waist string.

Cut two circles of card about the size of the pompon required. Cut out a circle in the exact centre of each. Lay the two circles together and wind the wool as in *Fig. 84*. When the centre circle is full, thread your loose end between the cards and fasten securely. Cut round the edges of the circles and the pompon will fluff out.

FANCY TOPS FOR STOCKINGS AND SOCKS

Thick sports socks are much improved by having a row or two of colour worked as a stripe round the top. Socks for a schoolboy will be more appreciated if they have a turn-back of a pattern in several colours, or merely a broad band of one colour, chosen from your old balls. It is hardly worth while to buy yarn specially for the purpose unless it is possible to obtain quite small quantities, and this is often only feasible in thin wools.

COLLARS AND CUFFS

Children's jumpers and coats may be very prettily finished by the addition of collar and cuffs in a contrasting shade, and remnants may be made use of for this purpose, as well as for buttons for the garment itself.

CROCHET EDGING

Many articles may be finished off with a row of chain stitch, or a more elaborate edging of several rows of treble, and it is often an effective method to use wool or other yarn of a different colour.

CARE OF WOOL

Take care to keep your oddments of wool in some place where they will not be accessible to moths. They can be packed in a tightly fastened polythene bag or even kept in a cake tin until wanted.

KEEPING THE WORK CLEAN

This is a very important point, especially with light-coloured or white garments. It is surprising how quickly white or cream will gradually darken in the course of a few weeks if precautions are not taken to protect the work.

Always keep it wrapped up when not in use, either in a polythene bag or a large white handkerchief. Wash the hands before starting any light-coloured work, even if they seem quite clean. Rough hands will also make the work fluffy and spoil the garment so it is wise to keep them smooth with a hand cream.

If you are knitting an article of some length, such as a scarf or jumper, keep the part already worked rolled up, or you will find that it gets dirty and rubbed and begins to look worn before the garment is even finished.

FINISHING OFF YOUR WORK

Many a well-made garment has been spoilt by being carelessly finished off, without due attention being given to all the small points which count for so much in the finishing. This is often caused by ignorance as to how to proceed when the actual knitting or crochet is completed.

Pressing

Before any attempt is made to sew up the various pieces of the finished article, they should be pressed separately. Lay a clean damp cloth on the wrong side of the work, and press gently but firmly with the iron, which should be of a moderate heat (or use a steam iron). Stocking stitch may be ironed on both sides, if necessary, as the more it is pressed the better it looks; but this does not apply to the more raised types of knitting and crochet, such as garter stitch, moss

stitch and treble stitch. It is best to press these rather lightly on the wrong side only.

The same applies to fancy patterns. It is not advisable to make them too flat, or it is apt to take the character out of the work. Ribbing should be left untouched, as ironing does nothing to improve its effect, and there is always danger of pressing it too much, so that its elasticity vanishes.

Making-up

Before sewing up, see that all the ends of yarn are neatly darned in on the wrong side. Then lay the two edges to be sewn side by side, and draw the loops of each together, using matching yarn. This should be done rather loosely, to allow for the stretching which the garment will be subjected to. Press all the seams after they are joined.

Brushing the Surface

Sometimes you may want to give a raised surface to the work, as in the case of babies' clothes or collars and cuffs of jumpers. A teasel brush should be applied, and the wool lightly brushed up to produce a 'fluffy' surface, but care must be taken that this process is not done too roughly, or the material may become torn or damaged. Make sure that the brush is quite clean before use, by rubbing it briskly on a piece of white cloth.

If angora or 'fuzzy-wuzzy' wool is used, the surface will be raised of its own accord, and little or no brushing will be necessary.

Washing

This is a most important subject, as the whole future usefulness and appearance of the article in question depend on how it is washed, especially the first time. Subsequent washings are less vital, because the first immersion of the garment in water determines its character, and if this is done carelessly, no amount of further washing

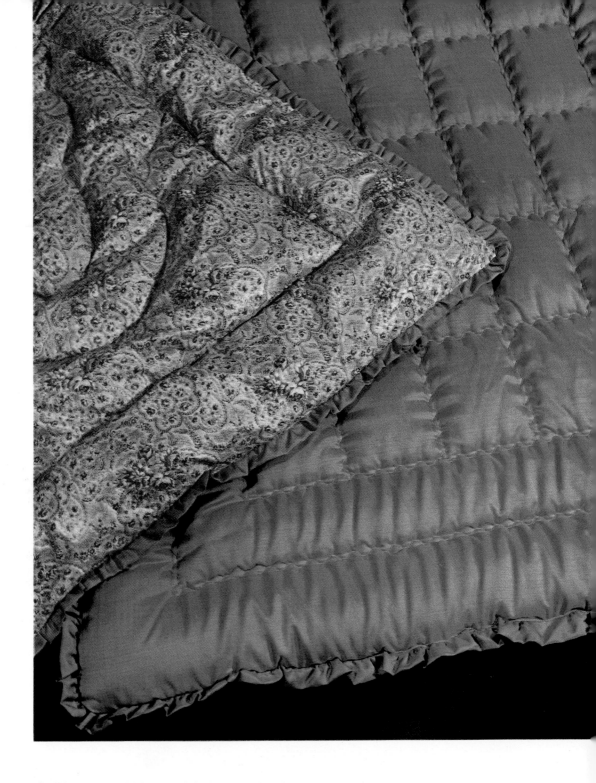

Quilting can add its special charm to home-made eiderdowns. Here an unfussed simple square pattern is used on the green eiderdown while a curved pattern is stitched through the traditional floral cover

Tapestry work adds distinction and a touch of period flavour to this reproduction Chippendale chair

will remedy any defects—in fact, it will only tend to exaggerate them.

White Garments must be treated rather differently from coloured ones, as there is always a danger of their losing their whiteness and becoming yellow. This is often caused by having the water too hot, which has the effect also of shrinking any wool garment, though cotton or man-made fibres are unaffected.

Make a good lather of warm water (it should be of a temperature in which the hands can be very comfortably borne). Gently move the garments about in the suds, avoiding rubbing, merely squeeze them carefully, seeing that each portion has equal treatment. Rinse in clean warm water of about the same temperature.

Coloured Garments require the water a shade cooler, as there is always risk of the colours running. A good plan to prevent this is to give an extra rinse in water to which about a tablespoonful of vinegar has been added.

In no case use soda when washing any type of knitted or crocheted article. It not only plays havoc with the dye, but also destroys the surface and 'mats' the wool.

Drying must be carefully carried out, or the shape of the garment may be ruined. When removing the washing from the water, place at once in a clean dry cloth and press out the moisture. Never wring, as this is bad for the texture of the wool.

Woollen things must not be hung up to dry, even on a wooden hanger, as the weight of the water-soaked material pulls the garment out of shape and ruins it for ever. The best way is to lay it out flat on a clean towel and allow it to dry in the air or in a warm room.

Woollen articles, especially, should not be left to lie about in a damp condition, but must be dried immediately, or shrinkage may occur and colours may run.

The success of washing knitting or crochet will partly depend on the way in which the article has been worked. For example, it is much more difficult to wash a loosely knitted garment well, as it will stretch more easily than a closely-woven one. The latter has the disadvantage of being liable to 'mat' or 'felt' and lose some of its surface that way.

REPAIRING

If a garment becomes torn or worn in one place, it is useful to be able to repair it so that there will appear to be no break in the pattern. The moment a hole appears, the stitches round it should be secured temporarily, or they will unravel very quickly and worse damage will be caused. Then, on the other side, the following process can be carried out:

Undo the temporary stitches and run a horizontal thread across in place of each broken thread, securing it in the uninjured part of the garment some way from the edge of the hole. Now push your needle through on to the right side and, starting at the top left-hand corner take up each horizontal thread in turn, putting the needle through from below upwards. On the ascending line, which makes the other half of each stitch, put the needle from above downwards. Push the stitches tightly in place with the needle, and continue till all the space is filled up.

This method is suitable for a large rent, but if only a small tear has been made, the damage can probably be righted by careful darning (*see page 145*). In this, however, it is always best to try to copy the arrangement of the stitches as far as possible.

COMMON MISTAKES IN
KNITTING AND CROCHET

Varying the Tension

It has been said that no two people knit in exactly the same way, and certainly there is a great amount of variation in different people's work. The work of any one person, however, should be uniform throughout; that is, the tension should be the same, provided the same sized needles and the same thickness in wool is used. If this is liable to vary, there will be unevenness of work, which will spoil the whole of the finished effect. A little practice will soon show you at what tension it is easiest for you to work.

Good durable knitting or crochet is fairly tight, but the stitches should run readily along the needles without being inclined to stick at all. Very loose work has the great disadvantage of stretching too much, and so getting quickly out of shape. On the other hand if it is too tight, a good deal of the elasticity of the wool is spoilt.

Get into the way of doing your work evenly, and half the difficulties of getting a good fit to the garment will disappear.

Another point to bear in mind is that breaking off in the middle of a row rather conduces to uneven work, as the stitches often get pulled out of shape by the needles. Always lay aside your knitting at the end of a row, and do not place the spare needle through the work already done, nor into the ball of wool as it can split a thread; it is best to put the end into a cork.

Stretching of Ribbing

Ribbing is always carried out in places where there will be a good deal of stretching; but, nevertheless, there must be a limit to the amount of pulling it is subjected to, or it will be drawn out of shape. There are two ways of avoiding this:

1. When starting with ribbing at the beginning of a garment, knit the first row into the back of each stitch, thus forming a firmer edge or cast on in the corded manner (*page 161*).

2. Carry out the ribbing on needles one or even two sizes smaller than those used for the rest of the garment. The smaller stitches have less power of stretching than the larger ones, and so the shape will be preserved.

When ribbing is cast off, there is some danger of the edge being too tight, as the cast-off edge has less stretching power than the ribbing itself. To avoid this, cast off RATHER LOOSELY, a good plan being to use needles one size larger than the rest of the knitting.

Knotting Wool

When wool or cotton or any form of yarn has to be joined, it should never be knotted. Not only does this process stretch the thread, but the knots, even if they are arranged on the wrong side, give the work an uneven surface, and, particularly in things like socks and stockings, may rub the wearer in inconvenient places. Always join wool by the method advised on *page 162*.

Dropped Stitches

These are naturally more the mistakes of a beginner, but quite experienced knitters and crochet-workers are liable to drop a stitch now and again. If this is not discovered at once, a lot of trouble follows, so from time to time it is as well to count your stitches while doing a row, to see that all is well.

If a lost stitch is discovered, use a spare knitting needle or crochet hook to pick up the loop, being careful to work it into the loops in all the rows missed. If it is garter stitch, the loop will have to be twisted alternately in and out; for one row the wool will be brought under then over, and for the next vice versa. In the case of stocking stitch, the loop is taken over then under in every row.

Picking up a lost crochet stitch is often a troublesome matter, and it is sometimes less work, in the long run, to undo several rows until the mistake is reached.

Size of Needles

In all patterns of knitted and crocheted articles the size of the needles or hook used is plainly given. It is most important to use the size recommended, as the whole appearance and fit of the garment depend upon it. A different-sized needle will make it either larger or smaller, unless, of course, you have worked out the tension and altered the number of stitches accordingly. This may lead to trouble when it comes to a complicated part of the pattern, as the number of stitches will not correspond, and you may have some difficulty and not a little exercise in mathematics.

The safest plan is to abide by the size given you, and to see also that the yarn is of the recommended thickness. It is not by any means always necessary to obtain the exact make of thread mentioned in your pattern, provided it is the same ply, and in general a similar class of yarn.

Untidy Seams

The way in which a seam is sewn up is of vital importance to the finished garment. If it is bunchy or uneven, it will be an obvious part of the article instead of being practically invisible. Shoulder seams and others which are specially in evidence need the maximum of care.

Never sew knitting or crochet as you would a seam in needlework, by putting the two edges together and running your thread along. This would give much too thick a seam, and would be very difficult to iron flat. Nor ought the edges to be oversewn, as this also produces a clumsy finish.

The correct method is described under the heading of Making-up (*see page 192*).

It is not uncommon to find when sewing the side seams of, say, a jumper that the two edges do not exactly correspond, even though you know that they each have the same number of rows. If this is the case, one side will have to be eased in a little, so as to make it the same size as the other. It is not difficult to do this, but care must be taken to make the easing very gradual, to avoid having any puckers.

Occasionally the whole look of a sweater or coat is spoilt because the armhole seam fits badly, and is several inches down the sleeve instead of being on the shoulder. This may be due to bad work and mean that the shoulder has been made too wide. However, there is still some hope of a moderately good fit if the armhole seam is judiciously dealt with, so as to take off some of the width from the shoulder. It is never advisable to try to shorten the sleeve by taking into your seam an extra bit of it, as the shaping is awkward to cope with, and you will probably spoil the set of it altogether.

RE-USING OLD WOOL

If you have a hand-knitted garment that has been outgrown or that has become shabby in parts (such as worn elbows or underarms) the wool may be unravelled and re-used. A child's garment may be made from an adult's jumper or cardigan, or the wool from two small garments may knit up attractively into a new bi-coloured garment. Before unravelling make sure the garment is clean, either hand-washed or dry-cleaned.

If large quantities have had to be unwound and a 'crinkly' appearance results, the unevenness will show in the result unless you know what to do. In such a case, wind the wool round the elbow and hand into a skein, lay it flat on the ironing-board, and press with a damp cloth, when a straight thread will once more be produced. It is never advisable to knit up crinkled wool and then try to make it straight afterwards.

DICTIONARY OF ABBREVIATIONS AND DEFINITIONS

Abbreviations in knitting patterns. K. = knit; P. = purl; KB. = knit into back of stitch; PB. = purl into back of stitch; st. = stitch; sl. = slip; stg.st. = stocking stitch; w.fwd. = wool forward; p.s.s.o. = pass slip stitch over; tog. = together; t.b.l. = through back of loops; inc. = increase; dec. = decrease; beg. = beginning; alt. = alternate; rep. = repeat; C.2.F. = Cable 2 Front by working across next 4 sts. as follows: Slip next 2 sts. on to cable needle and leave at FRONT of work, knit next 2 sts. then knit 2 sts. from cable needle; C.2.B. = Cable 2 Back, as C.2.F. but leaving sts. at BACK of work; m.1k. = make 1 knitwise; w.r.n. = wool round needle.

Brackets, thus (——). Portion between to be worked number of times stated or shown as *.

Brushing To raise the surface with a teasel brush.

Casting on Making the initial loops on the needle in knitting.

Casting off Finishing off stitches at the end of a piece of work.

Chain (ch.) A series of loops forming a chain, used at the beginning of most crochet patterns.

Double crochet (d.c.) A stitch formed by a double action of the crochet hook.

Double knitting wool Thick wool of unusual strength, used for heavy sweaters and jerseys.

Double treble (d.tr.) A more elaborate form of treble, the thread being wound twice round the hook instead of once.

Fingering Often called Scotch Fingering, a suitable yarn for all general purposes, especially for socks and stockings.

Knitting plain (k.) Making the ordinary knit stitch, with the wool behind the right-hand needle.

Knitting in rounds Applied to the use of three needles, a fourth being used to work with.

Making a stitch The taking up of an extra loop from the back of a stitch to make one more.

Ply Applied to wool to signify number of strands used in its make-up, e.g. 3-ply, 4-ply.

Purling (p.) Making a stitch with the wool forward, and the needle inserted into stitch to be knitted from above.

Ribbing Alternate sections of plain and purl, such as 2 plain, 2 purl, or 4 plain, 4 purl.

Seam stitch A seam or line produced by making, in each row, one purl stitch in otherwise plain knitting. Used chiefly in socks and stockings.

Single crochet (s.c.) Made by passing hook through stitch and drawing it through both loops on hook.

Slip loop or slip knot A loop which can be drawn to any size, used as the first stitch in crochet.

Slipping a stitch Passing stitch from one needle to another without knitting it.

Slots Holes made for the purpose of holding threads.

Tension Elasticity of knitting, usually reckoned in number of stitches to the inch when the work is laid flat, without stretching.

Treble (tr.) Ordinary treble stitch, made by winding thread once round hook before inserting it into stitch.

Triple treble (t.tr.) A still more elaborate form of treble, the thread being wound three times round the hook, instead of once or twice.

HOME UPHOLSTERY AND HOUSEHOLD LINEN

Home furnishings are a very costly part of any household budget. New curtains, new chair covers as well as cushions and other smaller items are expensive to buy or have professionally made and they can be tackled and made quite successfully at home given the time and the patience.

By making them yourself you can allow rather more for the cost of the material which is always worthwhile as such large items should give a great many years' good service. When choosing the fabrics for, say, curtains or chair covers do take the advice of a senior assistant in the shop. It is, for instance, a waste of time to use a light, thin material for a chair cover, however pretty the pattern, though it might be suitable for an unlined curtain. For curtaining it is important that the material should be guaranteed fadeless particularly if it is to hang in a sunny room.

THE EQUIPMENT YOU NEED

Little, if anything, beyond ordinary sewing equipment is necessary. Your sewing machine will be your best friend, and you will also need a tape measure, cutting-out and smaller scissors, tailor's chalk, sewing needles and pins. A yardstick is practically an essential in curtain-making, and you will find a set square (which you can buy at any shop selling carpentry tools or artists' materials or even at many stationers) a great help in getting good right-angles for pelmets and cushion covers. Slip-on paper clips are useful instead of pins for certain stages of pelmet-making.

SPECIAL STITCHES

There are just three special stitches worth learning. All are extremely easy, and you will master them in five minutes.

Catch Stitch

This is used for catching down raw edges to interlinings, chiefly in pelmets. It is worked over a raw edge, so single-turn hems are sometimes made with it on bulky materials such as velvet and velours, which would not turn in flatly twice.

To work Bring up the needle from the wrong side of the edge to be caught down, well inside that edge. From there pick up horizontally a thread or two of the inter-lining, just below the raw edge of material; moving diagonally forward again, this time upwards, pick up a short horizontal stitch in the material, again well inside the edge. Continue alternately picking up a horizontal stitch in the interlining and in the material and pulling the thread taut, so that the material and interlining are firmly held by a continuous series of open V stitches.

Locking

This special variation of buttonhole stitch has only one upholstery use—to hold together and 'lock' curtain and lining when making lined curtains. Work it with cotton exactly matching the curtain material, then the stitches will be unnoticeable when the curtain is hung.

To work Thread the needle with a really long length of thread. Double back the lining lengthwise as described for curtain-making on *page 201*. All down the length catch the fold of the lining to the single thickness of curtain lying beneath it with a buttonhole stitch which is tiny, but very widely spaced. In fact, each stitch should be about 4 inches apart, with the long thread connecting it with the next lying along the lining fold. Velvet curtains, how-ever, require the locking stitches to be only 2 inches apart.

Napery Hem

As its name implies, this is used for hemming household linens. It is also known as the French hem, top-sewing, or upright hemming. The direction of its stitches makes it blend specially well, on both right and wrong sides, with the rather coarse weaves (as compared with dress materials) used for household linen. Conse-quently it is the ideal invisible hand hem for table linen, linen runners, cretonne, printed linen curtains and handkerchiefs.

To work Double-fold the material for a hem. Then crease the whole hem backwards to lie along the right side of the material. Overcast finely along the new crease, through all three thicknesses, i.e. the two of the hem and one of the main part of the material. The needle must always be in-serted right ACROSS the crease, so that on the right side the stitches are minute vertical ones and on the wrong side they are slanting.

PIPING

Piping is a process which occurs in so many upholstery jobs that it is more conveniently described here than under any particular one. It differs slightly from piping in dressmaking. Cord, sold in hanks of several yards, is always used.

Shrink piping cord before use by boiling it, or it may cause puckering when the article containing it is washed. As piping strips to cover the cord use either ready-made bias tape (first ironing the prepared creases out of it) or bias-cut strips of self- or contrasting material. Cut and join these as described under Binding on *page 119*, making them from 1 to 1½ inches wide. Double the strips lengthwise over the shrunk piping cord and with matching thread tack them together, closely enclosing the cord.

To apply this prepared piping, lay it along the right side of the edge of the material, cord inwards, and the cut edges lying flush with and over the cut edges of the material. Pin it in position, nicking the piping cover almost to the cord at corners or curves so that it will lie flat. If only a single thickness is being piped, first tack and then machine on the piping, in both cases stitching as close as possible to the cord. When piping a seam, after pinning down the piping, pin the other half of the seam over it, right side

thicknesses together. To neaten single-thickness piping, *see page 119.*

CURTAINS FOR YOUR HOME
(Pl. 81)

The very first glimpse a visitor has of your taste and skill in home furnishing is when, still in the street, she sees the curtains hung at your windows. They also matter, more than any other home upholstery item, in the general harmony and cosiness of your rooms. In the case of the heavier lined curtains, especially, very great economies result from making these yourself rather than ordering them from a shop. Curtains, though large, are very straightforward work, and (except when lined) may be made quickly by machine.

Measuring and Making

Whatever the type of curtain you want to make, certain general rules will need to be followed.

1. Accurate measurement is most important in buying curtain material and making it up. Here your yardstick is invaluable for it will reach up to the top of the window-frame without your climbing on steps, and it will not stretch or flop like a tape measure. Use it for measuring both the actual windows and the bought material when cutting out.

2. When estimating the quantity of material needed, remember that very liberal turnings are needed for curtains. Draperies of any kind need relatively deep hems to give enough weight for graceful hanging, and allowance must be made as well for casings (and often headings) at the top. For long curtains allow an average of $\frac{1}{4}$ yard per curtain (unlined), or 6 inches (lined); for pane or casement curtains with a casing and heading, from 4 to 6 inches. This turning allowance is, of course, in addition

Plate 81

An overlooked window may have short curtains under a frilled pelmet with a half curtain across the lower part

downwards and edge flush with the other edges. Tack, and then machine the three

to the length from the top to the bottom of the space the curtain is to occupy. The heavier the material, generally speaking, the greater the turning allowance should be.

3. The correct length for short curtains, when finished and hung, is to the window-sill. As, however, most short curtains are washable and the materials of which they are made (especially net, lace, and voile) may shrink when laundered, they should hang at least 2 inches below the sill when first made. Add on this shrinkage allowance, in addition to the turnings allowance, when estimating the quantity of material needed. Terylene curtains may be made to the exact length required.

4. If the curtains are to be hung on a rod or wire run through a casing (a favourite plan for short pane curtains) you will save yourself much work after each laundering if you make the casing twice as wide as the rod, so that the latter will slip through easily even if shrinkage occurs. If a rod is inclined to catch and stick in the casing, by the way, put your thimble or the cap of your fountain-pen over the end of the rod, or if it is a hollow one fill it temporarily with a cork. Another plan is first to open the casings flattened by ironing by running through them a plated fruit-knife.

5. Curtain fullness is reckoned much as for frills in dressmaking. (*See Frills.*) One and a half times the width of the window suits most fabrics, but for thin, soft ones, such as voile, $1\frac{3}{4}$ times is better. Don't be pernickety to an inch about this width; some allowance must be made for the relative widths of the window and the material and how they will fit in. Try not to divide the material into less than half a width anywhere, and when joining a half-width to a whole one, place the narrower piece at the wall edge of the curtain, where it will show less.

6. The best seams for joining unlined curtain widths are a narrow French seam in thin, washable materials, a plain seam for joining two selvedges, or a flat-fell when a half-width is seamed to a whole width. (*See Seams on page 104.*) If they are lined, use plain seams.

7. To make a lined curtain, reckon length and width as for unlined ones, but allow 4 to 6 inches turning allowance—the latter only for heavy materials. Plain-seam necessary joins, but before seaming slash any selvedge edges every few inches with short SLANTING nicks. Press the seam out flat. Cut, slash and seam the lining similarly, quite separately from the curtain proper. Spread a curtain length out quite flat, wrong side uppermost. Lay the lining over it right side uppermost, matching the two exactly at edges and seams. Smooth the two materials out so that both lie absolutely flat and unwrinkled everywhere.

Now the two materials must be locked, so that they will hang together at the window as one material, not forming ugly separate folds. To lock, fold back length-wise one third of the lining width, leaving the curtain layer undisturbed. All down the length catch the fold of the lining with locking stitch (*described on page 199*). Fold the lining back similarly from the other side edge and lock again. Do the same for curtains a width and a half wide; but those containing two full widths must be locked three times—first down the centre seam, then half-way between it and each side edge. Turn in the sides of the curtain 1 inch or more, pressing the turn with a hot iron. Fold up the bottom the depth for which you have allowed when reckoning turnings. Turn in the lining edges to face the curtain ones, but $\frac{1}{2}$ inch inside them, and slipstitch the two together. Use the ordinary dress-making slipstitch but made with much longer 'slips' between the stitches. Finish the curtain top by turning down both curtain and lining together in a single turn.

Cover raw edges with tape, see overleaf.

8. To make a heading with casing below for a short curtain, allow on the top edge a turning equal to the depth of the heading plus the depth of the casing, DOUBLED, plus a $\frac{1}{2}$ inch turning. Thus, if the heading is the usual depth of 1 inch and the casing $\frac{3}{4}$ inch (total, $1\frac{3}{4}$ inches), double this to make $3\frac{1}{2}$ inches, add your $\frac{1}{2}$ inch turn, and make a total allowance of 4 inches. Fold down to the wrong side a $2\frac{1}{4}$ inch strip right across the width. One inch below the turn stitch through the two thicknesses to form the heading. Three-quarters of an inch below this stitching crease in your $\frac{1}{2}$ inch turn, and stitch the turn down, just above the fold, to the main part of the curtain. The space between the two lines of stitching provides the casing for the rod or spring wire.

Remember when making curtains that the material must be cut and creased very evenly. Straighten material if it has been stretched crooked when wound on its roll, and whenever possible draw a thread to guide you in cutting and creasing. To keep the crisp, fresh look of new curtains, tack the material as little as possible. Careful creasing, pinning and then pressing well before stitching, is the best plan.

Finish the top of the curtain according to the fitment from which it will be hung. On modern fitments the labour-saving curtain tape, fitted with slots for the hooks, is stitched along both edges to the wrong side, a little below the top. The strings in the tape are drawn up so that the curtain, when closed over the window hangs in nice folds. The strings are then knotted off and the ends tucked out of sight. It is better not to cut away the string ends as if the curtains are to be washed it is much easier to iron them flat and draw up the tape again afterwards.

Finishes and Trimmings

In the case of unlined curtains which have an unnoticeable selvedge, it is usual to leave this selvedge untouched for the sides of the curtains. If a width and a half is used, the cut edge of the half-width is joined to the full width in order to have a selvedge on each side edge.

However, in some fabrics the selvedge is not presentable, being either white on a coloured material or in some way conspicuously different from the body of the fabric. In this case it must be turned out of sight; cut off and the edge hemmed, or some finish must be used which will hide it. Again, a curtain with a good selvedge may need the decoration or the contrasting colour obtained by using a definite edge finish. There are several which are both easy and effective.

Binding (*see page 119*) in a contrasting colour, patterned on a plain curtain or plain on a printed fabric, generally looks well. Apply it entirely by machine. When finished, the bind should be from $\frac{1}{4}$ inch to $\frac{3}{4}$ inch wide.

Facing gives a rather more noticeable edge than binding. Make a right-side, machined facing, as described under Facings on *page 126*. Its finished width should be from $\frac{1}{2}$ to 2 inches.

Fringe is sometimes in fashion. It may be bought in varying widths in wool, silk or cotton, and stitched to the edges of either lined or unlined curtains. Unlined curtains, of a material with threads that pull easily, may be trimmed with a simple self fringe. Machine-stitch the distance away from the edge (after cutting off the selvedge) that the depth of the fringe is to be. Then pull out all threads up to the stitching, which will prevent any further unravelling in wear. Fringing gives a soft, informal edge suitable for curtains at fairly small bedroom or kitchen windows.

Frilled edges suitable for net, voile, or muslin curtains, are also very soft in effect. The frills should be straight strips gathered and from 1 to 3 inches wide. (*See under Frills on page 129.*)

Ric-rac or zigzag cotton braid made in white only, is a very effective ready-made edging for the cottage-type of curtains. It looks specially well with check gingham. Stitch it down its centre over selvedges or narrow tacked hems.

When the side edges of curtains are finished in any of these ways, it is usual to finish the lower edge to match.

Weighting long curtains is sometimes necessary if the material is light enough to blow about or clings to pieces of furniture. Use weighted tape inserted in the bottom hem, as single round weights make the curtains sag at the corners.

For bathroom curtains Gaily coloured or patterned plastic fabric is a good choice. As this material does not fray, only single seams and single turnings are needed. It can be stitched in the ordinary way, and curtain tape drawn up to the required width can also be stitched down across the top.

Other pretty bathroom curtains can be made from the bright printed terry towelling available by the yard. This is not affected by steam any more than your bathroom towels, and is easily washed when soiled.

For valance frills and pelmets for curtains *see Pelmets page 220.*

CUSHIONS AND PADS
(Pls. 82, 83 and 84)

A room without cushions looks very bare indeed but a good cushion is quite expensive to buy though really very easy to make.

Cushions and cushion covers can often be made from remnants of furnishing materials bought at sale time; pieces left over from curtains and chair covers can also be used. A set of new 'scatter' cushions, small and bright, can often make all the difference to a room when it is not proposed to do a major renovation of the furnishings. (*See Patchwork, page 149.*)

Many women make only cushion COVERS, and it is true that the cushions themselves can be cheaply bought. But as you may want a cushion which is an odd shape or size and not obtainable ready-made, you should know how to make it efficiently. If you like the luxury of feather cushions, too, these are cheaper to make than to buy. The feathers from old pillows may be used.

Making Cushions

The making of a feather cushion is described on page 206 when dealing with a round boxed cushion cover. Ordinary workaday cushions should be made from two squares or oblongs of cheap cotton material, such as casement cloth or unbleached calico, seamed together with $\frac{1}{2}$ inch turnings on three sides, filled with from 1 to 2 lb. of kapok or some sponge foam filling and the fourth side then sewn up securely.

Boxed cushions are sometimes preferred, as their surface is flat instead of rounded, and thus displays well any embroidery or other trimming on the cover. To make one, cut two squares or oblongs, and join them by means of a straight strip (usually $1\frac{1}{2}$ to 2 inches wide) long enough to go right round the four sides. The cover of such a cushion must be boxed in the same way. Remember that the squares of a boxed cushion should be considerably smaller than those of an ordinary cushion which is to hold the same amount of stuffing, owing to the extra area given by the strip joining the squares.

Plate 82 Day, *one side of a gaily embroidered nursery cushion (see plate 83, opposite)*

Bolster cushions are a form of boxed cushion, consisting of two relatively small circles joined into a cylinder by a very deep strip of material which forms the length of the cushion (*see Fig. 85*).

Pads are flat cushions used to give extra height or comfort to uncushioned chair seats, stools or box ottomans. Instead of being stuffed they are filled with several layers of material cut the shape and size of the upper cover but without turnings. They

usually have tapes at each corner by which they are tied to the chair legs. Cheap underlay carpet felt is sometimes used for filling, but it is difficult to find an equal to rough terry towelling of a cheap quality, as

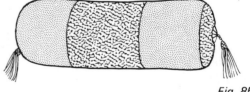

Fig. 85

Night, *the reverse side of the cushion shown in plate 82* Plate 83

this is so easily washable. Use from four to six layers.

Some Attractive Cushion Covers

Don't have all your cushions of equal size and shape. One or two small oblong 'tuck-ins', measuring about 16 by 10 inches (or alternatively 12 inches square), are such a comfort for the hollow of a tired back.

You need not necessarily buy new material for cushion covers. Odd pieces left from loose covers and cushions, taffeta and velvet remnants or wide ribbon—all these provide attractive and inexpensive cushion cover material. When pieces are small, two or more can be put together in panels or diagonal corners and joined with gimp or braid.

Bolster and Round Boxed Covers

To make a cover for a bolster cushion Make a tube of material just the width to pull over the bolster, but with enough extra length to cover the ends when gathered up. Turn in and tightly gather ends to fit a small circle of matching or contrasting

Scatter cushions in different colours picking up the tones of the cretonne for the divan of a bed-sittingroom

Plate 84

fabric, from the centre of which hang a tassel. You can leave the main tube part plain or trim it with two wide bands of ribbon or contrasting material.

If preferred, the cover may be made, like the bolster itself, from a cylinder or tube joined at each end to a circle. This gives a more tailored effect than the gathered ends. An even easier form of cover, suitable for cretonne or other simple materials, is to make the tube the whole width (45 to 50 inches) of the material, so as to have a selvedge at each end. Seam up the tube, put the bolster centrally inside it; then just outside each end of it draw the cover together tightly with three rows of gauging, letting the selvedge ends fall gracefully loose. This is a particularly good plan for the day-time ornamental bolster of a bed.

Round Boxed Cushion and Cover (feather stuffed). Feathers work through ordinary material, so make the cushion itself of $1\frac{1}{4}$ yards of downproof cambric or of unbleached calico which has been well beeswaxed on the wrong side and round the seams before filling. Make a boxed cushion, as already described, from two 20 inch circles joined by a 4 inch wide strip. Tack first and leave $\frac{1}{2}$ inch turnings; then stitch by machine. Overcast the turnings together. Stuff it with $\frac{3}{4}$ lb. of feathers and sew up the opening. If you sew the open edges of the bag containing the feathers to the opening in the case and pump and push the feathers through, there will be no risk of their flying about the room.

To make a handsome velvet boxed cover for this cushion, cut two 20 inch circles and a boxing strip half as long again as is required to go round the circles. Pipe each circle and trim the top one if desired. Gather the boxing strip along each edge to fit the circles and machine-stitch it in place between them.

Finishing Cushion Cover Edges

A cushion cover is nearly always the better for a definite trimming edge of some kind. The following are good and simple:

Cord This may be bought, or made at home by plaiting together three thicknesses or colours of rug wool. Sew over the seams with matching thread, making one or more loops at each corner. Slip each end of the cord inside the cover.

Fringe Use ready-made fringe or, if the cushion material is suitable, cut the top half larger all round than the bottom, and fringe it to the required depth before joining on the under side.

Embroidery Stitches Overcast cross stitch or twisted couching make a good finish for cushion edges. (*See pages 28 and 27 for these stitches.*)

Frills Consult this heading on page 129. Frills for cushion covers are usually made double and are best in thin materials such as muslin and organdie.

Piping is the most popular edge finish of all and suits almost every shape of cushion. The piping cover may match or contrast with the cushion cover; a contrast is usually better (*see Pl. 85*). Use a rather fine cord.

A bold design worked by couching a white piping cord over the simple outlines

Plate 85

Simulated piping gives a matching effect only. It consists simply of reversed French seams (first stitching on the wrong side, second stitching on the right) so that they stick out all round the cover like an unobtrusive piping.

Cushion Cover Openings

As cushion covers frequently need cleaning or laundering it is wise to make them easily removable. An opening should therefore be left along one edge of a square or oblong cushion and the turnings neatly hemmed. This opening should of course be on the underside, behind fringe, frill or piped edge. Large press fasteners should be sewn on at intervals to close the opening.

On a round cushion, if it has a plain back and embroidered or fancy front the opening is best made across the centre of the back and a small zip inserted through which the cushion pad can be inserted and removed when necessary.

DRESSING-TABLE DRAPERIES
(Figs. 86, 87 and 88; pl. 86)

A very cheap way of contriving a dressing-table is to use any odd shabby table and to turn it into a graceful piece of bedroom furniture by providing it with frilled 'petticoats' and a spongeable top of P.V.C. cloth or, if you can afford it, of plate glass cut to shape. These draped dressing-tables are necessarily small, and therefore take less room than one belonging to a suite. In fact, when space is very precious they may be fitted into a corner or made from a broad shelf screwed to a window sill.

A corner wardrobe fitment, fixed at table level, is also a good dressing-table foundation, as it is already provided with rods and rings to take the draperies. But when using an ordinary table, this mostly has a projecting rim which will successfully conceal a plastic wire rod run through top hems in the drapery and hooked together out of sight at the back.

Begin by covering the table top smoothly with P.V.C. Fix this with matching drawing-pins rather than tacks; then it is easily removed when it needs renewal. If a plate-glass top is being used (you can get this cut to fit by a picture-frame maker) you will need a foundation of the skirt material on the table to show through the glass. When the table has a projecting rim, cut the material covering large enough to go over the rim and be fastened invisibly on its under side.

The draperies are merely curtains. (*Refer to this heading on page 200 for width and turning allowances and other details.*) As their tops come up against the rim of the table, do not make them with a heading, but merely with a top hem to serve as a casing for the spring wire. If you like a two-tiered effect, you can use bordered material that is deeper than you want, turning over one border deeply to make the upper tier and stitching a casing in the fold. For a small dressing-table this is less bulky than two separate hems at the rim.

When nothing is being kept under the table, a continuous drapery, made by seaming together two or more widths of fabric, is best, as it does not get disarranged. But if there is a shelf or shoe-rack underneath which must be accessible, arrange the petticoats to divide at the centre front.

A front drawer sometimes complicates matters. A good solution of this difficulty is to make the draperies draw back as curtains each side of it.

Glazed chintz is an excellent choice for the draperies, because it keeps clean so long and can be brushed down. Other good materials are small-patterned cretonnes, sprigged dress cottons, plastic fabric and organdie flouncings with their pretty ready-made edge. Thin fabrics like the last one

Home furnishing is a great saving of expense. Curtains, cushions and seat covers combine to convert a half-landing into a cheerful study

Aprons as gifts are always welcome—and look at the colours and styles one can choose! All are quickly and simply made

Fig. 86

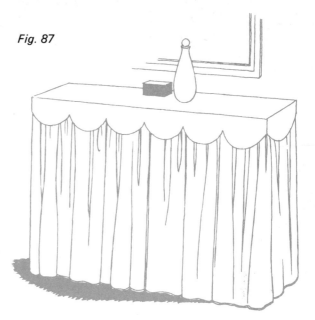

Fig. 87

should be backed by a straight, ungathered foundation or stiffened by an under-layer of pink chintz.

A stool stained and padded to match may accompany a draped dressing-table. For the making of stool pads, *see Cushions page 203*.

Ready-to-slip-on petticoats can transform an ordinary card-table instantly into an emergency dressing-table for the unexpected guest. Simply cut a square the size of the table top and add a deep frill to hang from it all round. The cover slips on in a moment, without fastenings, and is as easily taken off and packed away.

HOUSEHOLD LINEN AND ACCESSORIES

The contents of the linen cupboard are not home upholstery, but as they are home furnishings of another sort it is convenient to include them here. Some women still like to make at home such things as sheets and pillowslips as coloured sheeting is often available at advantageous prices. Few women do not enjoy making for themselves the more ornamental accessories, such as

Fig. 88

afternoon tablecloths, lunch-sets, runners and traycloths.

The sizes given here for various items are

Plate 86

A simple dressing table drape attached to the edge of the table cover with Velcro fastening

only approximate. Remember that dimensions can vary a good deal without being incorrect and that those quoted are intended only as a general guide.

Bed Linen

Mattress (Overlay) Covers It is wise to keep the permanent fixed cover of the overlay clean by using over it a loose, washable cover. Make this from unbleached calico or ticking in the form of a huge boxed cushion (*see Cushions page 203*), with this difference, that instead of one long boxing strip going right round there should be two strips the length of the cover and two its width, with enough turnings to allow of a plain or French seam at each corner. Leave one end open, and provide it with large

press-studs for closing or sew tapes to tie together.

Sheets With a machine these are very easily and quickly made. Use the specially wide sheeting sold for the purpose. If you want to economize, the unbleached kind is cheaper and after a few launderings becomes beautifully white. Sizes vary according to the bed size. Allow from $\frac{1}{2}$ yard to $\frac{3}{4}$ yard longer and wider than the mattress and you are sure of good hems and tuck-ins. Use the untouched selvedge for the side edges, and machine-stitch a 2 inch hem along the top and a 1 inch hem along the bottom of the sheet.

The top hem of a sheet may have embroidered decoration, either a trailing pattern worked along the machine stitching or a larger design worked in the centre about 3 to 4 inches below the stitching. Remember that the sheet top will be turned over and the motif or monogram must be placed to face towards the hemmed edge.

Pillowslips The average size of a pillowslip is 20 by 30 inches. It should be made of the same sheeting as the sheets if a set is intended. Pillowslips may also be made from old damask tablecloths not now in use or any smooth firm material with a fine surface.

The usual shape is known as the 'housewife'. It is made as a completed oblong 20 inches wide and 30 inches long with one end having a tuck in flap to hold the pillow in place. It may be made from one long piece of material 70 inches by 21 inches or from two pieces measuring 39 by 21 inches and 31 by 21 inches. If two pieces of material are used first join them into one long strip with a French seam. Hem both short ends of the strip.

Embroidered sheets and matching pillowcases are an elegant luxury

Plate 87

Turn in the flap of 8 inches (on the longer portion of the joined strip) and catch the sides of the flap into the side seams of the pillowslip.

Pillowslips may be embroidered with simple motifs or more elaborately embroidered ones in *broderie anglaise* (*see page 48*), but keep all decoration well to the outside edges or top corners as it is not comfortable to lie on.

Bolster slips are made like pillowslips, but are longer and without embroidery; 58 by 20 inches is a usual double-bed size.

For bedspreads, *see Spreads, page 224*.

Table Linen
Tablecloths Gay and hard-wearing cloths may be made easily at home from check gingham or seersucker. Two sides will probably be selvedged; simply machine-stitch narrow hems at each end. Another idea is a white cotton cloth finished with a wide right-side facing (*see Facings on page 126*) or double hem in checks or a plain colour.

For afternoon tea or other informal occasions a lace-trimmed cloth is decorative. Either crocheted lace (*see page 184*) or coarse bought lace may be used. A yard square of lined or unbleached calico finished with a wide edging of cotton lace, fulled or mitred at the corners, makes a pretty cloth for a small tea-table.

An embroidered cloth may very well become a treasured possession and a good linen should be used if fine work in counted thread embroidery is to be worked. It should be remembered that the centre of the cloth will be seen far more than the corners so that the embroidery is best worked in a pattern surrounding the centre. Small matching motifs can also be worked in the corners if liked.

Machine embroidery lends itself very well to decorating the larger surfaces of a table cloth. A simple leaf design worked in white thread on a plain blue or green material is most effective (*see Pl. 41*).

Table napkins may in all cases be made to match the cloth. For breakfast or lunch these should be approximately 17 inches square finished. Tea napkins may be smaller, about 14 inches square.

Table mats may be round, square or oblong in shape according to the shape of the table, the type of material used and the decoration if any. The material should of course be washable. On a round or oval

Plate 88

An elegant set of table mats are decorated with a rose design worked mainly in couching

On a cream linen tray cloth the flower motifs at each corner are appliquéd in alternate pink and blue linen. Buttonhole stitch is used on the outside edges but the inner edges are overcast

table, round mats are preferable; they should measure approximately 8½ or 9 inches in diameter. Small mats to accommodate a glass may be 4 or 5 inches in diameter. On a large table it is usual to have a centre piece to put under the bowl of flowers or fruit: this may be about 12 inches in diameter.

Circular mats may be finished round the edges with scalloping (*see page 39*) or more simply and speedily edged with braid or bound with a contrasting bias binding (*see page 119*). An embroidered circle may be worked with decorative stitches as an inner ring.

If you prefer a five-piece set with right-angled edges instead of curves, you may like a linen one, made up of short central runner, cut 30 inches by 12 inches, two large plate mats (12 inches by 9 inches), and two glass mats (6 inches square). Each piece could have large and small corner sprays embroidered in outline stitches.

Another good table-mat set is the runner and large mat type, for four or six people. The plan in this case is to avoid a number of small pieces. A runner 15 inches wide goes the length of the table, each of its ends serving one person as a place mat large enough for dinner plate, bread plate and glass. Oblong mats of the runner width serve those seated at the sides of the table.

Table mats may be edged with lace, bound in a colour or have their edges, if square or oblong, fringed out. Many ideas for embroidering them will be found in the embroidery chapters.

Breakfast or early morning sets consist usually of tea-cosy cover, traycloth, 12 inch napkin and egg-cosy cover. They may be made and trimmed in any of the ways suggested for table mats.

For monograms on household linen, *see Initials and Monograms on page 63*.

Runners, Chairbacks and Arm Rests

Runners protect the polished wood of tables and sideboards from being scratched by anything placed upon them. They may be washable or non-washable, and of almost any material from linen to suede.

Sizes vary a great deal. They may be long enough just to reach from end to end of the item of furniture they protect or may hang over considerably at each end. The width may be anything from 6 to 18 inches.

A co-ordinating idea is to make a runner from the same material as the curtains. If the curtains are cretonne or printed linen the runner may be made to match, either binding it with plain coloured material or edging it with a braid (if the runner material is washable be sure that the braid is also washable). Or a plain material may be used for the runner and cut-outs from the cretonne appliquéd on the ends. Remnants of furnishing materials bought at the sales are often suitable for a table runner and, if large enough, for one or more cushion covers as well. Remnants of furnishing braid may be found for the edging.

Chairbacks are a useful protection against soiling by people's heads. They are similar to runners and may be made in many of the same ways; but they are trim-med or embroidered only at one end. An average size is 15 inches wide by 21 inches long.

If the chair has a loose cover, especially if of a patterned material, it is a good idea to make the chairback of the same fabric. The oblong of material needs only to be hemmed all round, but it is usual to make the hem on the front end about 2 inches deep. A plain flat braid can then be stitched over the machine stitching as a neat finish.

On a plain chair, especially if there is no cushion, the chairback may be made in the same fabric or in a contrasting colour. A bold embroidered design carried out by machine or in appliqué on the front end would add an interesting decorative note to the room.

Arm rests are also useful protection as it is often the ends of a chair's arms that wear more quickly on a loose cover, or soil most on an upholstered chair. Arm rests should be about 9 inches wide but the length will depend on the width of the arm to which

A fitted divan cover for a bed-sittingroom is large enough to conceal the bedclothes.

Plate 90

you will have to add about 5 inches on each side to hang.

Where there is a loose cover the arm rest may be made of identical material. It can be a plain oblong as above or it may be made to fit the end of the arm. In this case it should be cut out similarly to the same parts of the loose cover and finished with piping (*see page 199*).

LOOSE COVERS
(Pls. 90, 91 and 92)

No household job is a more substantial economy than making your own loose covers. It seems a large order, but is actually a good deal less complicated than it appears, especially if you start by covering a very simple piece of furniture, progressing to a sofa only by degrees.

To initiate you gradually, given below are the various types of loose covers in order of difficulty.

Cover for a Bed-Settee

This is a very easy job, as bed-settees have wooden rails round three sides which are left as they are. The cover thus resolves itself merely into an oblong frilled along each long side.

Use a 50 inch cretonne or plain material. You will need about $4\frac{1}{4}$ yards, including enough for piping, as this type of cover looks far more professional with a piped edge.

Cut an oblong of material large enough to cover your settee (with bedclothes added if it is usually made up as a bed), plus 1 inch turnings. Pipe this all round with a self or contrasting piping. (*See page 199 for details.*) For the frills, cut strips 12 inches deep, or whatever fits the height of the settee, and join them to get half as much length again as that of the couch for each frill. Machine-hem the bottom edges.

To ensure uniform gathering, with pins divide both the sides of the oblong and the top edges of the frills into even quarters.

Gather each quarter of a frill on a separate thread, pulling this up to fit the corresponding quarter of the oblong. Lay the gathers over the piped edges and tack and seam through the three—frills, piping and oblong. Neatly overcast the turnings. Finish each end of the cover by stitching tape over the raw edges and felling it down invisibly. For a more tailored effect box pleat the frills instead of gathering them (*see page 135*).

Divan or Box Ottoman

Make either of these just as for the bed-settee, but frilled on all four sides, the frill all round being continuous. In the case of a bed with ends cut down so that it can be used as a divan, it may be easier to frill only the end where the foot formerly came.

If frilled all round, about 5 yards of 50 inch material will be required for a divan. Piping may be omitted if preferred.

A luxurious tapestry furnishing fabric makes a wall hanging with a fringed edge. A slip cover for the seat and back of a straight chair has a knotted fringe trimming

Plate 92

An Easy-chair without Arms
(Figs. 89 to 92)

Here we come to loose covering proper in its simplest form. Follow the instructions given stage by stage, and you will find the job easy and successful.

1. Measure your chair for the amount of 31 inch cretonne or other material required. The measurement from the floor up the front of the chair, across the seat, up the back and down behind to the floor again, will give you the amount. As a guide, the small armless chair illustrated in *Figs. 89* to *92* took $2\frac{1}{2}$ yards for the tailored cover, 3 yards for the frilled cover and $\frac{1}{2}$ yard extra if it has a small loose cushion. Bias tape (two 6 yard cards) may be used for piping. If you prefer self-piping, allow $\frac{1}{4}$ yard more material. For large chairs, buy double-width material (usually 48 inches).

2. To cut out, put the material on each part of the chair in turn, mark with tailor's chalk the correct outlines of the various pieces, which are: seat and 'collar', inside back (shown chalked for cutting) and outside back—but do not cut this last just yet. The collar—the depth piece below the seat—does not go right round, but joins the full-length outside back. Cut out all pieces with full $\frac{1}{2}$ inch turnings, but allow several inches tuck-in where the inside back will join the seat portion. Remember when cutting to centre any motifs nicely on seat and back, or to arrange that stripes join neatly down the inside back, seat and collar.

3. Make short seams in the collar, which is too long to come out of one width, avoiding one at the centre front and matching the pattern carefully. Press open the seams.

4. Prepare the piping as described on *page 199*. Pin it round the chalked outline of the seat portion; pin the collar edge, right side downwards, over it. Tack and

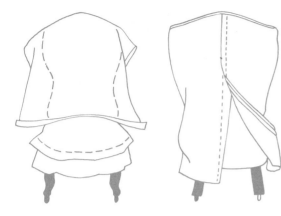

Fig. 89

Cretonne for a loose cover to a small chair chalked and partly cut out

Fig. 90

For easy taking on and off make a placket in the back of the loose cover

Fig. 91

The finished cover in a tailored style giving a smooth formal look

Fig. 92

For a bedroom the cover may be finished with a frill for a lighter effect

machine-stitch all together. Pin more piping round the inside back portion, A GOOD ½ INCH OUTSIDE THE CHALK LINES, to allow for the thickness of the wood. Pin it in correct position on the chair.

5. Cut in half lengthwise the outside back piece of material, and pin the two halves, overlapped about 2 inches, to the outside back of the chair. Chalk the correct outline and cut it out. It should reach just to the ground. Seam the top quarter of the two widths together. Turn in and stitch hems down the remaining material.

6. Pin the inside back and outside back together on the wrong side and try them on the chair for fit. If satisfactory, tack and machine the pieces together.

7. If making the frilled cover cut strips for the frills, allowing nearly double the collar length. Machine-hem the bottom edge. Tack piping along the lower edge and gather the frills by quarters to fit. Stitch them in place and overcast the raw edges.

A more tailored look may be given to a loose cover by box pleating the frill (*see page*

135). If, as is usual, the furnishing material is rather thick, the box pleat does not need to meet in the centre underneath. It is often better to space the pleats at 2 to 3 inch intervals leaving from ½ inch to 1½ inches between each set of pleats.

8. Put the two portions of the cover—seat and collar, and back—on the chair wrong side out. Carefully pin the join of seat and inside back, allowing a liberal tuck-in. Continue the join each side down the collar (and frill, if any), pinning these to the outside back. Tack and machine.

9. If making the tailored cover the bottom collar edge should not be piped until now, so that the piping may continue unbroken along the lower edge of the outside back. Face the wrong side neatly with tape. If the cover is frilled hem the bottom edge of the outside back level with the bottom edge of the frill.

10. Sew press-studs every 4 inches down the overlapped open part of the outside back. A small matching cushion cover may be made from left-overs.

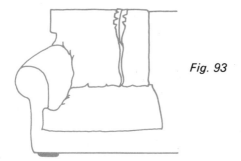

Fig. 93

Build up the loose cover pieces as they are cut on the chair or couch itself

Armchairs and Sofas *(Fig. 93)*

In a general way you should follow for these the detailed instructions already given for an armless easy-chair. But they will vary in several important details. For instance, the method of measuring must allow for the covering of the arms, which add extra pieces to the structure of the covers.

Taking measurements First measure as for the small easy-chair, noting down the amount. Then pass a tape-measure from the seat up the inside of one arm, over and down its outside to the floor. Double the measurement so obtained and add to it the amount already noted down, plus ½ yard for turnings and tuck-ins. This is for an armchair, the width of which will come out of the width of the material. In the case of a sofa unless it is a small-sized one, two widths will be required. So when measuring, double not only the arm measurement, but the up-and-down-the-chair measurement as well, and add ¾ yard for turnings and tuck-ins. Allowances for frills and piping are extra in all cases.

Furniture varies a great deal, but usually the pieces required for an armchair or sofa are: seat, seat collar, inside back, outside back, thickness of back, inside arm, outside arm, thickness or top of arm, front of arm and frill. On well-rounded arms the inside piece is usually carried over the arm to meet

the outside piece just under the roll-back, thus eliminating the thickness or top of arm piece. Keep the join well under the roll, so that it does not show from the front of the chair. Pipe all seams except the tuck-in joins of seat with inside back and inside arm.

Measure separately for any loose cushions and make boxed covers for these, piped along all seams.

When cutting out, cut the large pieces, particularly inside back, seat and outside arms, first, to make sure the pattern is displayed well on these prominent parts. The narrower pieces, such as the thickness of back and front of arm, can be taken from the left-overs of the larger portions. On the chair itself shape pieces to cover one entire arm, using double material to allow for the second arm. Take care the under layer is the right way up.

As each portion is cut out, place it wrong side upwards in position on the chair, thus gradually building up the whole cover. Pin it together to get a good fit, then chalk along the pin marks as a guide for seaming.

The best position for a placket is not down the centre back, as in the case of the armless chair, but in the seam at the corner of the left back and side. Frills, if used, should be about 9 inches deep and just clear the floor. They may be gathered or box-pleated. (*See pleats on page 135.*) If there are no frills, end the cover with a piping just above the tops of the castors.

Wing armchairs Armchairs which have a right-angle corner to the top of the back, to form a cosy nook for the head and keep out draughts, need two extra pieces to cover the front and back of each wing. Cut these to shape in position on one wing, using double material as for the arms, so that the second wing is provided for. Cut so that the seam joining front and back pieces comes well on to the outside of the wing, in order not to make discomfort for any one

Extra pieces are needed for the wings when making a loose cover for a large winged chair

sitting in the chair. Remember, too, when cutting the inside pieces, to tuck the material well into the crevice between the wing and the chair back. Ample turnings will be needed in this crevice (*see Fig. 94*).

When making up the cover, join back and wing pieces together before seaming either of them to the seat and arm pieces.

Open-armed chairs. Many chairs are not overstuffed (upholstered all over the frame-work) but have instead sprung and stuffed seats and backs with wooden or plastic open arms (*see Fig. 95*). A chair of this type should have an armless loose cover and looks best without any bottom frill. You will, therefore, need much less material —sometimes not more than half—than is required for an overstuffed chair and a remnant of cretonne can often be used. A three-piece suite with open arms also requires less fabric. Take measurements as for the armless easy-chair on *page 216*. Four yards of 30-inch material is an average amount for a fairly large chair of this type, but before buying check this by actual measurement of your chair.

The pieces required for open-armed chairs (unless they have wings) are inside and outside back, seat, collar for the front depth of the seat and side strips. These last run below the arms from the collar in front to the lower part of the outside back, where they form the lower part of the placket on

one or both sides of the chair.

Cut out direct on the chair as described for the previous loose covers. If using 31 inch material, this will usually cut economically. Double-width material goes further if placed on the chair so that there are sufficient turnings on one side and a surplus strip which can be cut off on the

An open-armed chair has the cover fitted to back and seat but arms left bare

other. These surplus strips from the seat and back can be used later for the side strips of the cover, thus economizing material. This method is only possible when cutting a plain, striped or all-over patterned fabric. With a large, centred design you MUST put the middle of the fabric to the middle of the chair, or the result will look lopsided.

Follow the instructions on *page 216* for cutting the two back pieces, the seat and the collar. The only difference to note is that where the arm joins the chair back, the inside arm piece must have a more or less circular piece lopped out of it to accommodate the arm. Cut all the rest of the inside back first. Then very cautiously slash at the fabric creased round the arm till, little by little, you get it to lie smoothly. Be very careful to make the incision not quite large enough, because it will increase a little in size when the raw edges are folded in and neatened. Take care not to narrow the fabric below the arm, because it must go round under it to meet the outside back piece.

From narrow pieces (if possible) cut straight strips to fit the portions of the frame at the sides under the arms, with $\frac{1}{2}$ inch turnings along the top edge and $1\frac{1}{2}$ inch ones along the bottom edge—2 inches in all—also inch turnings at each short end. As the pieces are cut, pin them together where they join, still on the chair, to get the general effect and be sure you are leaving ample turnings for seams.

Before removing the pinned-up cover, open one or both joins (according to the shape of the back) of the inside and outside back pieces, unpinning only enough, from the bottom upwards, to enable the cover to be removed easily from the chair. These unpinned portions of the seams will be your placket or plackets, so mark their termination with a pin placed crosswise or a tacking.

Make enough piping (*see page 199*) from oddments of self- or contrasting material to pipe all seams, except those which tuck out of sight round the seat, and for the top edges of the two side strips. Seam the various pieces together with piping inserted. Before joining inside and outside back pieces, either face in or bind with bias strips of self-material the cuts made to accommodate the top of the arm. Before joining the side strips to the collar, pipe their top edges; then on the wrong side cover the piping raw edges with a straight-cut facing and hem down the free edge of this.

Continue the piping between inside and outside back pieces unbroken down the upper edge of the placket and face this in as for the side strips. Fit the under side of the placket with a hem (if it is straight enough and there is sufficient width of material) if not, give it a projecting wrap. Sew on press studs or hooks and eyes, or the two alternating, every three inches. The placket, of course, will continue right

down to the bottom of the side strips. Before sewing on the lowest of these fastenings, turn and stitch an inch-deep hem right round the bottom of the cover.

The side strips, which have nothing to keep them up along the top edge, are improved in appearance, if the chair, has a middle panel to the arm, by arranging a supporting strap round it. This should be a short length of black tape. Sew it to the strip at the front edge of the panel, pass it round the panel in the seat side and fasten it with a press stud to the strip on the panel's other side.

PELMETS, FRILLS AND VALANCES

Top headings are not suited to long, heavy curtains. Something, however, is required to finish them off neatly along the top and to hold the general effect together as a frame encloses a picture. According to the type of window and curtains, either a pelmet or frill is used.

Pelmets *(Figs. 96a and 96b)*

These are dignified in effect but they are not washable. They are, therefore, suitable for long or imposing windows in rather large rooms, and for most sash windows, and to accompany curtains of heavy, non-washable material. They look best with three-quarter or floor-length curtains. They are fixed with nails to a pelmet-board erected by a carpenter at the top of the window-frame. The board is a few inches wide, so that the pelmet, when tacked to its projecting edge, will hang outside the curtains and not impede their free movement.

Pelmets have no fullness. They are cut to shape, lined and stiffened. Though they look rather important and professional they are really quite easy to make at home from the same material as the curtains. A very simple pelmet for a small window can be made from a straight strip of material without any shaping. This is suitable where the pelmet is not more than 5 to 6 inches deep.

Patterns are seldom available for pelmets, as windows vary so much, so you must begin by making a design for the bottom edge. The top, which is fastened to the pelmet-board, will be quite straight. Remember when planning your design that any extra depth it has should come at each side, so that it will hang over the pulled-back curtains and not in the centre, where it

Cut out the pelmet three times: in material with 1 inch turnings; in brown upholsterer's buckram without turnings; in lining with $\frac{1}{2}$ inch turnings. Unless the pelmet is small and the material wide, more than one width will be needed. Match the pattern accurately and make and press this join preferably BEFORE cutting out.

Now put the three layers together. Lay the cut-out material, right side downwards, flat on a large table or the floor. Lay the buckram shape over it, with the fabric turnings projecting evenly beyond it all round. With a sponge damp (not soak) the

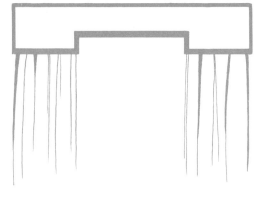

Fig. 96a

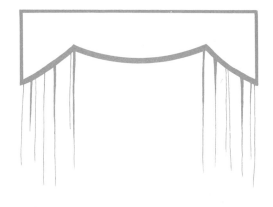

Fig. 96b

would block the light. Either straight lines or curves may be used; the former, of course, are easier to draw. A simple but always effective pelmet edge which you can easily rule out on joined sheets of newspaper is a straight horizontal edge in the centre, dropping to a deeper square at each end.

When calculating the depth of the pelmet, make it at its deepest point about $\frac{1}{6}$th of the total length from the top of the window to the floor. When calculating the width, remember that the pelmet should turn the corners of the board and go sideways along it until the wall is reached. This adds 6 inches or more (the width of the pelmet-board plus turnings) to the front length.

buckram edges all round to a depth of 2 inches. Take a hot iron and at once press the fabric edges down to the damped buckram. They will stick to the buckram, for this type contains glue, which is released by the heat of the iron—a much quicker method than stitching.

This ironing-down method only succeeds with yellow-brown upholsterer's buckram. If using any other stiffening you must catch-stitch the turnings down to it.

Lay the lining, right side upwards, over the buckram, crease in its turnings, and slip-stitch them down to the material turnings. As they were cut smaller, they will come well inside these and not show from the right side. The lower edge of the pelmet may be finished with fringe or a binding, or a braid may be stitched one inch from the edge.

Frills

These are soft and informal in effect, so they are used on small cottage type windows. As they also wash easily, they are to be preferred when the curtains are of material that needs frequent laundering. Use frills for casement or small, unimportant windows, such as those of the kitchen, bathroom and landing. They look best with sill-length curtains. *See Frills on page 129 for details of cutting and making.*

The best way to finish curtain frills is with a casing, if they are to be strung on a rod, or with curtain tape if a modern rail fitting is used. The usual plan is to hang the frills on a separate rod or rail from the curtains, this fitting projecting an inch or two further into the room than the one holding the curtains. A double rail fitting especially for frills is obtainable in most makes of modern rail fittings.

Valances

The frills which sometimes hang round a bed, from the mattress level to within a few inches of the floor are known as valances. Make them as for frills for a bed-settee cover (*page 215*) but attach their gathered or pleated top edges by a plain seam to an oblong of hessian or unbleached calico the exact size of spring mattress or top of box spring. To neaten the join on the inside stitch a tape over the raw edges or overcast strongly.

POUFFES

A pouffe is a very handy fireside seat, especially in small rooms, for it is so easily tucked away under a table or couch when not in use. It is a simple and inexpensive matter to make a pouffe at home that, with an occasional new cover, will give sterling service for years.

There are two good types—the straight-down, which has a somewhat severe, tailored look; and the four-ear kind, more informal-looking and rather easier to make. It is as well, therefore, to choose the four-ear style for your first attempt at pouffe-making.

The Four-ear Pouffe

For the case which holds the stuffing you will need ¾ yard of hessian 50 inches wide or twice the amount of a narrower width. From it cut two 16 inch circles and a strip the full width of the material and 10 inches deep. A round tray makes a good pattern for the circles, or you can draw a circle with a pencil by tying string the right length to it and pivoting the string from a drawing-pin which fixes it down at its other end.

Join the two circles by seaming up the strip into a cylinder and then seaming it between the circles with machine-stitching. Leave full ½ inch turnings. One circle must

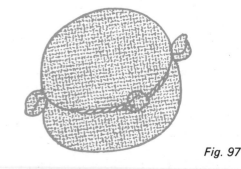

Fig. 97

be left half open for filling.

You have a choice of several stuffings. If you can obtain it easily, sawdust or the cork dust used for packing grapes both make firm and very economical fillings. Perhaps better than either is sawdust to give weight and firmness, with a top layer of kapok or foam cuttings for greater comfort and softness.

Should you have any dilapidated chair with some good stuffing in it, you could put this into the pouffe and so save money.

Never use all kapok for pouffes. It is much too soft.

Whatever filling is used, it is very important to stuff AS TIGHTLY AS POSSIBLE, not attempting to economize your filling. Just ram in as much as the case can possibly hold; otherwise it will soon sag and go limp in wear. Strongly sew up the opening, then thump and coax the pouffe to an even, true shape all over.

Give the pouffe a waist by tying a piece of thick string or cord round it as tightly as you can, getting a second person to help you if possible. If you can get the top half rather bigger than the bottom, all the better, as it will make a more comfortable seat.

For the four-ear cover you will need two 25 inch squares, either matching or different. Cretonne, poplin and repp are all suitable.

Seam the squares together on three sides as for a cushion cover. Slip them over the pouffe, centring them nicely, one over the top and one over the bottom. Sew up the open side. To hold the squares in place, secure 1½ yards of fancy unholstery cord round the waist. Where each corner or ear of the cover occurs, untwist enough of the cord to pull the ear through it tightly, thus drawing up the cover nicely taut. Sew each ear securely to the cord. The ears serve as convenient handles when the pouffe is moved about. (*See Fig.* 97.)

Straight-down Tailored Pouffe

This is made just like the four-ear one until stuffing is completed. But it is not provided with a waist and it is finished with a tight-fitting cover made just like the hessian case, from two circles joined by a strip. These must be cut a trifle larger than the case, so that they will go over it. For this cover use any of the materials suggested for the four-ear one, or heavier fabrics such as velour or velvet. The top circle may contrast with the rest, if preferred, and may be piped to accentuate its line, or be joined direct to the strip.

SCREENS

A screen is almost indispensable when there is a baby in the house, and is very useful also in either a temporary or a permanent sick-room. It is an expensive item to buy, and not every housewife realizes how simply and cheaply it can be made at home.

Wooden frames for screens can sometimes be bought ready for staining and covering or a home handyman will make them. Sometimes a shabby existing screen only needs re-covering. Again, a fair-sized wooden clothes-horse makes an excellent screen frame, if brass hinges are substituted for the webbing straps that join the panels. Enamel or stain the frame any colour desired. Yet another idea is to hinge together the frames of two old deck-chairs to make a four-fold screen.

The most practical covering is the 'French door' curtain, as this is so easily removed for laundering when required. Use any suitable washing material such as cretonne, printed linen or check gingham. Make a curtain for each panel, with a heading and casing at both top and bottom (*see Curtains on page 200 for details of cutting and making*), arranging the length so that the casings will come against the top and bottom edges of the frame, with the headings extending beyond them. Through each casing run a light plastic wire rod, screwing this in position on each upright of the panel; or, if the screen is small, run a tape through, and fix this to the frame with matching drawing-pins stuck at intervals through both tape and casing.

For a baby a screen with pockets in which

toilet articles are kept is useful at bath-time. Plastic curtain material should be used for this as it is both draught proof and also easily sponged over and kept clean. An acrylic-proofed Terylene which is light and flexible is also available. Only single turnings are needed on these materials which simplifies and speeds up the making.

Cut the screen panels to the size required and make up with heading and casing as described above. Now mark out with light pencil lines the sizes and position of the pockets required. Cut them to size allowing a small hem turning along the top. Stitch the hem on each pocket, place the pocket on the curtain as pencil outlines and stitch in place. If fullness is required in one or more of the pockets this should be achieved by a box pleat down the centre of the pocket. Hem the top of the pocket, then fold and stitch the pleat across the bottom and also across the stitching of the hem.

SPREADS, CURTAINS AND COVERS FOR YOUR BED

The most important mass of colour in a bedroom is the bedspread. The curtains may actually take more material, but they do not catch the eye so strikingly as the horizontal stretch of the bed covering. For this reason you should make the bedspread one of the first items in planning your room —in fact, it is often a good plan to make a handsome spread and then build the colour-scheme up round it. You should certainly do so if you have the luck to possess, or the energy to make, a fine patchwork quilt, of the kind described under Patchwork (*page 149*).

A home-made bedspread is particularly satisfactory, as you are sure then of getting exactly the material, colour, and type of decoration best suited to your room.

The approximate sizes for bedspreads are: for single beds, 108 inches by 72 inches; for double beds, 108 inches by 90 inches. The ideal plan is to use material 72 inches wide, so that single bedspreads, at least, may be made without a join. Some net and muslin curtaining material is made in this width. If this is used it is better to line it with a coloured taffeta to give it 'body'. The lining will of course have to be joined to get the necessary width and two 36 inch widths joined along their selvedges in a centre seam is the most satisfactory. If the outside of the bedspread is a washable material make sure that the lining is also washable, using a taffeta of man-made fibre for instance.

Unbleached calico soon washes white and makes a sturdy foundation for patch-work or the coarser kinds of embroidery. A coloured linen sheet, suitably trimmed or embroidered, also makes a handsome spread. If the bedroom has floral cretonne curtains, the spread may repeat the fabric, with a wide plain border round it for contrast, as in *Pl. 84*.

If you are using narrower material, either you can eke it out with wide con-trasting borders, neatly mitred (*see Mitres on page 133*) or you can use two widths (31 inch for a single bed, 50 or 54 inch for a double bed), joining them in some decorat-ive way. This may be by means of a veining stitch, such as linked buttonhole stitch (*see page 24*), or faggoting (*see page 105*), or plain seams may be made on the RIGHT side, the turnings trimmed rather narrow and covered with braid or bands of bias tape.

When joining two widths, avoid making the join come down the centre. Instead, divide one width in half lengthwise and seam each half along one side of the second complete width. In this way the joins come more or less at the edges of the bed and look far better.

If the bed is a four-poster or in any other antique style, with a pillar at each corner, cut a square out of each corner of the spread, so that it will divide effectively round the posts. If for daytime the bolster or pillows are to be rolled up in the spread, the latter must be made $\frac{1}{2}$ to $\frac{3}{4}$ yard longer than the length given above. Low beds of the divan type, with foot-rails absent or no higher than the mattress, often look their best in spreads which consist of a flat top, from which frills hang all round. Make such a spread as described under Loose Covers for divans (see page 216).

Appliqué is a good bedspread trimming, because it covers the large space rapidly and boldly. Embroidered appliqué is too long a job, but a large floral spray may be cut from cretonne and attached to the centre of the spread by blind appliqué. Another effective idea is to cut motifs from a cretonne in a straight-line design and apply by machine to form a hollow square and a narrow border round the hem.

Bedspread Edges

Here are some good methods of finishing the edges, according to the type of spread and the material of which it is made:

Binding When a definite but not too pronounced contrast either of colour or pattern is wanted. Apply the binding entirely by machine, as described under Binding on page 119.

Right-side facing This looks much like a bind, but is rather more conspicuous. (See Facings, page 126.)

Piping A very useful and neat finish for almost any material. When piping a single edge like this, neaten the wrong side afterwards with a narrow facing which covers raw edges of material and piping. (See Piping on page 199.)

Ruching This is a luxurious-looking edging for spreads made of silk or taffeta.

Either the box-pleated or corded types (described under Ruching on page 138) may be chosen, but corded ruching is perhaps the most generally suitable. It may be of self- or contrasting material.

Scalloping This gives a graceful edge and may be combined with ruching; or the scallops may be cut out and bound, or faced. To face scallops, tack along the straight edge of the spread, right sides touching, a self strip an inch or two deeper than the scallops will be. Its free edge should be a selvedge or already have a narrow turn creased in and machine-stitched. Outline the scallops half round a plate on the tacked-on facing and stitch along their outlines through both thicknesses. Cut away both thicknesses round the scallops with $\frac{1}{4}$ inch turnings, and at each inner angle nick the turning. Turn the facing over to the wrong side and carefully press, keeping the curves of the scallops accurate. If necessary, slip-stitch the free edge of the facing to the spread invisibly.

Trimmings These, such as gold galon, fringe, ric-rac braid (for cotton spreads) or strips of self-material kilted or box-pleated also make effective edgings.

Bedhead Curtains and Covers

The wall at the back of a divan bed quickly becomes soiled from the rub of pillows and heads. This can be prevented by making a wall hanging or curtain to be fixed to the wall behind the bedhead. It will look well if it is made of the same material as the window curtains, or it may be made to match the bedspread or bed valances.

In a feminine room it is pretty to have the bed curtain frilled or pleated to match the valances. Make it as a curtain with a small heading. It may be hung on the wall on a small wooden bar fixed by a handyman.

A wall hanging can be a very decorative affair. It is particularly suitable for a child's room and may be made of appliqué shapes with embroidery. A Noah's ark with animals cut out quite roughly from any oddments of washable materials and stitched to the background of strong cotton material by machine or blind appliqué (*pages 72 and 48*). The hanging should be the width of the bed and in depth long enough to protect the wall when the child sits up, and to reach to the mattress. Make a casing at the top of the hanging for a rod. Attach cords at each end of the rod and hang on the wall as a picture behind the bed.

Bedhead covers are loose covers made to fit over a padded bedhead; they are easily taken on and off for laundering or dry-cleaning. The front of the cover should be made of the same material as the bed valances, the back may be any strong cotton fabric. Cut the front large enough to cover the padded side allowing good turnings. Cut the back to fit the plain back of the bedhead with $\frac{1}{2}$ inch turnings. The two pieces may be joined with a plain seam or a piping introduced between the edges (*see page 199*). Hem the bottom edges and stitch on hooks and eyes to fasten or tapes to tie at intervals under the bedhead.

WADDED QUILTS

Beautifully warm bed coverings which are also very colourful and decorative can quite easily be made at home, especially in single bed and cot sizes for children. This work is not difficult and the quilts will give years of warmth and wear.

The best filling is Terylene wadding which is light and very warm when quilted between two layers of material. It is of course also washable so that with a washable

material for the quilt cover the complete article is easily laundered. The usual width for this is 48 inches. Courtelle wadding which is thinner is also washable but is only about 38 inches wide. Depending on the thickness you require for your quilt you will need two or more layers of the wadding you choose.

Baby's Quilt

For a new baby this should be very dainty with a white or pastel coloured cover to tone with the cot draperies. As these are now often made in nylon, Terylene or Tricel or other of the man-made fibres the whole set is easily washed. A fine sprigged muslin may also be used for the quilt cover if it is pre-shrunk or shrink resistant.

The usual cot size for a wadded quilt is 3 feet long by 2 feet wide, but as cots and cradles are not standardized in their dimensions, measure first and make sure of the size that will fit your particular baby's cot accurately. Remember that a quilt, unlike a sheet or blanket, should reach only to the baby's neck. Therefore, though it should fit the width of the cot it will be considerably shorter than the cot.

For a quilt measuring 2 by 3 feet you will need $1\frac{3}{4}$ yards 36 inch wide material for the cover and the same amount of white nylon or Tricel for a bag to hold the wadding. (This may be omitted if liked and the wadding laid directly between the outer covers though in this case it is rather more difficult to finish the edges of the quilt neatly.) One yard of wadding will allow for two layers which would probably be sufficiently warm for a tiny baby.

Make up the inner bag first leaving one end open. Fold the wadding into a piece 36 inches by 24 inches and trim slightly to fit in exactly to the bag. With a long thread of Terylene yarn in the needle lightly tack all the thicknesses together round the edges so that they do not slip. Close the end of the bag enclosing the wadding inside it.

For the outside cover cut the material into two oblongs to fit the wadded bag allowing good turnings if the material is likely to fray. On the right side of the top piece lightly draw with a pencil a line about 4 inches in from the edges all round. In the centre of this draw an oblong shape. Some delicate embroidery may be worked in this oblong.

From left-over material and a fine piping cord make enough piping to go round the quilt. Insert it between the two edges of the cover and stitch round three sides. On one short end stitch the piping only to the top edge of the cover leaving the end open to take the wadded bag. Insert the bag, making sure that the corners fit exactly. Slipstitch the open end together.

Now quilt all the layers together taking your stitching along your drawn pencil lines. This may be done by machine using the quilting attachment or by hand using a back stitch.

Quilt for Child's Bed

This quilt should be made exactly as described above for the baby's cot but should be 4 feet long by 2½ feet wide. You would require 2¾ yards material 36 inches wide both for the outer cover and for the inner bag. Using a 48 inch wide wadding on the length you will need ⅞ yard for each layer. On this larger expanse it is more satisfactory to quilt the layers together in squares of 6 inches each.

Enlarging a Quilt

A single bed quilt can be enlarged to fit a small double bed with no great difficulty and will save you the expense of buying a new one in the larger size. Or it may happen that a child outgrows his cot or small bed and when he is moved into a single bed needs a larger quilt.

To enlarge a single bed quilt to double bed size requires only the addition of wadded 'tubes' each side along the length. For a 4 foot 6 inch bed you will need to add a 12 inch wide 'tube' each side to the existing single bed quilt. The new material must be similar to that of the quilt though it can look most attractive if in a contrasting colour. Make up the 'tubes' and stuff with the wadding then slipstitch them each side along the length of the quilt.

To enlarge a cot quilt to child's bed size the additional wadded section must be made up as a frame for the existing quilt. Make four 'tubes' to fit the outside edge of the quilt and join by mitring the corners. Fit the little quilt inside the frame and stitch. The join may be covered with washable braid.

Remember when making any kind of wadded quilt to iron all creases out of the material thoroughly before joining it to the wadding. Once padded, heavy creases are almost impossible to remove.

REPAIRS AND RENOVATIONS

As items of home upholstery are mostly fairly expensive to replace, it pays to keep them in good order and to repair or renovate them, whenever possible, when they get to the shabby stage. You will be surprised how much money you will save in a year if you look these items over from time to time, and tackle any weak spots before they have a chance to become really bad.

Many more things than perhaps you would imagine can be given a fresh lease of life at hardly any expense if you are willing to take a certain amount of trouble over them.

Cushions

Cushion covers often wear first round the edges, especially at the corners. A good plan then is to cut off the worn seams and re-seam ½ inch inside them, inserting a contrasting piping which will look effective and take much of the future wear. Many cushions which never fitted tightly into their covers or have shrunk with use will fit—rather more tightly—into these somewhat smaller renovated covers. If they refuse to do so, then before seaming cut the cover in half across both ways and insert into it a cross made of wide ribbon or coarse wide insertion or contrasting panels of material. Or fit the cover to a rather smaller cushion.

Eiderdowns

These bed coverings are made so often of beautiful but not particularly hard-wearing materials so that you will often find that the cover becomes worn or faded while the quilt still has plenty of warmth in it. When this happens a new cover is a great deal cheaper than a new eiderdown.

If the existing cover is only faded and not worn, it is sufficient merely to envelop it in another cover which will hide the discolorations. Extra strength and durability are not required, so, as eiderdowns should always be as light in weight as possible, it is best to make a thin, semi-transparent cover of such a fabric as voile or furnishing net. If the present eiderdown cover is of plain fabric, a delicately patterned voile sold for summer frocks makes an attractive cover. Another alternative is to use Terylene net which is hard wearing, either matching the eiderdown or contrasting with it; in the latter case you will get a rather delightful shot effect from the eiderdown colour being glimpsed through the net.

Transparent Covers

To cover a patterned eiderdown, net or a plain voile is best. Both these materials, thin though they are, are remarkably hard-wearing. If the eiderdown being covered is a striped one, the voile cover may have em-broidered sprays on it, giving a very pretty effect. For such a thin material use a light flowing design which can be carried out mainly in running stitch, lazy daisy and a few French knots.

The new cover is made like a very large cushion cover. Make it on the large and loose side for your eiderdown because both net and voile usually shrink when washed. You must allow too, for the amount taken up by the thickness of the feathers.

Seam up the cover on three sides and part of the fourth, inserting a narrow contrasting piping (*see this heading*) between the two thicknesses. Lay the new cover out flat on a large table and put the eiderdown into it, spreading it out well so that it fills the new cover evenly.

Pin here and there through eiderdown and cover to keep the eiderdown spread out, and sew up the open end.

Now secure the new cover permanently in place by fixing it down to the eiderdown along the original lines of stitching in the latter. There are two ways of doing this fixing. One is to put the whole thing in the machine and stitch through all thicknesses of both. This is a bit tricky if you work alone, as you must keep one hand constantly moving about underneath the eiderdown to see that the under-lay of the new cover is not getting creased or folded in the machine. If using an electric or treadle machine which leaves your hands free this matter is simplified.

The other method is to quilt by hand in running stitch. Of course this takes much longer, but is pleasanter and easier, and can be got through in odd half-hours.

Thicker Covers

If your eiderdown is wearing through, so that feathers are inclined to escape, the new cover you make for it must be of thicker material—say downproof sateen. Make it and fix it on the eiderdown in the same way as for the transparent cover.

Thin Borders

When an eiderdown has had long wear, it often goes very flat along the outer borders, owing to the gradual escape of feathers through the outside seams, which have weakened with wear. It is hardly worth while making an entire new cover in this case. A simpler remedy is to put in extra feathers along each border in turn. These feathers may be obtained from an old pillow or cushion or bought new; the same applies to vegetable down, if the eiderdown is filled with this.

Carefully unpick enough of the piped seam of a border to tack the cover, pillow or bag containing the extra feathers to it, and pump them through as described under Cushions (*page 206*). Pump in enough to plump out your thin border, nicely distributing the feathers evenly along the whole border by kneading and squeezing with your hands. Afterwards remove the feather container and firmly and closely sew up the opening in the eiderdown. Re-seam all round just inside the present outer seam. Repeat with each of the four borders in turn; or sometimes the feathers can be worked round the entire border from one opening.

For repairs to worn pipings on eiderdowns follow the instructions given under Loose Covers (*below*).

Loose Covers

If you can't have new loose covers at present, you can mend and freshen your present ones. Matching material for patching may be found in the ample tuck-away round the seat of a chair or settee. These big turnings don't show, so cut off a strip 2 or 3 inches wide, replacing it, say, with a bit of old shirt or curtain. It is necessary to replace it, please note—the tuck-away isn't there just as a way to use up material but to allow play when someone sitting down depresses the springs. Another plan is to deprive a frilled cover of its frill and use that for repairs.

Cut patches carefully so that they leave the pattern on the cover unbroken. Hemmed down neatly over a burn, tear or stain, and well pressed, they will hardly be noticed in wear.

If the piping cord rubs through at exposed edges and corners, remedy this. On a long worn stretch unpick the seam, re-cover the exposed cord and re-seam into place. For merely a small rub-through at a front corner, here's a quicker method. Cut a bias strip of self or nearly matching material $1\frac{1}{2}$ inches wide and an inch longer than the worn part. Fold one long edge in singly and hem it down to the cover just below the piping cord. Bring the strip tautly over to cover the cord closely and hem down the second edge as near to the seam as possible. If neatly done this repair is unnoticeable.

Overlays

Often the older kind of overlay mattress will lose one or two of the leather discs, known as tufts, which are set evenly all over its top and bottom surfaces and connected by a string which keeps the stuffing in place. If you neglect to replace missing tufts, the overlay will soon develop 'hills and valleys', owing to the stuffing having shifted.

To put it right is one of the simpler upholstery jobs. You will need to buy a mattress needle, about 8 inches long, and with a point at both ends. If you have not kept the tufts as they fell out, get a new bundle, from an upholstery department or shop or cut small circles from an old soft leather belt.

Thread the mattress needle with a long piece of thin smooth string. Push it straight through the overlay, from bottom to top, just where the tuft used to be. If you have inserted it straight, it will emerge also just where the top tuft used to be. You will have to use some force to get the needle through so much stuffing. Get it clear through for its whole length, but keep an end of string hanging on the underside.

Push the needle through again, this time from top to bottom, $\frac{1}{4}$ inch from where it came up. As it has a point each end, you will find it easiest to draw it through the second time eye end first. Before you draw the string tight on the top of the overlay, slip a tuft under its loop. The tuft gives the tightened string something to pull against, so that the overlay material is not worn through.

Back again on the underside, tie the two ends of string over a second tuft, tying tightly enough to make each tuft sink slightly into the overlay.

The firm, hard cushions used for window-seats are made in the same manner as over-lays, and if they lose tufts may be repaired similarly.

Pillows

Pillows, like eiderdowns, get limp with age and gradual loss of feathers. A good plan, if you have several such 'invalids' in the bedrooms, is to use the feathers from three of them to make two really plump pillows.

Nothing could be simpler than this job. Choose the pillow with the worst ticking to be emptied, and by the usual tacking together and pumping method, described under Cushions on *page 206*, add enough of its feathers to each of the two other pillows to make them plump and well filled again. You will probably have some feathers left over which you can either keep by you till next time a pillow needs replenishing or make into a feather-filled cushion.

If the ticks of the two pillows seem to be old and leaky, make new ones, which can be done very cheaply, as most of the cost of a pillow is in the feathers. Before filling the new ticks, turn them inside out and rub them over thoroughly (especially at the seams) with beeswax, to make them feather-proof. Transfer the contents of the two pillows into the new ticks, adding enough from the third pillow, as described above.

Rugs

Frayed rug edges are a very common trouble and are both unsightly and dangerous. They are easily mended by binding the worn edges with carpet braid as near the colour of the rug as possible. Fold the braid over the frayed edges and stitch it strongly down, both sides at once, with a carpet needle threaded with linen thread.

It is almost impossible to wear a hole in a hand-hooked rug, thank goodness, but occasionally one is burnt by a jumping coal or cigarette end, or it may be impossible to take out a stain. In either case remove the damaged tufts and replace them with new ones. You will need a rug hook, a wooden rug gauge and a small hank of matching rug wool.

Cut as much wool as you will need into short even lengths on the gauge. Working across the width of the foundation canvas, insert the hook under a horizontal ridge of the canvas and through the hole just beyond. Insert just so far that the ridge comes BEHIND the latch of the hook; the hook is then lying open ready to take a double loop of wool. Push this into the canvas, then push the hook through the loop, holding the two loose ends of wool with the other hand. Pull these ends through the loop and tighten them with the fingers, thus forming a knot firmly fixed to the canvas, with a two-ended tuft standing straight up.

Work a similar tuft in every vacant space. Clip the ends of the tufts evenly, and rub well with the hand to work out any loose fluff from the new wool. If the colour match is good the repair will barely show.

NEEDLEWORK GIFTS

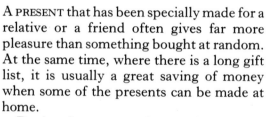

Fig. 98

A PRESENT that has been specially made for a relative or a friend often gives far more pleasure than something bought at random. At the same time, where there is a long gift list, it is usually a great saving of money when some of the presents can be made at home.

During the year one is sometimes called upon to donate something for a stall at a charity sale and 'Bring and Buy' sales are also very popular; it is useful therefore to have some small but useful gifts put by for this purpose. This is the kind of sewing that can be done at odd moments when there is nothing very important to be completed. The items can also be made from left-overs of dressmaking or soft furnishing and may cost very little indeed.

CAMPHOR SACHETS

Hung in a wardrobe or placed in drawers, these guard against the ravages of moths. Three, each in a different pastel shade, tied together or put in a pretty box, make a charming gift or sell well at charity sales.

Required : Oddments of organdie in pale colours; 1 camphor cube; $\frac{1}{4}$ yard of baby ribbon; and 1 needleful of stranded cotton for each sachet.

To make Cut two matching 4 inch squares of organdie for each sachet. One inch in from the outer edges, sew them together with large running stitches in stranded cotton. Before sewing the fourth side slip the camphor cube between the two thicknesses. Double the ribbon into a loop to hang the sachet by, and secure it at the fourth corner with the embroidery silk.

LAVENDER SACHETS
(Fig. 98)

These are not unlike the camphor sachets just described, and may be sold or presented also in sets of three.

Required : Oddments of organdie; 1 needleful of embroidery silk; $\frac{1}{4}$ yard of baby ribbon; 1 teaspoonful of dried lavender flowers for each sachet.

To make Cut two $3\frac{1}{2}$ inch circles for each sachet. Place them together, and 1 inch inside the edge all round work an inner circle of snail trail or coral stitch (*see page 26*) which is close enough to prevent the lavender working through. Before completing the circle put the lavender between the two thicknesses. Add a ribbon loop, putting its ends inside when completing the snail trail circle.

EMBROIDERED GUEST TOWEL

Required : ½ yard of pastel-tinted linen or huckaback; a small oddment of white linen; 1 skein of white stranded cotton; 1 needle-ful of yellow stranded cotton.

To make Cut the towel 16 inches wide and hem the long sides. To each end add a doubled white hem, 1 inch deep when finished. Pencilling round a penny, mark seven circles in a row 2 inches above one hem. Inside each circle work a lazy daisy flower in white, with a centre of yellow satin-stitch or French knots (*see Embroidery Section for these stitches*).

TEA OR LUNCH-CLOTH

Required : 1 yard of 36 inch linen, casement cloth or even unbleached calico; odd cotton scraps in bright colours from a piece-bag; oddments of embroidery thread.

To make Turn in a hem all round the square of material and run this with large black darning stitches. Cut circles 2 inches across from oddments of gay cotton; twelve circles will be needed, but they need not all be different. In each corner of the cloth arrange three circles of contrasting colours in a row, each overlapping the next, and buttonhole-stitch them down with coloured thread.

Napkins, 12 inches square may be made to match decorated with penny size circles.

A BIB FOR BABY

A set of three, with a different design on each, is a useful gift or soon sells at a charity sale.

Required : ½ yard of coloured linen or terry towelling (this will make three bibs); sheet of black carbon paper or three transfers; 1 skein of white embroidery cotton; 3 yards narrow white tape.

To make Divide the material across the width into three, to get three oblongs each measuring 15 inches deep by 11½ inches wide. Along the bottom of each bib make a 2 inch hem. Finish it with hemstitching if linen, or embroider a decorative line over the hem. At the top end scoop out the curve for the neck and bind the curve with cotton bias tape. A design (different for each bib) may be traced through black carbon paper from a child's picture book—a bird or animal is suitable, or use transfers. Work the design in bold outline stitches. (*See Outline Embroideries on page 72.*) Sew on tape ties.

HESSIAN MENDING OR KNITTING BAG *(Fig. 99)*

This can be very sturdy and inexpensive, yet decorative too.

Required : ½ yard of hessian (natural colour); oddments of bright-coloured embroidery wool.

To make Cut a piece of hessian 30 inches long by 12 inches wide. At each end turn over a 2½ inch hem on the RIGHT side and secure it with tacking stitches in coloured wool. Cut two strips, each 15 inches long and 4 inches wide, for the handles. Double them, with the raw edges turned inside, to make double handles 1½ inches wide. Over-lap them ¾ inch to the top hems of the bag, and overcast them down strongly with wool, continuing the overcasting as a decoration along both edges of the handles.

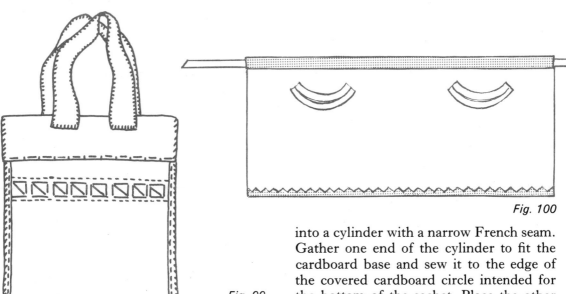

Fig. 99

Fig. 100

One inch below each broad hem on the bag work a bold border (*such as the one named Clip-clop on page 15*) in tacking stitch.

On each long side of the bag turn in a $\frac{1}{2}$ inch hem on the right side and secure it with tacking stitch. Double up the bag with hems and handles matching, and overcast its sides strongly together. To give more capacity, if you like you can add side gussets, making these 4 inches wide, including hems, and inserting them between the front and back halves.

TWIST HANDKERCHIEF OR STOCKING SACHET

Required : Round embroidery hoop, measuring 6 inches across; $\frac{3}{8}$ yard of soft silk in any pretty shade; a small piece of cardboard; an oddment of flannel.

To make Use one hoop ring only, the other will make another sachet. For each sachet cut two circles of cardboard the same size as the ring. Lay them together, pad them with a circle each of flannel, then cover each on one side with the silk chosen. They form the base of the sachet.

For the bag part, cut a strip of silk $11\frac{1}{2}$ inches deep and 27 inches wide. Make it

into a cylinder with a narrow French seam. Gather one end of the cylinder to fit the cardboard base and sew it to the edge of the covered cardboard circle intended for the bottom of the sachet. Place the other circle, right side upwards, over the raw edges, and stitch it down all round.

Finish the top of the bag with a $\frac{1}{4}$ inch heading and a casing below it, as for short pane curtains, but on a smaller scale. Insert the embroidery ring into the casing before stitching its lower edge.

This case will hold many handkerchiefs or pairs of nylons keeping them flat and uncreased on its firm cardboard base. To close the sachet, hold it with the bag part fully extended, and twist the ring half-way round before letting it drop. It will fall neatly in position, in a series of charming pleats, over the base, and keep the contents entirely free from dust.

TODDLER'S FEEDING PINAFORE
(Fig. 100)

When a toddler begins to feed himself he needs to be well covered, even a large bib is not as satisfactory as a cover-up pinafore. This is very easy to make from a plain oblong of material. It may be trimmed with braid, bias binding or embroidery.

Required : An oblong of any washing cotton 24 inches wide and 16 inches deep. A card of bias binding also ric-rac braid or embroidery cottons for decoration.

To make The only cutting out required are two half circle slits for the armholes (*see Fig. 100*). Fold the oblong so that the two shorter ends meet in the centre back. On the folds each side, 3 inches down from the top edge mark a point for the armhole. With pins mark an upward curve about 2 inches in from the fold. Cut along the curve through the double material on each side of the pinafore for the two armholes. Bind with bias binding round the lower curves which are the armholes and the upper curves which become cap sleeves. Hem the two side edges narrowly, and the lower edge. Bind all along the top edge or stitch a contrasting band to make a casing through which to thread a tape. Trim the pinafore with bands of braid or embroidery. Small patch pockets may be added with embroidery stitches if liked.

COOK'S APRON

An apron which combines as an oven cloth is a useful gift for the cook hostess. It may be made of plain material and embroidered, or of printed material and quilted. It is made as a plain apron with two large padded pockets into which the hands may be slipped to protect them when carrying hot dishes from the oven to the table for serving.

Required : ¾ yard of any strong washable cotton 36 inches wide; two pieces of wadding for padding about 10 inches by 7 inches; contrasting bias binding, and coloured braid for ties.

To make Cut an oblong 22 inches wide and 20 inches deep for the apron and two bands 4 inches wide by 17 inches long for the yoke. Cut two pieces 20 inches by 7 inches for the pockets (if using a patterned material plan the pieces before cutting out so that the pattern lies the same way).

Fold each pocket piece in half, slip a piece of wadding between and stitch round the edges to hold in place. If the pockets are to be quilted mark them into squares or diamond shapes and machine stitch as quilted. Bind one short edge and one long edge of each pocket.

Lay the pockets to the lower edges of the apron piece with the raw edges exactly to the edges of the apron and tack in place. Slightly gather the top of apron and insert in the yoke which has been joined along one long edge and the two short sides. Now bind all round the apron taking in all the edges firmly; the binding should be tacked in place and then machine stitched through all the thicknesses, this insures that the edges of the pockets are firmly held.

Add tapes for tying at each side of the yoke and embroider the front of the aprons between the pockets.

QUILTED TURBAN SCARF

An attractive turban to fit any head size is easily made from a square of silk or cotton or a head square.

Required : A 24 inch square of material and some wadding for padding.

To make First hem the edges of the square. Fold in half diagonally and mark off the centre 12 inches along the diagonal fold. Cut the wadding into a strip 12 inches by 4 inches and lay in the fold in the centre. Tack in place and stitch in straight lines ¾ inch apart along the length of the wadding through all thicknesses.

The ends of the scarf tie the turban in place and adjust the fit for individual head measurements.

FELT EGG COSIES

These are particularly good sellers in a Spring charity sale when eggs are plentiful.

They can be made in many different shapes and colours besides those suggested here.

Required : Small squares or scraps of felt from any needlework shop and coloured embroidery threads.

Baby Chicken

On two pieces of yellow felt 3 inches square draw a simple outline side view of the head and body of a baby chicken, shaping a tiny beak in the front of the head. Join round the shaped sides by overcasting. Embroider the beak with orange thread and embroider an eye. A narrow band of green felt may be added round the base.

Triangle

Cut three isosceles triangles each in a different coloured felt with a base of $1\frac{3}{4}$ inches. Join the long sides by overcasting or buttonholing in contrasting embroidery thread. A motley design of French knots may be worked on each triangle.

Flower Dome

From two pieces of green felt cut an oblong $2\frac{3}{4}$ inches wide by $3\frac{1}{4}$ inches deep. Shape the top into a curved dome. Embroider the top of each piece thickly with small flower heads and leaves using a thick embroidery thread or wool. Join the sides of the egg cosy and complete by embroidering a flower-head across the join each side.

DOLLY BAG

Useful to hold kitchen rags, scraps of string, oddments of knitting wools etc., it can be made of any fancy material with a head cut out of thick cardboard and painted.

Required : Two pieces of gay material 14 inches by 10 inches, scraps from an old nylon stocking for arms and legs, wool for hair; cardboard for head.

To make On the cardboard mark out a circle about 4 inches in diameter for the head, draw a short neck sloping the lines each side into 'shoulders'. Cut out round the outlines and paint the face. Make a miniature wig from wool to cover top of head.

Make arms of tubes of nylon about $\frac{3}{4}$ inch wide and 5 inches long and legs in same way about 8 inches long and stuff with the remainder of the old stockings.

Make a vertical slit in the centre of one piece of the bag material and bind it neatly. Join the sides with single or French seams inserting the top ends of the legs in the bottom seam and the arms near the top of the side seams. Turn in the top of the bag and gather up to fit round the neck.

Trim with a collar of a scrap of lace or *broderie anglaise*. Attach a loop of material to the top of the bag so that it can be hung on a hook.

GIANT SHOE TIDY

For a married couple living in a small flat this shoe tidy can be made to fit the inside of the door of a built-in cupboard.

Required : Hessian or strong cotton furnishing material is best for this as it must be durable. For binding use cross way strips of contrasting material. The amount required will depend on the size of the tidy.

To make For the back of the tidy cut a piece of the material divisible by 6 across the width plus 2 inches and by 12 down the length plus 4 inches. Cut strips for the pockets 9 inches deep by one and a half the width of the background. Bind one long edge of each pocket strip. Now mark the pocket strips off into 9 inch divisions and pin or tack a box pleat in the centre of each taking up 3 inches of material. Turn in the

The tulip flower tray set has a small matching
napkin tucked in the flower 'pocket'

Plate 93

raw edges and place across the background
strip at 12 inch intervals. Tack and stitch
in place across the lower edge of each and
at the sides. Complete by binding all round
the tidy taking in all edges at the sides.
Round curtain rings may be sewn at intervals
along the top to be hooked over cup screws
on the cupboard door.

The light shoes should be kept in the top
pockets and the man's shoes in the lower
pockets.

TRAY SET *(Pl. 93)*

A tray cloth with matching napkin is
unusual when the napkin is fitted into a
pocket on the cloth.

Required : A piece of linen approximately
27 inches by 12 inches and scraps of a
contrasting colour; embroidery
threads.

To make Cut the traycloth to the required

size (16 inches by 12 inches is a good size) and from remaining material cut a square for the napkin. Bind the edges of both or hem with some fancy stitch.

The pocket of the traycloth may be part of the design (*as in Plate 93*). It may be a flower shape, a large leaf, or more simply a coloured cube in a design of rectangular shapes. Draw the design on the cloth and from the contrasting scraps of material cut pieces for the appliqué pocket. Apply with buttonhole stitch, completing the open edge of the pocket with buttonhole stitch. Embroider the remainder of the design in simple surface stitches.

Complete the set by embroidering a tiny matching motif on one corner of the napkin.

DOOR STOP

An unusual and decorative door stop is easily made using a large straight-sided jar with screw top filled with sand. This can be covered in a variety of ways and decorated with embroidery and beads.
Required : A strip of felt as wide as the depth of the jar and as long as the circum-

ference plus 1 inch; also two circles of felt ½ inch larger in diameter than the diameter of the jar; embroidery threads, beads, etc.

To make Embroider the top circle and decorate with beads or buttons in an attractive pattern. Join the strip into a ring to fit the jar exactly, trimming away the surplus felt. Join the top circle into the top of the ring. Put in the jar and join in the remaining circle of felt as the base. The joins may be covered by couching a thick thread of contrasting wool round the edges.

DACHSHUND DRAUGHT EXCLUDER
(Pl. 94)

A long tube of fabric tapered off one end and formed into the long nosed head of a dachshund while the other end is stuffed with laddered nylons is a useful gift and a practical way of making use of old stockings.
Required : ⅜ yard of closely woven material 36 inches wide (felt is excellent); scraps of contrasting material from which to make eyes, nose, ears, legs and tail;

A dachshund draught excluder will be popular with all the family

Plate 94

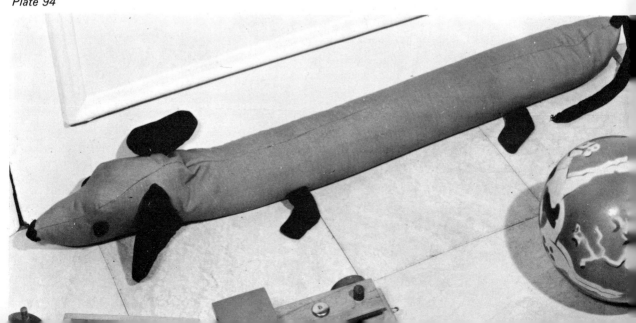

filling of old nylons, clean rags, foam rubber pieces or kapok.

To make The average door is 30 to 33 inches wide. Fold the strip of material in half, curving one end of the fold for the tail end and shaping the other end into a dog's head. From cut away scraps cut a long diamond shape for the front of the head fitting the long points to nose and top of head and the wider part across the 'forehead'. Stitch with single seams leaving the tail end open and also a small gap in the neck for stuffing.

Turn through to the right side. Cut ears, legs and tail from the contrasting material, cutting them double. Stitch all round and turn through. Attach in appropriate places to the body. Embroider the nose with black thread and stitch two circles of dark fabric in place for eyes.

Finally stuff the body and the head very firmly, continually adding more stuffing and pushing it down to fill out the tube and shape the head. When stuffing is complete neatly sew up the seams.

PLAYING CARD CUSHIONS *(Pl. 95)*

Simply made cushion covers are effective and gay with appliqué playing card motifs.

Fig. 101

Make two cushions in white with red motifs and two in red with black motifs.

Materials : For each cushion 2 pieces of felt 14 inches square, a 7 inch square in contrasting colour and 2 yards of cord; also a foam-filled cushion pad 14 inches square.

To make Cut out the playing card motifs from the contrast squares using the appropriate diagram design (*Figs. 101* and *102*) drawn out on paper ruled into 1 inch squares. Mount each into the centre of one cushion cover side in simple hemmed appliqué (no turnings are needed on felt). Stitch three sides of each cover and insert pad, slip-stitch the fourth side to close. Stitch cord all round over joins, finishing each corner with a little loop of the cord.

CHILD'S ONE-PIECE PINAFORE

Required : ¾ to 1 yard (according to the size of the child) of 36 inch zephyr, checked cotton or linen; embroidery threads; two buttons.

To make No pattern is needed. Cut an oblong 32 inches wide by 20 inches long, and out of one of the long edges cut the armholes, 9 inches deep, leaving a point at

Fig. 102

*This set of playing card
cushions is made from
felt squares in red and
white with the appliqué
card motifs boldly cut
from black and red felt*

Plate 95

each end that will just take a buttonhole.
This leaves between the armholes a centre-
front about 10 inches wide, out of which
you must hollow the neck, 4 or 5 inches
deep, and sloping up to two more points
between it and the armholes. These points
will take buttons to fit the buttonholes on
the back points, giving a cross-over back
and fastening on each shoulder.

Hem all edges and trim them with
bright-coloured feather stitching or some
other suitable embroidery bordering (*see
Embroidery Section*), make two buttonholes
and sew on two buttons. The pinafore
measurements given are toddler's size, but
they are easily enlarged for older children.

GINGHAM CLOTH AND
COSY COVER

Just the thing for a tea-table set in the
garden, to take on holiday at a country
cottage or for the children's meal—very
hard-wearing, cheerful and quick to make.

Required : $1\frac{3}{4}$ yards of green gingham; an
oddment or left-over of plain green
cotton; a skein of green embroidery
cotton.

To make Cut the cloth a yard square in
gingham. Then decorate it and make it a
little larger by adding a broad double hem
in the plain green material. Make a cover
to slip over an average-sized tea cosy in the
gingham, with a 2 inch bottom hem of plain
green.

Trim both items with simple pine-tree
appliqués. No transfer is needed for these—
just cut three 3 inch squares of the plain
green. Divide each in half diagonally and
you have two tree appliqués. Place three
in each corner of the cloth, on long thick
trunks made of green chain stitch. The
middle tree should spring exactly from the
corner, with a shorter one each side of it.
Buttonhole-stitch the appliqués down to
the cloth. On the cosy cover there should be
three trees rising from the green hem in a
descending row, each a little shorter than
the last.

USEFUL HINTS

BE KIND TO YOUR SEWING MACHINE

As the sewing machine is used for almost every form of needlecraft described in this book except knitting and crochet, it seems more appropriate to give hints on the care of your machine here, under a separate heading, rather than in the dressmaking chapters.

As with every new sewing machine you buy there is a booklet of instructions relating to that particular machine, such information is not given here. But you must read these instructions carefully and go over all the points mentioned so that you become really familiar with the model which you will be using. Just because you have used a sewing machine before does not necessarily mean that you know all about the machine that is now in front of you. Each make varies slightly and new models are continually being introduced.

Storage

Your machine can no more thrive on damp and dirt that you do yourself. Dust is one of the worst enemies of all the delicate parts, which easily get clogged; so always put the cover on directly you stop using it, even if only for half an hour. Do not store it against an outside wall or in any other place likely to be damp. Preferably it should be kept in a room which is heated in winter, rather than a cold spare room.

Cleaning

Dust, fluff, and dirt of any kind getting into the works will cause the machine to run 'hard', squeak or develop some other little fault. Therefore, never let it get dirty. A suitable brush for removing dust and fluff often goes with the machine or can be bought from the manufacturers; or a SOFT typewriter brush serves very well. If the machine still seems dirty after a good brushing and dusting, inject paraffin oil, which is very cleansing, into all oil holes and where dirt seems to have collected. Leave it in for an hour or two, then you will find that the oil and dirt can be wiped away together.

Oiling

This lubricates the machine, and must be done from time to time if it is to run smoothly and without undue wear. Use only the best machine oil, putting it sparingly into all oil holes and any other place which your book of instructions tells you should be lubricated. Don't put in so much oil that it oozes out again all over your work. As a precaution, after the oil has had a little time to soak in, wipe away any surplus, and then run an odd bit of fabric through the machine, to work the oil in and absorb the stray drops on to something that doesn't matter. If your machine is to be put away for any length of time it is a wise precaution to oil it before storing.

Needles and Thread

Your sewing machine must be supplied with good needles and thread to work well. The needles made especially for your make of machine are best, and remember that any particular needle does not last for ever. Go to the trouble of putting in a new one if, after the one you are using has seen good service, the machine seems to work hard. If you cannot get a needle through even reasonably thick layers of material, it is almost certain that a new one is wanted.

If sewing with a No. 40 thread a No. 16 needle is recommended; if No. 50 thread is used then a No. 14 needle is best.

Tension

A new machine is adjusted to stitch at an average tension for a firm lightweight material. But the tension will have to be adjusted to suit different materials and threads. If stitching materials of man-made fibres a lighter tension is usually required. Consult your instruction book to see how adjustment is made on your particular machine. The tension is at fault on either the under or upper thread if either of these threads lies straight along the material, instead of locking properly in the thickness of the material.

Sitting Comfortably at your Machine

It is most important that you should sit comfortably at a correct height at your machine. Not only does it give you better control but it will save back-breaking fatigue if you are doing any long jobs. If you have your machine on the dining or kitchen table then you will find that the dining or kitchen chair is probably the correct height if you are of average size.

Sit well into the chair so that the base of the spine is supported but do not bend over your work in a round-shouldered fashion; keep your spine straight and lean forward a little from the hips.

If you are using an electric machine with foot control and you are inclined to be short raise the pedal on books or a box so that it is within comfortable reach. Should you be working a treadle machine you may find you have to sit rather lower to your work to have proper control.

If using a hand-operated machine it is less tiring to sit rather high (as for type-writing) so put a firm cushion on your chair to raise yourself.

Remember that your machine cannot be better than its operator. If your results are not perfect at first don't blame the machine which probably isn't at fault at all, but go on practising until you get better stitching due to your greater experience.

Some Common Troubles

If needles break, suspect one of the following causes and set it right: (a) wrong threading; (b) incorrect tension; (c) a blunt needle or one put in wrongly; poor cotton or cotton too coarse for the needle; (d) wrong adjustment of the presser foot.

If the thread keeps breaking, it may be caused by: (a) incorrect threading; (b) tension too tight; (c) bobbin wound too tight or too full; (d) thread caught round the looper (on a chain-stitch machine); (e) stiff, obstinate material which requires soaping.

Puckering may be due to: (a) tension too tight; (b) wrong amount of pressure on the presser foot.

Heavy or hard working of the machine may be due to: (a) clogging by dust or fluff; (b) a blunt needle; (c) the machine needs oiling; (d) threads caught in the shuttle or bobbin case (lock stitch) or between the wheel and the connecting rod (chain stitch).

REPLACING TORN-OUT BUTTONS

Sometimes, especially on children's clothes, a button is torn away, bringing a piece of fabric with it and leaving a hole in the garment. The best method of mending is first to sew a fresh button on to a square of material larger than the hole; or cut such a square, with a button attached, from an old garment of the same colour. From the back push the button through the hole, leaving its square of fabric on the wrong side to form a patch which is hemmed down and the torn edges of the hole caught to it.

WHEN COTTON KNOTS

If cotton keeps knotting, probably you are threading it from the wrong end. Try threading the loose end on the reel into the needle before cutting it off. Then put your knot in the cut-off end.

SHRUNKEN BLANKETS

If carelessly washed, blankets sometimes shrink so that there is not enough left to tuck in well all round. A good remedy is to add wide strips of either flannelette or old sheeting down both sides. This will tuck in, leaving all the warmth where it is wanted—on the bed. Blankets are too thick for ordinary seams, so turn in the added material singly and lap it over the blanket edge.

MENDING LACE

Torn lace can often be neatly mended by machine. Lay a piece of paper under the lace, bringing the torn edges as nearly together as possible. Thread the machine with very fine cotton, stitch backwards and forwards irregularly till the tear is firmly held, and then carefully tear away the paper. The mend will hardly show, if the cotton used is a good match to the lace.

WHEN SCISSORS ARE BLUNT

It is so important to keep both scissors and cutting-out shears really sharp that you should take prompt action as soon as they seem the least bit dull. Here are three simple home remedies. (1) Try fifteen or twenty times to cut off the neck of a glass bottle with your scissors; the slipping of the blades on the glass will sharpen them. (2) Use the scissors several times to cut a piece of coarse sandpaper. (3) If your scissors are new, they may be screwed up rather tightly, so that they work a little stiffly. Just draw your finger or thumb gently up the inside of each blade two or three times, thus dusting and slightly lubricating the metal from the natural oil in your skin. You will be surprised at the difference in smoothness that this makes. It will only work, of course, with scissors that are comparatively new.

PRICKED FINGER MARKS

The chief trouble about pricking a finger when sewing is that you are apt to stain your material with a drop or two of blood. Deal with the mark at once by soaking it in tepid salt water and afterwards washing it in soapy tepid water. On silk it is best to try peroxide of hydrogen; but, as this sometimes removes the colour as well as the stain, test its effect first on a cutting of the material.

REALLY EFFECTIVE TEA-COSIES

For lining a tea-cosy, nothing is better than ordinary chamois leather, for this is remarkably good at holding in the heat.

DAMPING BEFORE PRESSING

Whenever possible, use warm water for damping press-cloths or seams which are to be pressed. The warmth penetrates the fibres of the material more quickly than cold, with the result that damping is quicker and more even.

NEEDLE POINTS

To sharpen a sewing-machine needle, a good plan is to do a few inches of stitching through a piece of sandpaper, the grit of which sharpens the point. Finish by holding the flame of a match to the needle point.

Chamois leather is a good choice for the leaves of needle-books, instead of flannel, as it keeps the steel from rusting.

MAKING VESTS LADDERPROOF

While the vest is new and unworn, use a fine mercerized embroidery thread to work round the bottom edge; one double crochet, two chain. This keeps the edge unbroken, and it is broken edges which start ladders.

KEEPING THE DOOR OPEN

When going to and fro setting a meal, or if listening for a sleeping child, you may need to keep a door ajar without its banging in every breeze. A good way of doing this is to make a sausage buffer. Cut a strip of woollen material measuring 12 by 8 inches. Join into a tube, gather up one end tightly, and stuff loosely with bran or tightly with cut-up rags. Close the other end by gathering, and to each end sew loops of cord or ribbon which will slip over the handles, one on each side of the door, thus holding it ajar but stopping any swinging or banging.

A NET CURTAIN HINT

When making net curtains a great difficulty is that pins supposed to hold the hems only too easily drop out of the open mesh.

Get some packets of small fine hairpins and use these instead. They stay in, yet are easily drawn out when the job is done.

WORN RUG EDGES

Rugs usually go at the edges while the main part is quite good. An easy repair is to buttonhole closely over the edge with rug or a very thick knitting wool. To make a still stronger repair, do the buttonholing over a length of blind cord held along the worn edge.

COTTON REELS THAT STAY PUT

How often one has an interrupting search for a reel of cotton that has rolled under a chair or got hidden under one's work. Here are two good 'stay put' hints. (1) Hammer long nails at even distances into a small board, hammering them only a little way in. The board stands on your work-table and on each nail a reel of cotton stays securely, yet can be easily threaded from when hand-sewing or lifted off to go into the sewing-machine. (2) Buy two reels of each colour for a dressmaking or upholstery job—you usually have to, anyway. One of each goes in the machine. The other is threaded on to a length of tape, with other reels in common use. Make the tape long enough to double into a loop and knot at the top and hang it handily. When hand-sewing or tacking your cotton is never lost and yet can be cut easily from the suspended reel.

TRANSPARENT CURTAIN HEMS

Curtains made of transparent material, such as net, voile, muslin and organdie, should always have three-ply hems—that is, the first turn, that of the raw edge, should be the full depth of the hem. If it is narrower, as in an ordinary hem, the raw edge will show through the transparent material and look rather unsightly, especially if it is uneven in the slightest degree.

PLASTIC FABRIC

This non-woven, waterproof, reversible material is a radical departure from ordinary fabrics. It may be either thick and opaque such as P.V.C. material or almost transparent. Opaque plastic fabric makes up well for sponge bags and toilet cases which require to be waterproof. It is also used in fashion garments, and often printed with a design. The thinner semi-transparent variety, which is lighter in weight, may be used for softly draped curtains, waterproof hoods, women's and children's mackintoshes, aprons and similar articles.

Remember when using this fabric that it must not be ironed, hand-hemmed, or gathered. Stitch hems on a sewing machine if possible, making only a single turn a good $\frac{1}{4}$ inch deeper than the hem is to be and stitching it that $\frac{1}{4}$ inch away from the cut edge. Don't cut away that $\frac{1}{4}$ inch afterwards or your hem may pull out in wear. Plastic does not fray, so raw edges are perfectly safe. With the transparent variety there is no objection to a double hem if you prefer it.

If you haven't a sewing machine, secure the hem with fairly large running stitches in matching thread. The top hem of a curtain, which has to take a considerable weight, should have two rows of running stitches close together, with the stitches in the two rows alternating. Plastic material should only be used for curtains which stay in place and do not have to be drawn open and closed, as the fabric does not take well to constant strain and jerking.

Pins leave permanent marks in this fabric, so when pinning seams together before stitching them place the pins along the seam line, where the stitching will afterwards cover them. There is no weave or grain to guide you when cutting out plastic, so to keep lines straight use a ruler and pencil.

Though it is best stitched by machine, this material is very hard on machine needles unless precautions are taken. Whenever possible, bind edges rather than hem them and use a cotton or rayon bind, not a plastic one. Double the bind over the cut plastic edge, first pin and then tack it in place, then stitch both sides on at once, so that the bind is always between the machine and the plastic. If you tack with cotton matching the bind, it is often unnecessary to remove the tackings afterwards, as the stitching largely ploughs them in unnoticeably. When stitching plastic, don't hold it down firmly with the left hand. Pull it slightly instead.

When you have to stitch direct without any intervening material, here's a valuable tip. Keep by you, as you work, a saucer containing a few drops of sewing-machine oil. Moisten a finger-tip in oil and run it along your seam line before starting to stitch. This lubrication makes the working easier and your needle lasts far longer.

Plastic tends to stick and become difficult to handle if exposed to heat. So make it up away from the direct warmth of a fire or summer sunshine.

When soiled, plastic may be cleansed by sponging over with slightly warm sudsy water. Rinse by sponging a second time with clear water and let it dry naturally, away from a fire.

INDEX

American: Block patchwork, 153–156; pleated rag rugs, 158–159

Appliqué: 24, 27, 45–48, 238, 239; blind, 48, 78; for bedspreads, 225; *broderie anglaise*, 48–49; Chinese, 48; embroidered, 46–48; machine, 72; patchwork, 153, 154; ribbon or tape, 77–78

Apron: cook's, 234; patch pocket for, 137; zig-zag machine embroidery on, 72

Babies' clothes: casings for, 131; cross-stitch for, 28; embroidery for, 57

Bead work: 90

Bedhead: covers, 226; curtains, 225–226

Bedspreads: appliqué for, 45, 48; binding, 225; corded ruching for, 138; edges, 225; facing, right-side, 225; foundations, 224; initials & monograms on, 63; piping, 225; ruching, 225; scalloping, 225; size of, 224; trimmings, 225

Belts: 118–119; holders of, 119; mending of, 147

Bias tape: 119–120, 123, 125, 131; for piping, 134

Bibs: 232

Bindings: 119–120, 123, 124, 129; bound, 131; diagonal joints of, 133

Bishop sleeves: 139

Bolster cushions: 204; cover, 205–206; corded ruching for, 138

Bolster slips: 212

Borders: crochet, 185–186; lattice, 185–186; open, 185

Broderie anglaise: 10, 11, 12, 24, 27, 29, 39, 41, 141, 235; method of, 48–49; pressing, 87; laundry of, 88; for pillow-slips, 212

Buffer: sausage, 243

Buttonholes: 120–123

Buttons: 127–128; replacing of, 147, 242

Candlewick: 98

Casings: 131; babies' clothes, 131; curtains, 201; dressing-table cover, 208; frills, 222; underwear, 131

Chairbacks: 15, 32, 37, 64, 214

Chair-seats: tapestry for, 83

Children's clothes: cardigan pattern, 173–174; embroidery, 15, 29, 30, 35, 37, 38, 42, 43, 44, 72–73, 80; jumper pockets, 136–137; machine embroidery, 70–72; patch pockets, 137; piping, 134

Christmas Bride, quilt: 154

Cleanliness of knitting & crocheting: 192

Clothes-horse: as frame for quilting, 156; as screen, 223

Coats: 131, 133, 137; knitted, 172

Collars: 123–124; mending of men's soft, 148

Corded quilting: *see* ITALIAN QUILTING

Cosies: tea-, 242–243; felt egg, 234–235; gingham, 239; knitted chick egg, 178–179

Coton à broder: 56, 64

Cotton reels: fixing, 243

Crochet: abbreviations, 196–197; bedroom slippers, 189; blanket, 182–183; borders, 185–186; braid

edging, 188–189; buttonholes, 168; decreasing, 181; definitions, 196–197; double, 182; drying, 193; edging, 191; errors, 194–195; finishing, 192; hooks, 161; increasing, 181; joining threads, 182; lace, 184–185; lace for tablecloths, 212; lace edging for towels, 186; making up, 192, 195; method, 179–180; motifs, 186–188; puff stitch, 182–183; ribbed double pattern, 182; shell stitch, 184; slots in, 168; stitches, 180–181; tensions, 181–182; treble stitch, 183–184; tricot stitch, 183; washing, 192–193

Crosses & Losses, quilt: 154

Curtains: bathroom, 203; bedhead, 225–226; binding, 202; braid, 203; casings, 201; facing, 202; finishes, 202–203; frilled edges, 203; fringes, 202–203; heading, 202; hems of transparent, 244; length of material, 200–201; lining, 201; measurement 200, 201; net, 243; seams, 201; tape, 201, 202; weighting, 203; width, 201.

Cushion covers: 205; appliqué, 45; embroidery, 32, 37, 64, 72, 79, 205; openings, 208; patchwork, 152–153; pile, 156–158; smocking, 80–82; tapestry, 83

Cushions: blind appliqué for, 48; bolster, 204; bolster cover, 205–206; boxed, 203–204; corded ruching for bolster, 138; feather, 203, 206; finishes, 207; pads, 204–205; patchwork, 150; pile, 156–158; piping, 207–208; playing card, 238; renovation, 227–228; repair of window, 230; round boxed, 206–207

Dachshund draught excluder: 237–238

Darning: 145–146; hoop, 71; stitch, 28–29

Delectable Mountains, quilt: 154

Designs: barbed wire, 16; built-up embroidery patterns, 15–17; climbing roses, 15–16; clip-clop, 15; clover, 17; cornerwise, 16; creating own, 13–14; draw-round, 16–17; Eve's apple, 17; forget-me-nots, 16–17; inner circle, 17; rainbow wheel, 16; transferring to material, 14–15; up-and-down, 17

Dolly bag: 235

Door stop: 237

Dove-in-the-Window, quilt: 154

Dress: *see also* DRESSMAKING: preparing to cut, 111–112; accessories, 42, 48; forms, 100, 101

Dressing gown, patchwork: 152, 153

Dressing-table: card tables, temporary, 209; draperies, 208–209; mats, 79

Dressmaker's weights: 83

Dressmaking: *see also* FACINGS: PATTERNS: assembling garment, 114; basic dress pattern, 114–115; belts, 118–119; binding, 119–120; buttonholes, 120–123; casings, 131; collars, 123–124; cuffs, 124–125; cutting out, 112–113; darts, 125–126; equipment, 99–101; facings, 126–127; faggoting, 105, 148; fastenings, 127–128; fitting, 115–117; flares & flounces, 128–129; frills, 129; fur trimmings, 129–130; hems, 127, 130–131; lace trimmings, 131–132; linings, 130, 132–133; machine stitching, 118; mitres, 120, 127, 132, 133–134; new clothes for old, 142–144; order of work, 111; pattern marking, 113; piping, 134; plackets, 134–135; pleats, 135–136; pockets, 136–137; pressing, 117–118; Rouleaux, 119, 137–138; ruching, 138–139; sleeves, 139–140; slots, bound, 122; tucks, 140–141; underwear, 141; wristbands, 124, 125; wrist finishes, 125; zip fastener, 128, 141–142

Eiderdowns: renovating, 228; thicker covers, 228–229; thin borders for worn, 229; transparent covers, 228
Embroidery: *see also* DESIGN: STITCHES: Amager work, 90; appliqué, 46–48; Assisi, 52, 65–68; Blackwork, 90; *broderie anglaise*, 48–49; Bulgarian, 92; canvas work, 82–85; Catalan, 53, 92–93; church, 92–93; crewel, 93; cross-stitch, 49–52; cutwork, 21, 43, 52–53, 87; Czechoslovakian, 93; darned, 53–57; *Découpé*, 64; designs for, 12–17; drawn thread, 57–63; Egyptian tentwork, 93; equipment, 9–10; eyelets, 29, 48–49; finishing, 87; Gayant, 93; Hardanger work, 24, 93; Hedebo, 94; Hungarian, 92; initials & monograms, 63–64, 213; inlay, 64; Italian, 65–68; Jacobean, 12, 93; on knitting, 167; laid work, 94–95; landscape & map, 68–69; lattice work, 78; laundry of, 88; machine, 70–72; materials suitable for, 11; Mexican drawn thread, 60; needles, 9; outline, 72–73; patterns, 15–17; pressing, 87–88; Reticella, 96; ribbon appliqués, 77–78; ribbon work, 96; Richelieu work, 96, 98; samplers, 18, 96–98; shaded, 78–79; shadow, 33, 79–80; Sicilian, 59, 68; smocking, 80–82; spiders' webs, 98; spotless quality of, 11; Swedish weaving or darning, 57–63; tablecloths, 212; tapestry, 11, 82–85; transfers for, 12–13; tufting, 98; types of, 45–86; Venetian, 23, 29, 53, 98; white, 98; working threads for, 11; wool, 85–86; zig-zag machine, 72

Facings: *see also* DRESSMAKING, mitres: 123, 124, 125, 126–127; bedspread, right-side, 225; curtain, 202
Fair Isle jumpers: 167
Fan corner: 60
Fire screens: tapestry for, 83
Fisherman's rib pattern: 165–166
Foot-mats: 156
Footstools: tapestry for, 83
Four-poster bed: 224
French hem: *see* NAPERY HEM
Frills: 129; bed-settee, 215–216; curtain, 203, 222; cushion, 207
Fringes: curtain, 202–203; cushion, 207; making, 190–191

Glass towelling: 11

Gloves: darning, 146; flower motif, 174–176; knitting pattern, 174–176; three-sided needle, 146

Handkerchief linen: 57–58
Hem marker: 130
Hessian: foundation for ragcraft, 156, 235; mending bag, 232–233
Hooks & eyes: 128
Hoop frames: 10, 233
Household linen: darning, 145, 209–215; embroidery for, 35, 42, 48, 52–53, 57, 64; initials & monograms on, 63
Huckaback: darned embroidery on, 56–57; 232

Interlinings: 132, 133
International embroidery: 89–98
Ironing board: 100; folding, 101
Italian: embroidery, 57, 65–68; hemstitching, 53, 65; quilting, 75–77

Japanese kimonos: 78–79

Kapok: 203
Knitted garments: cardigans, 172–174; drying, 193; mending, 148; repairing, 193; washing, 192–193
Knitting: abbreviations, 163, 196; bag, 232–233; brushing surface, 192; buttonholes, 168; casting on & off, 161; collars & cuffs, 191; decreasing, 162; definitions, 196–197; different colour, 167; dropped stitches, 194–195; embroidery on, 167; errors, 194–195; finishing off, 192; grafting, 162–163; increasing, 162; joining wool, 162; making up, 192, 195; method of, 161–163; needles, 160; patterns, 163–167, 170–179; plain, 161; pockets, 168–169; purl, 161–162; ribbing, stretching of, 194; slots in, 167–168; stitches, 163–167; tension, 162

Lace: diagonal joints, *see* DRESSMAKING, mitres: edging for towels, 186; inserting motif, 132, joining yokes, 132; knitted, 166–167; mending, 242; stitch, 34–35; trimmings, 131–132
Lady of the Lake, The, quilt: 154
Laundry bags: 64
Loose linings: 132
Loose covers: 215–220; armchair, 218–220; bed-settee, 215–216; divan, 216; easy-chair, armless, 216–217; open-armed chair, 219–220; ottoman box, 216; renovating, 229; sofas, 218–220; winged armchairs, 218–219

Machine: *see* SEWING MACHINE
Madeira embroideries: 29, 40; laundry of, 88
Magyar sleeve: 140
Mark-stitching: *see* TACKING, tailor
Mattress: cover, 210; repair of overlay, 229–230
Measurements for dressmaking: 107–109

Mending: 145–148
Men's shirts: patching of, 147
Mitres: 133–134
Monograms: 51, 63–64, 213

Napery hem: 198–199
Needlepoint: *see* TAPESTRY
Needles: beading, 22; crewel, 9; mattress, 229–230;
    punch, 10, 35; size of knitting & crochet, 195;
    three-sided glove, 146; wool, 10
Nightgown: lace yokes, 132

Overalls: patch pocket for, 137
Overlays: 229–230

Padding: cotton-wool, 130; for quilting patchwork, 156
Paper patterns: *see* PATTERNS
Patch pockets: embroidered, 32; knitwear, 169; overalls,
    137
Patching: 146–147
Patchwork: 149–156; crazy, 30, 150–152; dressing
    gown, 152, 153; feather stitch, 30; as folkcraft in
    U.S.A., 149; geometrical all-over, 153; origins of,
    149; pram covers, 150; strip for bedcovers, 152–
    153; quilts, 149, 153, 154, 224
Patterns: *see also* KNITTING PATTERNS: adjusting paper,
    109–110; assembling, 114; basic dress, 114–115;
    cutting out, 111–113; marking, 113; marking
    pleats, 135; preparation for use, 111–112; sizes,
    107–108
Petit-point: 84
Picot-edged finishes: 131
Pile cushions: 156–158
Pillows: renovating, 230
Pillowslips: 210–212; initials & monograms on, 63
Pinafore: child's one-piece, 238–239; toddler's feeding,
    233–234
Pincushions: 79, 100, 101
Pinking shears: 100, 101
Piping: 134, 199–200; bed-settee, 215; bedspreads, 225;
    cushions, 207–208; simulated, 208
Plackets: 124, 125, 128, 134–135; one-piece, 135;
    one-piece sleeve, 139; side-seam, 135; wrap, 135;
    zip fastener, 141
Pleats: 135–136; box, 135; gauge for, 135; inverted, 135–
    136; pressing, 136; side, 135
Point turc: 102
Pompoms: making, 191
Pouffes: 222–223
Pram: appliqué covers, 45; blankets, 190; knitted covers,
    165; patchwork covers, 150
Press studs: 128
Pressing: damping before, 243; embroidery, 87–88;
    home-made garments, 117–118; pleats, 136;
    roller, 101; Rouleaux, 138; sleeves, 118; tucks,
    140
Pricked finger marks: 242
Princess feather, quilt: 154
Prussian binding: 131
Punch needles: 10, 35, 41

Punto quadro: *see* ITALIAN HEMSTITCHING

Queen Charlotte's Crown, quilt: 154
Quilted turban scarf: 234
Quilting: English, 74–75; Italian, 75–77; patchwork, 156;
    stitch, 20, 73–77
Quilts: baby's, 226–227; child's bed, 227; enlarging, 227;
    frame for, 156; patchwork, 149, 153, 154, 156;
    wadded, 226–227

Ragcraft: 156–159
Raglan sleeve: 140
Relining: 132; coats, 133
Renovating: clothes, 142–143; gathered skirt to straight,
    143; dresses, 143
Ribbing: knitted, 164
Ribbon: appliqués, 77–78; for casings, 131; for ruffled
    ruching, 138, work, 96
Robbing Peter to Pay Paul, quilt: 154
Ruching: bedspread, 225; box-pleated, 138; corded, 138;
    ruffled, 138–139
Rugs: 190; repairing, 230, 243
Runners: embroidered, 213–214; embroidery for, 15, 32,
    37, 64

Sachets: handkerchief, 79–80; camphor, 231; lavender,
    231–232; stocking, 233
Samplers: 18, 96–98; purpose of, 18; material for, 18
Scissors: 10, 100, 198; buttonhole, 100, 121; sharpening,
    242
Screens: 223–224
Scrim: 50
Seams: 101–102, 104–107; binding, 107; faggoting, 105;
    flannel fell, 105; flat fell, 105–106; French, 105,
    106, 124; lapped, 106; plain, 106–107, 128;
    single-stitch, 107; welted, 107
Sequins: 90
Sewing machine: appliqué, 72; attachments, 118; care of,
    240–241; different types, 100; embroidery, 9, 70–
    72; filling, 71–72; needles, 241; plain machine
    stitching, 70–71; problems, 241; sharpening of
    needles, 243; stitching, 118; tension, 241
Shears: 100
Sheeting: 48; coloured, 209; unbleached, 210
Sheets: 210; mending, 148
Shoe tidy, giant: 235–236
Shrinking: blankets, 242
Sleeve: -board, 100, 118; pressing, 118; setting in, 139–
    140; types of, 139–140
Slipstitching: 131
Smocking: 33, 80–82; double-cable stitch, 82; double
    wave stitch, 82; feather stitch, 82; herringbone
    stitch, 82; outline stitch, 82; single cable stitch,
    82; Vandyke stitch, 82; wave stitch, 82
Socks: fancy tops for, 191; method of knitting, 169–170;
    patterns for knitted, 170–172; strengthening of
    knitted, 170
Spanish silk shawls: 78
Spanish work: *see* EMBROIDERY, Blackwork
Stars: 63

Stiletto: 10, 15, 29, 81, 100
Stitch: *see also* CROCHET: KNITTING: back, 19—20; barb, 20; bars, 20; basket, knitting, 165; basket filling, 21—22; beading, 22; Bermuda faggoting, *see* lace stitch; blanket, 22; braid, 22—23; branch, 23; bullion, 23; buttonhole, 23; buttonhole chain, 23; buttonhole chain for glove darning, 146; buttonhole, long-and-short, 25; buttonhole-open, 25; buttonhole, stem, 24; buttonholed bars, 20—21; cable knitting, 166; catch, upholstery, 198—199; chain, 26; chain, twisted, 26; coral, 26—27; cord, 27; couched, 41; couching, 27; couching; twisted, 27; crewel, 72; criss cross overcasting, *see* cross-stitch overcast; cross, 27—28; cross-overcast, 28; darning, for embroidery, 28—29, for mending, 145; detached chain, *see* lazy-daisy stitch; diamond hemstitch, 9; dot, *see* seed stitch; double back, *see* herringbone stitch; double cable, for smocking, 82; double Turkish, *see* lace stitch; double wave, for smocking, 82; drawn thread, *see* needleweaving stitch; eyelets, 29; faggoting, 105; feather, 29; feather for smocking, 82, for patchwork, 152; feather, double & treble, 30; feather triangular, 30; fine satin, *see* cord stitch; fly, 30—31; four-legged, 62—63; French knot, 31; French running, 102; garter, knitting, 163; Gobelin, 84; hemstitch, 31—32; hemstitch, bar, 32; hemstitch, diamond, 32; hemstitch, single crossing, 32—33; herringbone, 33, for smocking, 83, in dressmaking, 102—103; honeycombing, 33—34; lace, embroidery, 34—35; lace, knitting, 166—167; ladder, 35; lazy-daisy, 35—36; lightning blanket, 22; locking, upholstery, 199; long-and-short, 36; long French knot, 23; loose loop, 36—37; Mignonette, *see* seed stitch; *mille fleurs, see* stroke stitch; moss, knitting, 164—165; needleweaving, 37; Oriental, *see* Rumanian stitch; outline, 37; outline, for smocking, 82; padded satin, 38—39; picot, *see* lazy-daisy stitch; puff, *see* blanket stitch; punch, *see* lace stitch; rambler rose, 37—38; rice, 85; roll, *see* cord stitch; rope chain, 26; Rumanian, 38; running, 16, 17, 27, 28, 29, 74; satin, 38; scalloping, 39; seed, 39; single cable, smocking, 82; snail trail, *see* coral stitch; split, 39—40; stem, 40; stocking, knitting, 164; stroke, 40; Swedish darning, *see* needleweaving stitch; tapestry chain, 85; tent, 40—41; tent, couched, 41; three-sided, *see* lace stitch; trellis, 68; Turkey, *see* French running stitch; Turkish, 41; twisted bars, 20; twisted feather chain, 41; useful, 18—44; Vandyke, for smocking, 82; vilna, 42; wave, 42—43; wave, for smocking, 82; wheat-ear, 43; wheels, darned, 43; wheels, overcast, 43—44; whipped running, 44; woven bars, 21
Stitch-holders: 161
Stool pads: *see* CUSHIONS
Straight-down tailored pouffe: 223
Strip patchwork: 152—153

Tacking: 103; arrowheads, 103; diagonal, 103—104; tailor, 104, 113, 126
Table linen: 45, 212—213, 232; appliqué for, 45; breakfast sets, 213; embroidery for, 17, 32, 35; initials & monograms on 63; tray set, 15, 78, 236—237; zig-zag machinery, 72

Tablecloths: initials & monograms on, 63; mending of, 148, 212
Tailored garments: bound buttonholes, 122—123; stand pocket, 137; skirt hems, 131; worked tailored buttonholes, 123
Tailor's chalk: 100, 101
Tape: appliqués, 77—78; bias, 199; for casings, 131; measure, 100, 101, 198; patches, 147
Tapestry: 11, 82—85; chain stitch for, 85; pressing of, 88
Tassels: making of, 191
Tears: darning, 146
Teasel brush: 192
Templates, metal: for patchwork, 153
Tendril embroidery: 65
Teneriffe embroidery: 26, 59, 60—63
Terry towelling: 232
Texas Rose, quilt: 154
Threads: types of for various fabrics, 100, 118
Topping & Tailing: 147
Top-sewing: *see* NAPERY HEM
Towel: huckaback darning for, 37; embroidered guest, 232; mending, 148; outline embroidery, 72—73
Toy rabbit, knitted: 176
Tracing wheel: 100, 113
Transfers: 10—14; choice of, 12; colour of, 12—13; to material, 14; removal of outline, 12; use of, 12—13
Tufting: 98
Tweezers: 10, 100, 101
Twist handkerchief: 233

Underwear: casing for, 131; embroidery for, 29, 35, 57; lace trimmings for 132; materials for, 141; plackets for, 135; seams for, 104
Upholstery: box-pleated ruching, 138; curtains, 200—203; cushions, 203—208; dressing-table draperies, 208—209; equipment, 198; frills, 222; home, 133; household linen & accessories, 209—215; loose covers, 215—220; pelmets, 220—222; piping, 199—200; pouffes, 222—223; repairs & renovations, 227—230; screens, 223—224; special stitches, 198—199; spreads, 224—226; valances, 222; wadded quilts, 226—227

Velcro: 128
Vests: reinforcing, 243
Victoria & Albert Museum: 89, 153

Wall hanging: blind appliqué for, 48
Windmill corner: 59
Wooden darning ball: 145
Wool: care of oddments, 191; embroideries, 85—86; knotting of, 194; needles, 10; pressing of embroideries, 87; re-using old, 195—196; using oddments, 189—191; winders, 161

Zip fastener: 128; inserting, 141—142